THE NEW CENSORSHIP

Columbia Journalism Review Books

COLUMBIA JOURNALISM REVIEW BOOKS

Series Editors: Victor Navasky, Evan Cornog, Mike Hoyt,
and the editors of the *Columbia Journalism Review*

For more than fifty years, the *Columbia Journalism Review* has been the gold standard for media criticism, holding the profession to the highest standards and exploring where journalism is headed, for good and for ill.

Columbia Journalism Review Books expands upon this mission, seeking to publish titles that allow for greater depth in exploring key issues confronting journalism, both past and present, and pointing to new ways of thinking about the field's impact and potential.

Drawing on the expertise of the editorial staff at the *Columbia Journalism Review* as well as the Columbia Journalism School, the series of books will seek out innovative voices as well as reclaim important works, traditions, and standards. In doing this, the series will also incorporate new ways of publishing made available by the Web and e-books.

~~THE~~
~~NEW CENSORSHIP~~

Inside the Global Battle for Media Freedom

Joel Simon

Columbia University Press
New York

Columbia University Press
Publishers Since 1893
New York   Chichester, West Sussex
cup.columbia.edu
Copyright © 2015 Joel Simon
All rights reserved

Library of Congress Cataloging-in-Publication Data
Simon, Joel, 1964–
The new censorship : inside the global battle for media freedom / Joel Simon.
pages cm. —(Columbia journalism review books)
Includes bibliographical references and index.
ISBN 978-0-231-16064-3 (cloth : alk. paper)—ISBN 978-0-231-53833-6 (e-book)
1. Journalism—Political aspects—History—21st century.   2. Censorship—History—21st century.
3. Freedom of the press—History—21st century.   4. Press and politics—History—21st century.
5. Journalists—Violence against.   I. Title.
PN4751.S56 2014
363.31097309′05—dc23
2014012961

Columbia University Press books are printed on permanent and durable acid-free paper.
This book is printed on paper with recycled content.
Printed in the United States of America

c 10 9 8 7 6 5 4 3 2 1

COVER DESIGN: Archie Ferguson

For Ingrid

Contents

Acknowledgments

The New Censorship was written over a three-year period, between 2011 and 2013. However, the book draws on my experience of more than fifteen years spent defending press freedom and on the insights, observations, and research of colleagues and collaborators over an extended period of time. Among the many leaders in the struggle for freedom of expression whose ides have informed my own are Agnes Callamard, Christophe Deloire, Annie Game, Jean-Francois Julliard, John Kampfner, Rony Koven, Alison Bethel MacKenzie, Julio Muñoz, Ricardo Trotti, and Aidan White.

While I have consulted a wide variety of sources and experts in framing my analysis, it should come as no surprise that I rely heavily on the press freedom research carried out by the extraordinary staff at the Committee to Protect Journalists. The contributions of CPJ experts are acknowledged in the endnotes notes of each chapter, but I would like to recognize the support of key individuals. Among them are Robert Mahoney, Bill Sweeney, Carlos Lauría, Elisabeth Witchel, Jean-Paul Marthoz, and Özgür Öğret, who all read drafts and provided commentary and insight. I'd also like to acknowledge the guidance and support of my predecessors as executive director: Anne Nelson, Bill Orme, and particularly Ann Cooper, who provided encouragement, support, and detailed feedback on various drafts.

During my time at CPJ, I have had the opportunity to work closely with four different board chairman, Gene Roberts, Dave Laventhol, Paul Steiger, and Sandy Rowe. All provided outstanding leadership, and they taught me from their own perspective what journalism means and why it matters. The support of CPJ's board of directors allowed me to explore the complex issues raised in this book. I benefited tremendously from debates and discussions at board meeting, over coffee, or while carrying out CPJ missions. I would like to recognize those board members who contributed directly to this project either by agreeing to be interviewed or by sharing insights and expertise, including Michael Massing, Sheila Coronel, Dave Marash, Jim Goodale, Franz Allina, Kati Marton, Josh Friedman, Rebecca MacKinnon, Rajiv Chandrasekeran, Clarence Page, Anne Garrels, Victor Navasky, and Jacob Weisberg.

Others members of the CPJ extended family who provided insights and support include Aryeh Neier, David Rohde, Eric Newton, Joel Campagna, Michael Shifter, Danny O'Brien, and Dan Gillmor. And I'm forever indebted to friends and colleagues who read chapters and provided feedback, including Andy Blauvelt, Lee Bollinger, Daniel Dombey, Nisid Hajari, Jonathan Lethem, Colum Lynch, Peter Noorlander, Eric Siblin, and Jon Williams. Finally I'd like to offer a huge thanks to Greg Fay, my research assistant on this book, who went beyond the call of duty over and over.

No one could ask for a more committed and dedicated agent than Richard Parks. I'm grateful to my editor, Philip Leventhal, who directed me with clarity and focus through various rounds of revision, and his colleagues at Columbia University Press.

Inevitably, this book was written on the fly in hotel rooms, airplanes, trains, coffee shops, and hotel lobbies. This is why I am particularly grateful to those who provided some stability and quiet time for writing and reflecting. They include Arlene Abramovitch (Montreal and Bretton Woods, New Hampshire); Jerry and Marcia Simon (Ashland, Oregon), and Barbara Simon (Los Angeles). I am also grateful to the writer-in-residence program at the Ace Hotel.

The last— and most profound—thank-you must go to my family: my amazing daughters, Ruby and Lola, and my wife, Ingrid Abramovitch. Ingrid contributed as an editor and a cheerleader, insisting always that I push on and never succumb to doubt or self-pity. This book would not have been possible without her love and support, and that is why it is dedicated to her.

THE NEW CENSORSHIP

INTRODUCTION
A Murder in Pakistan

We arrived in Pakistan's capital, Islamabad, on May 1, 2011, two days in advance of our scheduled meeting with President Asif Ali Zardari. Bob Dietz, a veteran journalist who had covered wars in Somalia and Lebanon and edited a magazine in Hong Kong before becoming the Asia program coordinator at the Committee to Protect Journalists, had done the advance work, arranging our schedule and preparing our agenda. Paul Steiger and I were the other members of the team. Steiger was the managing editor at the *Wall Street Journal* in 2001 when the reporter Daniel Pearl was kidnapped and killed in Pakistan. It was this terrible experience that led Steiger to become involved in the fight for global press freedom and eventually to become the chairman of CPJ. In May 2007, Steiger stepped down from the *Journal* and started up an innovative media nonprofit called ProPublica, which is dedicated to carrying out investigative journalism in the public interest. We hoped to capitalize on Steiger's personal history to shame the Pakistani authorities into action.[1]

While intensive international pressure had led to the arrest and conviction of several people involved in the Pearl killing, fifteen journalists had been murdered subsequently, all of them Pakistani. No convictions had been obtained in any of those cases. In order to reinforce this point, we had compiled a report on those murdered that we had provocatively labeled "A Dossier of Death."[2] Our plan was to deliver it directly to the president and secure from him a public commitment to investigate the crimes fully.

All of our careful planning was thrown into disarray when we awoke on May 2 to a huge global news story: A commando unit of Navy SEALs had infiltrated Pakistan and carried out a daring raid that killed Osama bin Laden. While we were not in Pakistan to cover the bin Laden raid, being in the midst of the one of the biggest global news stories in recent history gave me a fascinating window into the way our evolving system of global information functions.

Overnight, a Pakistani engineer in Abbottabad—the garrison town where bin Laden had holed up with his wives and children—had sent out a curious tweet about a helicopter crash at a compound on the outskirts of town. Much was made of the fact that the story of the bin Laden raid had broken on Twitter, but this was highly misleading. Without context the one tweet was essentially meaningless. It was only when Pakistani journalists arrived on the scene that information began to flow. Pakistan has several vibrant and powerful cable news channels. Amid the burning wreckage of the downed helicopter, I watched breathless correspondents deliver standups in Urdu. Occasionally, tidbits of information in English would appear on the crawl at the bottom of the screen.

As the morning progressed our hotel began to fill with international journalists making their way to Abbottabad, which was described in initial international news reports as "just outside the capital of Islamabad" but was actually a two-hour drive away. The raid had clearly caught officials completely off guard, and in the disarray journalists swarmed the city, interviewing neighbors and climbing hillsides to take photos of bin Laden's compound and the remains of the crashed helicopter.

We also saw from our close-up vantage point how international media coverage distorted and misinterpreted the local reality, and this lack of clear information made it more difficult for us to make informed decisions about basic issues like our own security. The initial coverage suggested that throngs of Pakistanis were about to pour into the streets to express their outrage and indignation over the U.S. raid and their support for bin Laden. Not surprisingly, we received flurries of e-mails from home suggesting that as foreigners we were in imminent danger and should hightail it out of town.

But by working our contacts in the Pakistani media we were quickly able to discern that street protests were unlikely. Such protests are not generally spontaneous outpourings but are organized by political parties, factions, or religious groups who mobilize their supporters. The political environment was not conducive to such mobilizations at a time when most of the public anger was directed not toward the United States but toward the Pakistani military and intelligence establishment that had been humiliated by the raid. While the streets of Islamabad were in fact empty, the international cable networks I watched from my hotel room used images of a small public protest in Karachi on heavy rotation. When I visited Karachi a few days later, a friend and journalist who lives there took me on a sightseeing tour of the city. He was dismissive of the media portrayal. "There are protests in Karachi every day," he told me.

The Pakistani government's strategy, meanwhile, was to project an atmosphere of business as usual. So our May 3 meeting with President Zardari was reconfirmed. The pressing desire for normalcy was highlighted by our hotel restaurant, which went ahead with its scheduled "Mexican night," featuring tacos and enchiladas—but not Coronas, this being Pakistan.

The role of Pakistani journalists in covering the bin Laden story reinforced the importance of our presidential meeting because it gave us a close-up view of their absolutely critical role. Pakistani journalists were the first to record the dramatic events in Abbottabad, and Pakistani reporters, after the deluge of foreign correspondents had gone home, were left to report on subsequent developments, to analyze and agitate, and to interpret Pakistan for a global audience. This was not to say that the Pakistani media is exemplary—far from it. The press features plenty of rumor mongering, shoddy reporting, drivel, and craven attacks orchestrated by political forces. But at least the information was flowing, debate was raging, and powerful institutions that had escaped criticism were facing heightened scrutiny. Pakistani journalists recognized just how vulnerable they were in this environment. Several prominent media figures had called the president on our behalf to lobby for our meeting. We owed it to them to extract as much as we could.

The next morning at the appointed hour we climbed into a rented Toyota Land Cruiser and drove all of five minutes through silent streets lined with the usual barricades and police checkpoints. At the presidential palace, we were escorted into a large reception area and from there into the formal receiving room where chairs had been lined up in two facing rows. The government delegation, consisting of the interior minister, the information minister, and a number of other advisors, filed in and took their seats on one side. We sat opposite.

President Zardari entered and sat in a raised chair placed between the two rows. Steiger introduced our delegation and spoke about the comfort he took from the vigorous investigation that the Pakistani authorities had carried out into the killing of Danny Pearl. While making clear that many suspects in that case remained at large, Steiger contrasted the response to the Pearl killing with the complete lack of investigation into the murders of fifteen Pakistani journalists killed subsequently, all of them local reporters. Dietz handed the president the "Dossier of Death" report, which reinforced our point that Pakistan not only was one of the most deadly countries in the world for the media but also had one of the world's worst records for bringing the murderers of journalists to justice. These two facts were linked, because the failure to solve previous crimes perpetuated the climate of violence.

The president seemed surprised, and over the course of our meeting he spoke about the considerable challenges that Pakistan faces— from the lack of resources to the ongoing threat of terrorism. Zardari asked us what other countries confronting violence against journalists had done. I told him that a firm commitment from the country's leadership was a prerequisite to addressing the issue and spoke specifically about Colombia and Brazil, two countries in Latin America that had made progress in achieving convictions.[3] The president responded by asking Interior Minister Rehman Malik to provide us with detailed information on the status of the outstanding cases. He also asked his cabinet members to work with parliament to develop new legislation to strengthen press freedom. The president then shook hands and quickly left the meeting.

The commitment from the head of state was significant, although we were well aware that Zardari was politically isolated and that real power in Pakistan rests with the military and the shadowy Inter-Services Intelligence, or ISI. Complicating our efforts was the fact that the ISI is alleged to have been involved in a number of targeted attacks on the media, including the December 2005 kidnapping and murder of Hayatullah Khan. Khan, a photographer, writer, and stringer for a number of international news organizations, was abducted in North Waziristan after taking photos showing fragments of a U.S.-made Hellfire missile used to kill the al-Qaeda militant Hamza Rabia. The photo and the story Khan published along with it contradicted the official Pakistani government explanation that Rabia had died when a bomb he was building in his house exploded.[4]

A few days after our meeting with President Zardari, I traveled to Lahore to visit my friends Najam Sethi and Jugnu Mohsin, two of Pakistan's best-known journalists. They were living under threat of death, and their elegant brick home had become a virtual fortress surrounded by armed guards.[5] Despite this, I found them in a state of high excitement. Sethi had flown in that afternoon from Islamabad, where he and eighteen television news anchors had been given a briefing by the top military brass, including the army chief of staff General Ashfaq Parvez Kayani and Lt. Gen Ahmed Shuja Pasha, then head of the ISI (Pasha retired in March 2012, and Kayani retired in November 2013). Shockingly, Sethi recounted, the generals first heard about the U.S. raid when a journalist from the national cable broadcaster GEO TV called the ISI to find out if one of their helicopters had crashed in Abbottabad. ISI officials then called the army, and only when they both realized that the helicopter did not belong to either of them did they deploy troops to the scene. By that time the U.S. ground operation was over. The Pakistani air force scrambled fighter jets with an order to attack the intruders, but the Americans made it back across the border into Afghanistan.

For Sethi, the fact that top generals were compelled to explain themselves to the Pakistani media was an unprecedented and welcome development. The generals invited the nation's top anchors for a sit-down because in the aftermath of the bin Laden killing they had completely lost control of the country's information agenda. The nationalist commentators were attacking the military and the ISI as incompetent for failing to defend the country's sovereignty against the

U.S. invasion. They were calling for commissions of inquiry, questioning the military budget, and intimating that Pasha and Kayani should step down. Sethi's criticism was different. He believed that the government's policy of supporting militant groups, including the Taliban, was wrongheaded and detrimental to Pakistan's national interest. His personal anger focused on the fact that bin Laden was living comfortably in a military garrison town with apparent high-level protection.

Sethi and Mohsin had begun their journalism careers as editor and publisher (and founders) of the *Friday Times*, a leading English-language weekly aimed squarely at the country's intellectual elite. The paper had earned a respectable circulation and was read and discussed by the top political and military leaders as well as by the business and diplomatic communities, but to Sethi's great disappointment its political influence was limited. In 2002, the former Pakistani president Pervez Musharraf liberalized ownership rules for cable television channels, partly as a political move to counter the influence and popularity of Indian satellite channels that were widely available in Pakistan. The result was an explosion of television news channels across the country. Sethi was invited to host an interview and opinion program, and his television show gave him visibility, reach, and influence that he had never previously enjoyed.

Sethi's sense of being able to influence the national debate was amplified in the aftermath of the bin Laden killing when, for the first time in recent memory and perhaps ever, the press turned on the military and the ISI, demanding accountability. But while the generals were providing an unprecedented level of access, they were also sending a strong and ominous message about the limits of acceptable criticism. Pakistani journalists are routinely summoned to have "tea" with ISI officials, who criticize their reporting while simultaneously warning them of threats. In the aftermath of the bin Laden raid, the frequency and stridency of the meetings increased. The clear message was that the media had crossed the line and that their continued impertinence would not be tolerated.

On May 29, two weeks after the CPJ delegation left Pakistan, the journalist Saleem Shahzad was intercepted on the streets of Islamabad while on his way to a television interview. Shahzad, forty, was a veteran reporter who had started on the crime beat in Karachi in the 1990s working for the daily *Star* and later branched out into coverage of political and military issues. He was abducted a few days after his report was published on the website *Asia Online* detailing how al-Qaeda had infiltrated Pakistan's navy. After its double agents were exposed, al-Qaeda carried out a reprisal attack on May 17 against a highly secure naval base in Karachi that left ten dead and destroyed two surveillance planes purchased from the United States. Shahzad had also recently published a book on the militant networks and their links to the ISI, *Inside al-Qaeda and the Taliban*. Following an October 17 meeting with ISI officials in which he was threatened, Shahzad sent an e-mail to Human Rights Watch Pakistan director Ali Dayan Hasan to be made public in the case of his death.

Shahzad's body was recovered on May 30 in a drainage canal about two hours outside of Islamabad. He had been beaten to death. His liver was ruptured, and he had suffered two broken ribs. Widespread suspicion that he was abducted and killed by the ISI was confirmed by an unnamed U.S. official who told the *New York Times*, "This was a deliberate, targeted killing that was most likely meant to send shock waves through Pakistan's journalist community and civil society." According to Dexter Filkins, writing in the *New Yorker*, the order to kill Shahzad came from a senior officer on General Kayani's staff. The ISI denied any involvement, calling Shahzad's murder "unfortunate and tragic" but noting ominously that it should not be "used to target and malign the country's security agency."[6]

Over the next few weeks, several other prominent journalists were threatened and forced to leave the country.[7] Sethi, who had already been warned by the ISI that he was under threat, obtained specific evidence of a conspiracy to kill him involving the banned militant group Lakshi-e-Taiba, which had close ties to elements in the ISI. In August 2011, Sethi accepted a three-month appointment as a senior advisor with the New America Foundation, and he and Mohsin moved to Washington, D.C. There was no follow-up on the commitments from President Zardari, and we never heard more from Rehman Malik's office about the investigations into journalists' killings. The message the ISI seemed to be sending was that no amount of international and domestic outcry would deter them in their efforts to ensure that the media stayed within the boundaries it had drawn for acceptable criticism.[8]

I took the murder of Saleem Shahzad very personally because I felt his killing was the ISI's answer to our efforts to stand up for Pakistani journalists and keep them safe. It made me feel angry and helpless.

The efforts to control the news in the aftermath of the bin Laden killing also highlighted the complexity and vulnerability of the system of global information that has evolved in the Internet age. Yes, the Internet has spawned an unprecedented transformation in the way that global news is gathered and disseminated, and it has immensely facilitated certain kinds of reporting, specifically of protests and demonstrations, which are now routinely documented through social media. But the bin Laden raid, despite the excitement about the initial tweet from Abbottabad, was not reported on social media. It was covered the old-fashioned way by reporters on the ground who provided both firsthand accounts and informed analysis based on years of experience and deep contacts.

Journalists covering frontline stories are routinely murdered not just in Pakistan but in Russia and the Philippines.

Despite the communication revolution spawned by technology, collective access to the essential information we need in a globalized world to make informed decisions about our lives and our future is by no means assured. State repression of the media is on the rise, though often hidden behind a democratic façade. The Internet, which has obviously become the key piece of infrastructure in the global news system, is threatened by increasingly effective national censorship regimes in places like China and Iran and undermined by revelations of the unprecedented global surveillance effort carried by the U.S. National Security Agency.

Today we live in a world in which the old information order dominated by large and powerful media corporations has been upended, transformed by a new system in which technology has enabled individuals and loosely configured organizations to participate in the process of gathering and disseminating news on a global scale. The endless debate over which system is better is a massive distraction. The reality is that we live in a hybrid system in which the traditional media—local newspapers and radio, national broadcasters, magazines and dailies, and powerful global media organizations—exist alongside new forms of communications, including citizen journalism, blogging, and even more informal information networks, such as person-to-person texting. Each plays a vital role. The traditional media is certainly diminished, but it remains essential to bringing information to a mass audience. Meanwhile, precisely because there are fewer international correspondents, the frontline newsgatherers are increasingly freelancers, local journalists working in their own country, human rights activists, and average people with cell phones. It's not an either/or scenario, and it's not necessarily a pretty picture. But the reality is that we depend on the ability of both the old and new systems to operate simultaneously and interact with each other to deliver the news we need. The current system is jury-rigged and fragile, and the challenge of ensuring that access to global information is strengthened and expanded is exacerbated by the fact that the system continues to evolve.

The New Censorship describes this emerging global information order, analyzes threats, and proposes steps that need to be taken to keep the vital flow of information open. My goal is not to predict the future of the media (although I try to do it briefly in chapter 9) or to fit the current messy reality into some neat paradigm. Rather, I seek to describe the system as it exists today, identify the challenges, and outline the strategies that we can employ to meet them. We need to fight both to keep the Internet open and to ensure justice for journalists who are killed. We need to deploy new technologies to help people in repressive societies circumvent censorship and fight to get imprisoned journalists out of jail. More broadly, we need a robust international framework that recognizes the crucial role that information plays in the new global order and provides redress for people everywhere who are unable to access the information to which they are legally entitled.

Independent media of one form or another has played a critical role in many of the seminal events of the last half-century: the collapse of the Soviet Union, the restoration of democracy in Latin America, the economic transformation of Asia, and recent Arab uprisings. But in today's globalized, interconnected world, free and unfettered information is more essential than ever. It's essential for markets and for trade. And it's essential to empowering the emerging community of global citizens and ensuring that they are able to participate in a meaningful way in the decisions that affect their lives. Likewise, those who are deprived of information are essentially disempowered. We live in a world in which the abundance of information obscures the enormous gaps in our knowledge created by violence, repression, and state censorship. Ensuring that news and information circulate freely throughout societies and across borders is the challenge of our time.

~~ONE~~

~~Informing the Global Citizen~~

Throughout the 150-year history of the International Committee of the Red Cross (ICRC), the Geneva-based humanitarian organization that helps to alleviate the suffering of war has relied on journalists to serve as its eyes and ears on the frontlines. In providing firsthand accounts of wars and humanitarian emergencies, journalists have often risked their lives—and sometimes died—because they believed that their reporting would lead to action. Sometimes, a single image refocused global priorities, like the footage of emaciated Bosnian refugees filmed by an ITN television crew in 1992 or the Pulitzer Prize–winning photo of a vulture hovering near a starving child by the South African photographer Kevin Carter in a Sudanese refugee camp in 1993. From Central America to South Africa, over the last few decades journalists have helped set the humanitarian agenda.

And so it came as something of a shock when Yves Daccord, the director general of the ICRC, took the floor at a press freedom conference in Doha, Qatar, sponsored by the pan-Arab network al-Jazeera and, pointing to his iPhone, declared, "Nothing has changed our work more than this. The time when we had to wait for journalists to tell us what was going on is over. I have information. There is noise everywhere."

Daccord cited the civil war in Syria, where citizen-journalists and "media activists" aligned with rebel factions have used smart phones to document atrocities committed by the Syrian military. He also talked about the violence in the eastern Congo, a perennial battleground where the still-simmering conflict goes largely uncovered by the international press. As Daccord noted, international human rights organizations—not journalists—have provided the frontline documentation of that war.

Reduced budgets for international news organizations mean that journalists are too often absent from the frontlines of conflict. Daccord argued they are still desperately needed. While he is overwhelmed with information, Daccord struggles to understand its implications and formulate responses. "Where is the context?" he asked. "Journalists need to be closer. Armed groups understand that—and they don't want journalists to be closer."

Daccord's remarks served as a clear reminder that while professional journalists working for established media organizations continue to play a vital role, they are today just one element in a much larger and more complex media ecosystem. This is true in conflict zones, but it is also true in every corner of the world and on every major story. Journalists today amplify, contextualize, and synthesize information. But firsthand documentation is increasingly accomplished by anyone with a smartphone, including average citizens, bloggers, and activists.

Daccord, of course, is a special case because the work of the ICRC depends on its ability to access accurate and timely information from conflict zones. Yet we all have a stake in ensuring the free flow of global information because to a greater or lesser extent we are all global citizens whose well-being depends on policies and actions taken outside our countries. Information in all its forms is the engine of the global economy. It is what connects us across borders. It is what allows us to forge solutions to international challenges from global warming, to AIDS, to economic development.

Twenty years ago, most people got their international news from relatively well-established foreign correspondents working for agencies, broadcast outlets, and newspapers. Today, of course, the process of both gathering and disseminating news is more diffuse. This new system has some widely recognized advantages. It democratizes the information-gathering process, allowing participation by more people from different backgrounds and perspectives. It opens the media not only to "citizen journalists" but also to advocacy and civil society organizations including human rights groups that increasingly provide firsthand reporting in war-ravaged societies. New information technologies allow those involved in collecting news to communicate directly with those accessing the information. The sheer volume of people participating in this process challenges authoritarian models of censorship based on hierarchies of control.

But there are also considerable weaknesses. Freelancers, bloggers, and citizen journalists who work with few resources and little or no institutional support are more vulnerable to government repression. Emerging technologies cut both ways, and autocratic governments are developing new systems to monitor and control online speech that are both effective and hard to detect. The direct links created between content producers and consumers make it possible for violent groups to bypass the traditional media and reach the public via chat rooms and websites. Journalists have become less essential and therefore more vulnerable as a result. This is a subject that is explored in chapter 3, which examines the effects of terrorism on the press.

Many predicted that the quantity, quality, and fluidity of information would inherently increase as time went on and technology improved, but this has not necessarily been the case. While mass censorship has become more difficult, new and highly effective models of repression have emerged in response to the rapid changes in the way news and information is gathered and delivered. Statistics indicate that even as information technologies have proliferated, the situation for journalists on the ground has gotten worse, not better. The number of journalists killed and imprisoned around the world has reached record levels in recent years and, according to several studies, press freedom is in decline. At the beginning of December 2012, there were 232 journalists in jail according to CPJ research, the highest tally ever recorded.[1] While historically repressive countries like Iran and China contributed to the upsurge in imprisonment, the world's leading jailer of journalists was Turkey, a country with a relatively open media and aspirations to join the European Union. Most of those jailed were being held on antistate charges, and over half of all journalists in jail around the world worked online, including a majority of those imprisoned in China.

In 2012, seventy journalists were killed while carrying out their work; this is close to the record highs recorded at the peak of the

Iraq war.[2] The Syrian conflict has proved devastating for the press, with twenty-eight journalists killed in a single year.[3] The tally once again reinforced the hybrid nature of frontline newsgathering, with high casualties among both established international media organizations and citizen journalists. Two renowned war correspondents, Marie Colvin of the *Sunday Times* and the French photographer Rémi Ochlik, were killed when their improvised media center in Homs was targeted by Syrian forces in February 2011. Meanwhile, at least thirteen citizen journalists who reported on the conflict from an activist perspective and provided devastating video images of the carnage and savagery of war also perished, some at the hands of Syrian government snipers.

The leading historical press freedom index compiled by Freedom House, based in Washington D.C., shows that global press freedom has waned in recent years.[4] "After two decades of progress, press freedom is now in decline in almost every part of the world," Freedom House noted in its 2011 *Freedom of the Press Index*, which tracks the state of media freedom in over 190 countries and has been published since 1980. "Only 15 percent of the world's citizens live in countries that enjoy a free press."

Covering Mexico in the 1990s

How did we get here? Why has it become more dangerous for journalists and other information providers even as technology has made it easier to communicate and access information across borders? This chapter seeks to answer these questions.

The best place to start is to look at the way international correspondents operated twenty years ago, at the dawn of the Internet revolution. While each country and each situation is different, my own experience as a freelance correspondent covering Mexico in the 1990s gives some insight into how the process worked.

I started my work as a journalist as a graduate student in Latin American studies at Stanford University. While carrying out research in Mexico and Guatemala on the voluntary repatriation of Guatemalan refugees to a country still ravaged by war, I would send occasional dispatches to newspapers and wire services like the *San Francisco Chronicle* and Pacific News Service. After completing my graduate work, I lined up some more regular journalism strings and moved to Mexico City full time to cover the debate over the North American Free Trade Agreement, or NAFTA. The Internet existed but was not an important part of my life.

In the early 1990s, Mexico City was a sought-after posting for international reporters, and there were dozens of correspondents representing everyone from the BBC to the American broadcast networks; wire services ranging from the Chinese Xinhua to the Italian ANSA; national dailies like the *Guardian* and *El Pais*; and local and regional newspapers like the *Baltimore Sun* and the *Sacramento Bee*. We reported the news by interviewing government officials, analysts, and people in the street; we traveled from dusty small towns to the urban slums; we covered the collapse of the Mexican peso and the Zapatista uprising. Nearly all of our reporting was done face to face. Phone interviews were unusual. Most sources did not trust the phones and were reluctant to discuss matters that were remotely sensitive. We sometimes still filed our stories by dictation. We also used fax machines, later modems, and finally e-mail, which was often balky and erratic.

An important part of our job was to read carefully the Mexican press each day (we would watch TV as well, but the national broadcasters at the time were largely mouthpieces for the government). We relied on the Mexican media to track national developments, spot stories and trends, and compare perspectives. Occasionally, an international correspondent would break a major story not covered in the domestic media, but much of our daily coverage was derived from Mexican media reports. When we traveled to a provincial city, we would often seek out a journalist from the local newspaper and ask for a briefing and introductions to officials. Usually such arrangements were informal, but sometimes we hired local reporters as stringers and essentially paid them to be our guides. Some of the reporters who helped us were threatened as a result. Indeed, my awareness of the risks that these local journalists took on our behalf is one of the reasons I took a job as the Americas program coordinator at the Committee to Protect Journalists, where I began in 1997.

For the most part, the dozens of international journalists based in Mexico City covered the same stories in largely the same way. Foreign editors often asked their correspondents to "match" what the wires were doing or follow up on a particularly compelling story published in a rival publication. Some reporters were more connected and more entrepreneurial than others. Some were better interviewers or more stylish writers. But in the end most of us made a living not necessarily by differentiating our coverage but by tailoring it to local markets. As a freelancer, I always sought new angles and new perspectives, particularly the perspectives of average people, including slum dwellers, small farmers, factory workers, and activists. That kind of reporting took time, which was my competitive advantage since I did not have daily filing deadlines. I am amused to recall that I was able to sell the same story (or a slight variant) to multiple newspapers. This was done with the full knowledge of the foreign editors at places like the *Fort Worth Star-Telegram*, the *San Francisco Chronicle*, the *Detroit Free Press*, and the *Toronto Globe and Mail*, who all told me that I was free to repackage the material for "another market." While the editors were reading the wires, in the pre-Internet era I did not have direct access to the work of my competitors. I learned what my colleagues had been up to at the Friday "cantina night," at which several dozen foreign correspondents would regularly gather. If I wanted to read their stories, I had to go to a local coffee shop called Sanborns that stocked international magazines and newspapers. I spent hours doing this each weekend despite the fact that everything was between a few days and a few weeks out of date.

Like a lot of businesses, freelance journalism was "disrupted" by the Internet. By the end of the decade, the *San Francisco Chronicle* and the *Fort Worth Star-Telegram* were no longer in separate markets. When it came to national and international news they were competing not only with each other but also with the *New York Times*, the *Wall Street Journal*, and the BBC and any other news website accessible over the Internet. This undermined the value not only of freelancers but also of the full-time correspondents employed by second-tier U.S. newspapers like the *Boston Globe* and *Newsday*. Some of the journalists who worked for these publications were extraordinarily talented, but their positions were expendable once readers were able to use the Internet to obtain easy access to national and international news organizations with more correspondents and more resources. This made closing the bureaus an easy call, particularly as the same technological forces that suddenly forced regional newspapers to compete against one another also ravaged their economic model, with advertising migrating online and circulation plummeting.

The role that international correspondents in Mexico City played as a conduit for the Mexican media also become less essential as interested readers gained the ability to access the websites of local newspapers like *La Jornada* or *Reforma* directly through the Internet. Of course, this was before Google Translate, so Spanish-language skills were required.

The trend of closing and consolidating bureaus in Mexico City accelerated after the 9/11 terror attacks, when news organizations retooled to cover the wars in Afghanistan and Iraq. Today Mexico remains a vital global story, but there are far fewer international correspondents operating in the country. Those international reporters who are left continue to play a vital role by covering sensitive stories that might be too dangerous for local journalists, particularly on drug trafficking. They are also generally able to report with greater independence and to provide specialized context that make their stories more appealing and accessible to their readers, viewers, and listeners.

While the decline in foreign correspondents in Mexico and in so many other countries around the world is in many ways lamentable, it also must be acknowledged that the Internet exposed some of the inefficiencies of the old structure, in which dozens of reporters filing for different media outlets essentially produced the same story. Certainly, informed and committed observers of Mexico can go online and find infinitely more information than I could access as a correspondent covering the country in the 1990s. Does that mean people are better informed? It depends. If information were apples, then the role of international journalists back in the 1990s was to select the best fruit and "export" them to the international market. Now, using the Internet, international news consumers can buy wholesale. They have access to more information, but they also must sort through it on their own, deciding what is most important and most useful. What has changed is the marketing and distribution systems. But much of the information about Mexico that the world needs is still produced by local journalists on the ground. Their role in the new international media ecosystem is therefore even more crucial.

Keeping It Local in Iraq

There was another reason that local journalists took on a more direct role in informing the global public, and that was safety. In Iraq, the risk of specific targeted attacks on international journalists became so great that at the height of the violence many well-staffed international bureaus in Baghdad were forced to rely on Iraqi journalists to carry out nearly all street reporting. These reporters became the eyes and ears of the world; they also paid a terrible price in blood.

Initially, the U.S.-led invasion of Iraq in 2003 was covered almost exclusively by international media. The Iraqi media under Saddam was one of the most censored and controlled in the world, and there was virtually no independent information inside the country. Seeking to facilitate coverage of the invasion from the perspective of the allied forces, the U.S. military established a program to "embed" journalists with the invading militaries. The idea was to give reporters frontline access to the combat operations but also to manage coverage of the war. In addition to the thousands of embedded journalists, several hundred "unilateral" reporters converged independently in Baghdad. They clustered in high-end hotels, like the Hamra and the Palestine. The Iraqi government tolerated them because it wanted journalists in Baghdad to help get its message of resistance and defiance out to the world. It also wanted Western journalists on the scene to document the collateral damage from U.S. bombs. International journalists were accompanied everywhere by Iraqi government minders.

As the Saddam Hussein regime disintegrated, the system of minders and controls began to break down, and the journalists began to slip away. The two sets of reporters—the embeds who accompanied the U.S. military and the unilaterals who covered the war from Baghdad—converged on Firdos Square, just outside the Palestine Hotel, as the U.S. Marines rode triumphantly into Baghdad. But the concentration of international media did not necessarily produce an accurate portrait of events. The actions of the Marines and journalists on the ground in Firdos Square, amplified by editors in newsrooms in the United States, turned what was a relatively minor and ambiguous moment in the conflict, the toppling of the statue of Saddam Hussein, into a triumphalist image, according to an account by the journalist Peter Maas published in the *New Yorker*. Maas, who accompanied the Third Marine Battalion as it rolled into Baghdad, was technically a unilateral rather than an embedded reporter because he had made contact with the Marines after driving across the border from Kuwait in a rented car.[5]

In the immediate aftermath of Saddam's fall, international news organizations moved to a system of bureaus and journalists began to operate freely. During this brief period, they moved about the entire country, delving into areas of Iraqi life previously unexplored. "We entered Iraq during a fleeting golden age of modern war time journalism," recalled the *Washington Post* reporter Rajiv Chandrasekaran, who established the newspaper's bureau in Baghdad in April 2003.[6] "In the early weeks and months there were minimal security threats. You could put fuel in the tank, find a willing driver, and go anywhere. The biggest risk was getting into a car accident or being invited into someone's home and served tea, since drinking water was pumped directly from the Tigris. Journalists were seen as neutral, sympathetic figures and people were anxious to engage with us."

But there were ominous signs. On July 5, 2003, an Iraqi gunman approached the twenty-four-year old British freelance cameraman Richard Wild and shot him in the head as he was reporting outside Baghdad's natural history museum. The circumstances remain murky—it was unclear whether Wild was carrying a camera or whether he was working on a story about looting—and journalists in Baghdad paid the incident little heed, seeing it as just a random act.

But as the conflict intensified, so did violent attacks on the media. As Internet access expanded rapidly in Iraq, insurgent groups developed their own online information networks, relying on websites and local and regional news outlets to communicate externally and on chat rooms to engage with their supporters. These groups had little interest in influencing international public opinion but had a strong interest in disrupting the emerging civil society and consolidation of the American-backed government. Attacking journalists was an effective method for achieving this goal.

As journalists were kidnapped and in some cases executed, bureaus added fortifications, and journalists were forced to move around in armored vehicles accompanied in many cases by armed guards.

"In mid-2004, as Al-Qaeda elements began taking over leadership of the insurgency from the nationalist good old boys of the Baath party, things changed dramatically," Chandrasekaran recalled. "Journalists were no longer seen as neutral actors and people to talk to. Instead, they were people to apprehend and kidnap. The tenor of the interviews changed among those Iraqis not supportive of the American presence. People were less interested in talking, and harder to get a hold of. The interviews were far more uneasy. Journalists stopped talking to those people."

Because Western reporters could only move around in carefully planned operations, Iraqi reporters—many of whom were initially hired as translators and fixers—took over many of the frontline reporting activities. Unlike Westerners, they could disappear into the crowd, particularly at the scene of suicide attacks. When they went home, Iraqi journalists did their best to keep their profession a secret. But there were casualties. On September 19, 2005, the *New York Times* reporter Fakher Haider was seized from his home in the southern Iraqi city of Basra by men claiming to be police officers. His body, with a gunshot wound to the head, was recovered the next day. On December 12, 2006, the AP cameraman Aswan Ahmed Lutfallah was shot dead by an insurgent who spotted him filming clashes in Mosul.

The increased dependence by international media organizations on local Iraqis to carry out street reporting created challenges with the U.S. military, which was suspicious of Iraqis carrying cameras since the insurgents often sought to document their attacks. Accredited Iraqi reporters were regularly detained and accused of having ties to terrorists. Some were held for extended periods.

The effect of the violence on the coverage of the Iraq conflict is examined in chapter 3. But one point is clear: The violent censorship of the media carried out primarily by insurgent groups and sectarian militias had a devastating effect on the quality and quantity of information coming out of Iraq. Reporting on the nature and structure of militant and sectarian groups, their relationship to government security forces, the role of Iran in the insurgency, and the scope of government corruption were all vital—and underreported—stories. Despite the vast resources invested in covering Iraq, the strategy of imposing censorship through violence was extremely effective. More than 150 journalists and media workers were killed during the Iraq war, the highest number ever documented in a single conflict. Eighty-five percent of them were Iraqis.[7]

From Curated Search to Social Media

When I was a freelancer covering Mexico and Latin America, international news was "curated." This meant that if you were a news consumer outside the country, you had to rely on the judgment of the journalists on the ground and the editors who selected what stories to publish to stay informed. By the time the second Iraq war rolled around, people got their news in a different way: Search. Yes, they might read their local paper or watch the news from the BBC or CNN, but if they got interested in a particular story, they could use Google to dig deeper. A few keystrokes would direct them to the most detailed coverage of a specific incident or to an investigation or analyses that shed light on a certain aspect of the story.

By the time the Arab revolts broke out in January 2010 a new method of following international news had emerged: social media. Again, many people around the world watched the events unfold on television or read about them in their local newspapers. And as during the Iraq war, they used search engines to dig deeper. But social media—notably Twitter and Facebook—became the most efficient way to follow developments minute by minute and gain access not only to the perspectives of journalists but also eyewitnesses and informed observers. I followed developments in Egypt while sitting in my office in New York. I streamed al-Jazeera on my desktop while simultaneously monitoring Twitter. I followed the feeds of journalists that I knew were present in Tahrir Square. Their tweets led to bloggers and activists who were also on the scene. I was generally aware of every major development within minutes. Even though news websites were updated perhaps hourly, I turned to them the way people used to read weeklies like *Time* or *Newsweek*—not for breaking news but for context and analysis.

The evolution from curated to search to social media is tracked by Ethan Zuckerman in his 2013 book *Rewire: Digital Cosmopolitans in the Age of Connection.* One of the great benefits of using social media to share news is that it provides a forum for local journalists to bring specific stories and issues to the attention of a global audience. Plus, the same channels used to spread the news can also be used to defend the rights of the reporter who is subsequently threatened or put under pressure. Take the case of the Liberian journalist Mae Azango. In March 2012, Azango published a story entitled "Growing Pains" in *Front Page Africa*, a Liberian newspaper that also serves the large community of exiles through its active website.[8] The story blew the lid off a taboo subject in Liberia, female genital cutting. The practice is carried out by the secret Sande society, which is also a powerful political force in Liberia, particularly at election time. This is why the country's Nobel Prize–winning president Ellen Johnson Sirleaf was reluctant to stand up to the Sande and tackle the issue of cutting, which is practiced on an estimated 60 percent of Liberian girls. In her report, Azango interviewed a woman who described being held down by five women while her clitoris was cut out with an unsterilized knife. The account was brutal and shocking. Azango chronicled the health risks and social consequences of the practice, interviewing medical professionals. The story sparked a fierce debate in Liberia and in the exile community. But it also put Azango at risk. Death threats poured in, forcing Azango and her daughter into hiding.[9]

Neither Azango's original report nor the threats against her were covered by traditional media. What gave the story life were social media networks that helped spread the word. Once the threats emerged, this same network was mobilized. Eventually, the *New York Times* columnist Nick Kristof took up Azango's case and used his Twitter feed, which has over one million followers, to draw international attention that led to action. President Sirleaf, who had responded with seeming indifference, eventually agreed to provide physical protection for Azango. As a result of the international attention, she also took steps to challenge the Sande, and her government imposed a temporary ban on genital cutting while it studied the issue.

While social media has had a profound effect on news consumers and journalists, it has also changed the way governments manage information. Activists celebrated when the effort of Egypt's President Hosni Mubarak to control information during the Tahrir Square revolt failed, and he was eventually toppled. But governments around the world learned a different lesson from those events. Recognizing the threat posed by new information networks, they began cracking down on online speech. The battle to control online communication is the focus of chapter 5, which looks closely at China's information policies. While some countries seek to hide their repressive policies beyond a façade of democracy, China is quite public about its efforts and takes pride in its ability to monitor and censor information online—and no wonder. With more than 564 million Internet users at the end of 2012, China has more people online than any other country.[10] Many are highly active on social media.

The Chinese government has developed strategies combining traditional forms of repression with high-tech techniques, like using software to filter out prohibited content. Newsgatherers in China face myriad restrictions. Foreign reporters are often unable to obtain visas to enter the country, and those based in China are sometimes blocked from traveling to certain areas, notably Tibet. Photographers often find their work obstructed by security forces, particularly when documenting demonstrations. Chinese employees of international newsgathering operations face constant monitoring and government pressure. International human rights organizations are for the most part unable to operate inside mainland China. Meanwhile, Chinese journalists working for the domestic media must follow regular government directives on what to cover and not cover. Failure to follow these guidelines is likely to result in dismissal or worse.

While dissident journalists in China face the possibility of arrest and imprisonment, CPJ research suggests that the number of journalists imprisoned has not increased in recent years and stood at thirty-two at the end of 2012.[11] Given the size of China's population—and the size of its press corps—imprisonment is clearly not the preferred strategy. In fact, most of those imprisoned are not traditional journalists but online dissidents and activists who straddle the line between journalism and activism.

The real threat as China sees it is the way in which the growing number of people who use social media share information and links. The program of domestic monitoring—using electronic surveillance and tens of thousands of paid government supporters who patrol chat rooms and read posts—has been expanded.[12] Filtering has become more pervasive and effective. But China's ultimate goal is to transform the current structure of the Internet, converting it from a decentralized global system to one in which national governments exercise effective control. If China succeeds in its efforts, the Internet as we know it would come to an end.

Quality Control

The ability of governments to manage, control, and manipulate information undermines the creation of a global civic culture and shields powerful institutions from public accountability. When Pakistan's government suppresses coverage of its military and intelligence operations, when China censors reports about food safety, and when Syria completely blocks access to international reporters, they are not only censoring within their own national borders. They are censoring news and information critical to people in many parts of the world. Without adequate information, global citizens are essentially disempowered. While the right of people everywhere to "seek and receive information through any media and regardless of frontiers" is enshrined in Article 19 of the Universal Declaration of Human Rights and other international legal instruments, the reality is that there are few effective means to fight back against censorship on an international level.

While the lack of institutional and legal protections is troubling, it is hardly surprising that governments would seek to censor and control information. But what happens if the media itself is doing the censoring? This is unquestionably a significant issue. In many countries around the world, the media is not independent. It is partisan, biased, corrupt, and irresponsible. It is beholden to powerful corporate interests, in some cases governments, in other cases opposition forces. These deficiencies in the global media structure provide a critical backdrop for much of the analysis in this book, but they are not the focus. While the quality of information clearly matters, the imperative in the current environment is to ensure that information of all kinds continues to flow within national boundaries and across borders. Governments, militants, and other enemies of freedom of expression cannot be allowed to restrict the flow of international news.

Poor media performance, while lamentable, is not a violation of international law. Article 19 guarantees the right of all people to express their ideas and prevents governments from prohibiting their expression. It does not guarantee that the ideas ultimately expressed will be thoughtful, considered, or responsible.

Clearly, journalists and media organizations should produce ethical, responsible journalism that serves the public interest. This is always the goal. But based on my experience as the executive director of the Committee to Protect Journalists, I am reluctant to combine the defense of freedom of expression with a discussion of strategies for improving the quality of information. This is because too often I have seen governments justify restrictions on freedom of expression or the press by arguing that certain kinds of information are harmful or destabilizing or that the media is biased, irresponsible, or beholden to "foreign" interests. I remember a debate with the Venezuelan ambassador to the United States, who argued that his government should use its authority to ensure that all news presented to the public was "truthful." One can acknowledge that the performance of the Venezuelan media has at times been woeful while still recognizing that this is a terrible idea.

I can remember another meeting I had with the interior minister of the Gambia, a tiny sliver of a country in West Africa where journalists have faced persecution and restrictions. He argued that government intervention was necessary because the Gambian media was reckless and irresponsible. My counterargument is that the media is generally no more biased, underdeveloped, or polarized than the rest of the society and that expecting the media to rise above all other institutions is unrealistic and unfair. Journalists everywhere too often fail in their responsibility to inform the public, to hold governments to account, and always to seek the truth. But such failures should never be used to justify legal action, control, or censorship. There are of course legitimate limits on freedom of expression in an international and domestic context. Incitement to violence is never protected, there must be legal redress available for libel and slander, and governments may take certain legally prescribed measures to limit speech to safeguard national security. There are also valid critiques of the media in nearly every country in the world. The U.S. media is dominated by corporate interests. The British media is distorted by invasive and scandal-mongering tabloids. Elements of the Pakistani media are infiltrated by state security agencies. The Turkish media is dominated by business interests beholden to the government. The Mexican media has been partially corrupted by trafficking organizations. Governments can help address these issues by supporting media development and investing in journalism education; they can take steps to end cronyism and break up monopolies. But a prerequisite for any government efforts to improve the quality of information available to the public must be a clear and unequivocal embrace of the full range of freedom of expression guaranteed under international law. Without such a commitment, governments in my experience that point to the media's shortcomings are looking to exploit them to justify restrictions rather than to ensure that people have access to timely and accurate information. Under international law, governments do not have the authority to restrict information because it is "biased," "false," or offensive, disruptive, or destabilizing. This is the essence of free expression.

Covering Mexico Today

While the work of the Committee to Protect Journalists is global, I maintain an intense interest in Mexico for both personal and professional reasons. I also make it a point to check in with my friends in the Mexican press whenever I can, especially those who are in danger as a result of their work. So when I attended a media conference in San Diego in April 2011, I took off one afternoon to cross the border to Tijuana and visit with Adela Navarro Bello, the editor of the weekly *Zeta*.[13]

Violence and murder are the primary means for controlling the news in Mexico. The dynamics are very different from Iraq, but like the insurgents there, Mexican drug cartels have targeted traditional journalists while using alternative means including social media to communicate with one another and the public. Of course the message they generally want to send is one of fear. Cartels now routinely post gruesome execution videos to blogs and social media sites, including a notorious example featuring decapitation by chainsaw. An estimated fifty thousand Mexicans have been killed or have disappeared in the ongoing drug wars.[14] Dozens of reporters have been murdered, and whole areas of the country are essentially off limits to probing media, particularly along the U.S.-Mexico border.

When I was a reporter working in Mexico, *Zeta* was always my first stop in Tijuana. Over the years, I'd seen how violence had devastated the paper. In 1988, the columnist and *Zeta* cofounder Héctor Félix Miranda was gunned down by two employees of Jorge Hank Rhon, the scion of the prominent political family who was eventually elected mayor of Tijuana. In 1997, not long after I started at CPJ, the other founding editor, Jesús Blancornelas, was ambushed on his way to work by gunmen from the notorious Arellano Félix drug cartel. Blancornelas survived, but a bodyguard, Luis Valero, died trying to protect him. In 2003 another *Zeta* editor, Francisco Ortiz Franco, was murdered by an Arellano Félix cartel hit team. While returning from a doctor's visit, Ortiz Franco was shot through the window of his car as his two young children watched in horror from the back seat. I considered Ortiz Franco a friend, and in November 2004 my CPJ colleague Carlos Lauría and I published a detailed investigation into his murder.[15] Several of those involved in the killing were later arrested and sentenced to long prison terms in the United States on drug trafficking charges.

Blancornelas died of stomach cancer in 2006, and today *Zeta* is coedited by his son César René Blanco Villalón and Navarro Bello, a feisty and fearless reporter utterly devoted to the news. The paper is a tabloid and lives on scoops. Every Friday afternoon *Zeta* vendors snake through the streets of Tijuana hawking the latest edition. Most weeks, the paper sells around fifty thousand copies. When there's a good crime story, circulation doubles.

Tijuana is somewhat less violent than many other border cities, and when I met with Navarro Bello in the paper's fortress-like office she assured me that while the risks were real she also felt safe. But I was not reassured. Over many years of working with threatened journalists all over the world, I've found sadly that those who are most vulnerable are often least able to appreciate the danger. This is because of what I call the normalization of risk, a nonchalance that develops after years of living in an environment in which threats and violence are routine.

When I expressed some skepticism, Navarro Bello decided it would be helpful to give me a primer on the evolution of drug trafficking in Tijuana since the September 11, 2001, attacks on the United States. That date is not necessarily considered a milestone in Mexico. But in fact the attacks had a profound effect on the country because of actions taken by the U.S. government, which virtually shut down the border. Traffic crossing from Tijuana to San Diego ground to a halt. The shutdown badly disrupted the Tijuana economy, which is dependent on U.S. exports and tourism. It also devastated the cash flow of the drug cartels, which could no longer move large quantities of drugs through the border hidden in tractor trailers.

One might think this is a good thing, and in many ways it was. But it had enormous unintended consequences for Mexican society, consequences that continue to be felt today. The drug cartels had developed into major organizations with huge infrastructures and large payrolls. With the trafficking routes shut down, the cartels had to come up with another strategy to generate revenue. Using their idled "security units," they moved into extortion, kidnapping, and selling drugs inside Mexico. In essence, they morphed from trafficking organizations to criminal organizations along the lines of the mafia. And as they expanded into organized crime, the cartels were no longer satisfied with the control of a main road or border crossing. Instead, they sought to control entire territories and assert authority over key institutions ranging from municipal governments to the police and the media itself.

In fact, the cartels viewed control over the media as critical and developed elaborate strategies to manage newsrooms through bribes and threats. It was during this period that journalists started dying and disappearing and massive self-censorship among the media began to take hold. The killing of two reporters from *El Diario de Ciudad Juárez*—the veteran crime reporter Armando Rodríguez in November 2008 and a young photographer, Luis Carlos Santiago, in September 2010—prompted the newspaper to publish a front-page editorial asking the traffickers, "What do you want from us?" and declaring them to be the de facto authority in the city. The editorial garnered international headlines, but the editors from *Zeta* were appalled by what they saw as an effective surrender by *El Diario* to the will of the traffickers. Indeed, Navarro Bello believes that *Zeta's* willingness to stand up to the traffickers and pay the costs created a different dynamic in Tijuana, where despite the efforts of the cartels the city's civic culture never entirely disappeared.

While Adela Navarro is proud of the newspaper's role, she does not necessarily think it contributed directly to the decline in violence in Tijuana. She also does not give much credit to the city's celebrated but controversial former police chief, who claimed to reduce the crime rate through his aggressive tactics.[16] Instead, she credits the completion of massive smuggling tunnels under the border that allowed the drugs to move freely once again. By the late 2000s, dozens of tunnels were believed to be in operation in Tijuana (the U.S. government says it discovered twenty-eight tunnels along the entire border in 2008 alone).[17] In November 2010, U.S. federal investigators discovered two half-mile tunnels equipped with rails, carts, and lighting and ventilation systems that connected drug warehouses in Mexico and the United States.[18] Authorities said the tunnel was built and operated by the Sinaloa cartel, which had battled the Tijuana cartel for years.

Navarro Bello believes that the tunnels have been largely successful in helping the cartels reestablish trafficking routes, and because of this success the traffickers stopped fighting one another and increased cooperation. They went back to their main business and dialed back on kidnapping and extortion, which had declined in Tijuana. It is deeply ironic that Navarro felt safer as a result.

What started out as an attempt by Navarro Bello to assuage my worry about her safety had turned into a tutorial on the immense value that the paper provides to the people of Tijuana, and those around the world who care about what is happening there, simply by doing what journalists do best: covering their community with depth, nuance, and understanding. It is not necessarily the job of the media to solve problems, and indeed *Zeta* has certainly not solved the problem of drug trafficking or violent crime. *Zeta*'s role is to help the people of Tijuana understand the forces that affect their lives. Without this understanding no solutions are possible.

While the emerging generation of journalists and activists in places like Egypt, Iran, China, and Turkey has used new technologies to break through censorship and media control, Navarro Bello was less positive about their effect in Mexico. Partially this skepticism stems from her perspective as an old-school journalist trying to run a business. "Every day newspapers—national, regional, or local like us—are losing readers to the Internet," Navarro Bello explained. "There are papers here in Baja California that are entering a crisis. In *Zeta*, it affects us as well, although not as much as others. That's because we have such loyal readers who have accompanied us from a difficult beginning through a process of growth that has been marked by blood, murders, and threats."

In other parts of Mexico where local newspapers are under cartel control, attempts to use social media have not always worked out well. On September 24, 2011, the body of the blogger María Elizabeth Macías Castro was found in Nuevo Laredo with a handwritten message. "OK. Nuevo Laredo Live and social media, I am the Girl from Laredo and I am here because of my reports and yours," the note read, a reference to her online moniker, NenaDLaredo. Nearby, her killers left a computer keyboard, with a pair of headphones on her decapitated head. Macías Castro's murder was the first case CPJ had documented in which someone was murdered in direct retaliation for journalism posted on social media.[19]

Informing the World

Technology has transformed the way that news is disseminated and consumed around the world. But we still need people on the ground in places where news is breaking out for the system as it is now structured to work effectively. There has been much excitement about the roles that citizen journalists and activists have played in providing firsthand accounts of unfolding events in Egypt, Iran, Syria, and China. That excitement is understandable. But for the moment the most important (and least heralded) figures in the global information ecosystem are local journalists working in their own countries, journalists like Adela Navarro Bello. Partly as a result of their increased importance in the absence of international correspondents, local journalists are more vulnerable. They are the ones informing global citizens—and they are ones being jailed and killed in record numbers.

The flow of information is undoubtedly increasing, so much so that we are often inundated and often unable to process it or put it into proper context. "The big question today is how we manage information," noted Yves Daccord, the ICRC president. In fact, the volume of information can even obscure what we don't know and prevent us from seeing the ways that governments and violent forces are disrupting the flow of news within countries and across borders. Deluged with data, we are blind to the larger reality. Around the world new systems of control are taking hold. They are stifling the global conversation and impeding the development of policies and solutions based on an informed understanding of the local realities. Repression and violence against journalists is at record levels, and press freedom is in decline.

~~TWO~~

~~The Democratators~~

Every dictatorship is based on the control and manipulation of information. Independent media is anathema, and journalists who challenge the state's information hegemony are routinely jailed. In a functioning democracy, the power of government to limit speech and the press is circumscribed by law or tradition based on a recognition that an informed public debate is necessary to ensure accountability. But what if the leader of a country embraces democracy while working surreptitiously to subvert it?

One of the most critical challenges to the media comes from a new generation of popularly elected autocrats—call them "democratators." Deprived of an ideological basis for state control of information since the collapse of the Soviet Union, the democratators have adapted to the new global reality. Instead of relying on brute force and direct control, they use stealth, manipulations, and subterfuge. A few old-style dictatorships survive—Cuba, North Korea, and Turkmenistan all exercise absolute control over their domestic media. But today's autocrats generally seek to hide their policies behind a democratic façade and thus become part of the international community. In an interconnected world, the democratators seek to develop trade, attract investment, and exercise regional influence.

Democratators have certain characteristics that distinguish them from the previous generation of autocratic leaders and also from countries like China that, while allowing considerable personal freedom, eschew democratic norms.

What are these differences between dictators and democratators? Dictators rule by force. Democratators rule by manipulation. Dictators impose their will. Democratators govern with the support of the majority. Dictators do not claim to be democrats—at least credibly. Democratators always do. Dictators control information. Democratators manage it.

Democratators win elections that are not necessarily fair but are free, meaning they are not decided by fraud. Democratators do not seek to exercise absolute control over the media because they recognize that to achieve this in the Internet age they would have to close their societies to the world. They tolerate, even encourage, private media but manage critical expression through diverse measures such as national security prosecutions, punitive tax audits, manipulation of government advertising, and seemingly reasonable content restrictions, like prohibitions on graphic violence or hate speech. When they do crack down on the media, they cast their efforts as consistent with international law.

It is unquestionably better to live under a democratator than a dictator. The fact that repressive governments are compelled to present themselves as democracies in order to gain international legitimacy tempers some of the worst abuses. Democratators are susceptible to carefully calibrated domestic and international pressure, and their societies can evolve. While it is nearly impossible to change the behavior of the leadership in Cuba, Turkmenistan, or North Korea, democratators can be forced to respond to pressure. Democratators can even lose power without revolution or rupture. It is for this reason that human rights and free press organizations devote so much of their energy to confronting these leaders. The work is difficult, but it can be successful.

Democratators span the globe and the ideological spectrum. They vary in the amount of repression that they employ. The list includes Latin American populists like Rafael Correa of Ecuador and Daniel Ortega of Nicaragua, European backsliders like Viktor Orbán of Hungary and Viktor Yanukovych, the former president of Ukraine who was deposed in February 2014, and African leaders like Paul Kagame of Rwanda and Jacob Zuma of South Africa. Even President Thein Sein of Burma has implemented a strategy of skin-deep democratic reform—including releasing all of Burma's long-imprisoned journalists and relaxing censorship rules—to garner international legitimacy successfully and ease sanctions.

But the most successful democratators are Turkey's Recep Tayyip Erdoğan and Russia's Vladimir Putin, as well as the late Hugo Chávez of Venezuela, who died of cancer in March 2013 after fourteen years in power. This chapter looks at the systems of media control as practiced in these very different countries. Each leader developed strategies of repression based on trial and error and their own historical circumstances. But there are essential similarities. First and most importantly, these leaders enjoy (or enjoyed, in the case of Chávez) genuine popularity and are able to compete in and win contested elections. They cast themselves as reformers, challenging the entrenched powers of the old order. In office, they use their majoritarian support to dismantle independent institutions including the media, which they claim are blocking necessary reforms. This argument has resonated with the public because it had some basis in reality. The compromised record of the media as an institution in Turkey, Venezuela, and Russia has been essential to the success of all three men.

Turkey's Managed Repression

Prime Minister Recep Tayyip Erdoğan has cast his ongoing crackdown on the Turkish media in legalistic terms. Indeed, amid the bars and cafes of Istanbul that overflow with late-night revelers, the sophisticated museums crammed with European tourists, and the once-decrepit downtown full of bustle and energy, it can take a bit of effort to find the repression. In a rundown office building in the Beyoğlu district on the fringes of the redevelopment zone, I ride a creeping, chugging elevator to the top floor where about a dozen editors and reporters from the pro-Kurdish daily *Özgür Gündem* have assembled around a table crowded with tea, sodas, and sweets. They have gathered to provide an update on the latest wave of arrests.

I am anxious to hear their story, but also wary. The government has accused the newspaper and its reporters of supporting terrorism based on its sympathetic coverage of the Kurdistan Workers Party, or PKK, which has employed brutal tactics, including terror attacks, against civilian and military targets in its decades-long battle for Kurdish autonomy. On December 20, 2011, Turkish police raided the office where I am now sitting and rounded up nine journalists. All told, forty pro-Kurdish journalists were arrested as part of a broad and ongoing crackdown that also included lawmakers and a leading international publisher.[1] Police actions extended from central Istanbul; to Turkey's capital, Ankara; to the Kurdish heartland in the southeastern part of the country. Turkish authorities claimed the police action targeted the PKK's underground network of supporters. Kurdish activists described the crackdown as an assault on Kurdish civil society intended to stifle legitimate—and legal—opposition to repressive government policies.

With the arrests, the number of the journalists in jail in Turkey at the end of 2011 swelled to over one hundred, according to Turkish press groups—more than China, more than Iran, in fact more than any other country in the world.[2] About two-thirds of those imprisoned worked for the Kurdish media. But the arrests were part of a broader media crackdown in Turkey. Scores of other journalists were rounded up for allegedly conspiring against the government; private media companies came under intensive political pressure, and some were subjected to punitive tax penalties; the Internet was widely restricted; and critical commentators were publicly excoriated by the prime minister himself.

But the ferocious assault on press freedom—which stifled critical debate and reshaped the media landscape—did not immediately have an effect on Turkey's international reputation. Erdoğan had succeeded in blunting international and domestic criticism through his considerable charisma and by pointing to his administration's significant political achievements. Erdoğan cast the arrests as a legitimate security operation targeting coup plotters and terrorists and never tired of highlighting Turkey's immense strategic value as a NATO ally and, given its critical geopolitical position, as a reliable partner to the West. Turkey's status as a popular international travel destination also helps soften the country's image. If you're one of the many tourists visiting Istanbul and heading to the beaches, Turkey just doesn't seem that repressive.

But once you get off the tourist trail, the country looks very different. Turkey's population is mostly religious and conservative, and across the country Erdoğan's pro-Islamist AK Party has won broad support that the prime minister has used to carry out a political transformation. Erdoğan has overseen the unprecedented opening and rapid expansion of the Turkish economy. He has advocated for Turkey's economic integration with Europe and challenged the power of the old guard among the military and the industrial elite. U.S. president Barack Obama for a time championed Turkey as a successful model for countries throughout the Middle East seeking to reconcile democracy with an Islamic outlook. But while much has changed in Turkey under Erdoğan, one thing has not. The prime minister has retained—and in some cases expanded—the authoritarian structures he inherited when he took office in 2003.

As I sat in the office of *Özgür Gündem* I pushed the editors to respond to the allegations made against them by Turkish prosecutors, specifically that its reporters had participated in PKK-organized "media training" conferences held in the autonomous Kurdish region of Iraq. The readership of *Özgür Gündem* is composed largely of Kurdish emigrants from their traditional homeland in southeastern Turkey who have resettled in urban centers. The newspaper is published in Turkish, not Kurdish. It has a history of providing detailed coverage of the military conflict in southeastern Turkey and highlighting human rights violations and discrimination. Because the PKK is never criticized in its pages, the government has long maintained that the paper is directly integrated into the organization's military structure and takes orders from the PKK leadership. But the paper's editors adamantly deny it. They say that while they have covered meetings of the PKK outside of Turkey, they do not take orders from the organization and certainly have not participated in "media training." Indeed, a review of the indictment suggests that there is virtually no evidence to support the government's allegations.[3]

In the 1990s *Özgür Gündem* was subjected to a wave of brutal repression. Its Ankara office was bombed and according to the newspaper's own records between 1992 and 1995, twenty-three of its staff members were murdered—writers, correspondents, and distributors. Today's *Özgür Gündem* is the heir to the original newspaper, which was forced to shut down after the bombing of its Ankara office in 1994, an act of terrorism the paper alleges was carried out on the orders of the Turkish military. After operating under various names for nearly a decade, *Özgür Gündem* was formally relaunched in April 2011 and was immediately hit with a wave of prosecutions. When asked to characterize what has changed over the last two decades, the paper's editor Bayram Balcı thinks for a minute before responding, "Before they were killing us," he says. "Now they are arresting us."[4]

Unquestionably Erdoğan took advantage of the post-9/11 antiterror environment to recast his crackdown on critical dissent not as "censorship" but as a legitimate response to a mounting threat to national security. The strategy resonated because Turkey does face threats from a variety of actors, including underground leftist groups and what are known in the Turkish context as "ultranationalists." (Why "ultra"? Because Turks will tell you, "We're all nationalists.")

The repression largely escaped international attention until March 2011, when Erdoğan overplayed his hand. Turkish prosecutors arrested two prominent journalists, Nedim Şener and Ahmet Şık, and accused them of conspiring to overthrow the government. The allegations were absurd. Şık, an investigative reporter, labor activist, and academic with a leftist pedigree, was accused of conspiring with a web of ultranationalists and military officials in a massive conspiracy known as Ergenekon. Prosecutors alleged that Şık, with the assistance of Şener, was working on an explosive investigation revealing that the followers of Fethullah Gülen, an imam and religious leader who lives in exile in Pennsylvania, had infiltrated portions of the government and the security agencies, including the police. According to the indictment, the purpose of the book was to foment an environment of chaos in order to pave the way for a military coup.

Şık was indeed working on a book about the Gülen movement, but he was doing it on his own, without Şener, whom he barely knew. His purpose was entirely journalistic. Şener, meanwhile, a leading investigative reporter and commentator, had recently published a book of his own about the unsolved 2007 murder of the Turkish-Armenian editor Hrant Dink, whose killing he revealed was part of an antigovernment plot carried out with the participation of the police, many of whom are reputedly followers of Gülen. The evidence against the two journalists was a draft of Şık's book—titled *The Imam's Army*—that was found on the computer of an ultranationalist website called OdaTV. Prosecutors alleged that the journalists at OdaTV were participants in the Ergenekon conspiracy along with retired military officials and civil servants tied to the secular establishment. In justifying the police action and arrests, Prime Minster Erdoğan publicly compared Şık's book to a bomb.[5]

When I met with Soner Yalçın, the founder of the OdaTV website in Istanbul in October 2013, he insisted that a forensic analysis carried out by outside experts had determined that Şık's book had been planted remotely on the OdaTV computer. He noted, however, that even if the government allegations were true, "I face a possible sentence of sixty-four years on terrorism charges for the crime of having a journalist write a book, a journalist I don't know." Yalçın had already served two years in prison on pretrial detention and was free on bond when I met with him.[6]

Most informed observers believe that the Ergenekon conspiracy does exist but that the authorities have expanded the scope of the investigation to encompass nearly all of the regime's political opponents. The entire legal process—consisting of indictments that run to thousands of pages, hearings that are repeatedly postponed, and trials that drag on for years before a verdict is rendered—is so bewildering that it is impossible to follow or comprehend. But the notion that Şık and Şener would have supported such a plot was laughable both because of the utter lack of evidence and because no one believed the two journalists would have associated with ultranationalist conspirators who were the target of several of their journalistic investigations. Both of them—along with Yalçin—note what the OdaTV defendants have in common is their criticism of the Gülen movement. They believe that their prosecutions were carried out on behalf of the movement, with government support.[7]

The arrests of Şık and Şener raised deep concerns among Turkey's journalism community and sparked street protests in Istanbul. They also vastly increased the level of international attention on press freedom issues in Turkey. Prior to their arrests it was easier for the Turkish government to cast the crackdown against the Kurdish media that began in 2009 as a part of a legitimate security operation. But after

Şık and Şener's arrests, human rights organizations, journalist organizations in Turkey, and even the media freedom representative of the Organization for Security and Cooperation in Europe, a regional security organization, began sounding the alarm.

In October 2012, after carefully reviewing all of the outstanding cases, CPJ weighed in with its own report that determined there were sixty-one journalists in prison for their work and another fifteen cases in which journalism was a possible factor.[8] The report was a detailed examination of the various strategies of media repression employed by the Erdoğan administration—the libel suits, the personal attacks, the legal harassment, and the prosecutions—but the overarching message was simple. With the crackdown, Turkey had become the world's leading jailer of journalists. The release of the CPJ report spawned a flurry of media attention both inside and outside Turkey. The mass arrests of journalists had given critics a golden opportunity to disrupt Turkey's narrative of progress. After all, how could a country that was liberalizing democracy jail more journalists than China, Iran, Eritrea, or Vietnam?

Soon after the CPJ report was released in Istanbul I had lunch with Şık at the university in Istanbul where he teaches. He had been released in March 2012 after spending a year in jail, and he seemed in good spirits, animated and engaged. "There are journalists in this country who believe that the solution is a coup d'état," he said. "But as much as I disagree with this government I would never choose that. Still, I know I will be convicted in this case. All the suspects will be. That's because the people running the trial are part of the government conspiracy."

The underlying problem in Turkey is the repressive legal structure developed over decades by military-dominated governments responding to security challenges from leftists, Islamists, and Kurdish nationalists. In fact, since the founding of the Turkish Republic by Mustafa Kemal Atatürk in 1923 the interests of the state have always taken precedence over the rights of individuals, ethnic groups such as Kurds, and, until recently, Islamists.

Like Chávez and Putin, Erdoğan came to power on a pledge to take on the county's political establishment. The key to forging a new coalition in Turkey was to shift the focus of the debate around religion.

Instead of pushing for more religion in government, Erdoğan flipped the argument by pushing less government in religion. His efforts to end anachronistic restrictions on religious expression dovetailed with a broader effort to modernize the Turkish economy and push toward European integration. Erdoğan casts as enemies of his political project the "deep state," the web of military officials, business leaders, civil servants, media, and government institutions dedicated to maintaining the secular, statist order.[9]

The media in Turkey is dominated by large conglomerates with diverse business interests, some with previous ties to the military establishment. Erdoğan harbors a deep mistrust of the media, and he has taken dramatic steps to tame criticism, lashing out at individual journalists and filing dozens of lawsuits for defamation. After the daily *Hurriyet* and other media outlets owned by the powerful Doğan Group began in 2008 to publish stories about a German investigation into a charity that was alleged to have channeled money to AKP leaders, Erdoğan fumed, telling his supporters, "Don't buy newspapers that print lies!" The following year, the government opened a tax evasion case and fined the company $2.5 billion. Doğan leaders were eventually able to negotiate a reduction in the fine to $600 million after they replaced the editor of *Hurriyet* and sold off two of its TV stations. But the message had been sent. "No one tells me not to criticize the government, but it's in the air," said a prominent newspaper columnist. "The prime minister has assumed the role of Turkey's press critic in chief."[10] In fact, the pressure has gone far beyond criticism. In 2013, according to a study by the Turkish Union of Journalists, nearly sixty journalists were fired or quit as a direct result of government interference.

Erdoğan has made no secret of his desire to place clear limits on public discourse, telling the journalist Christiane Amanpour in a September 2012 CNN interview that "Insult is one thing; criticism is another thing. I will never put up with insult."[11] He also lashed out at journalists covering the Kurdish conflict insisting during a live television debate that news about the PKK "must be ignored; there is no other way." He continued: "The most important target of terrorism is propaganda. . . . On whose side will the media be?"[12]

While pledging reform, Erdoğan—who was himself jailed for four months in 1998 for reading a poem with an Islamist theme—has availed himself of the existing legal structure to imprison journalists. Statutes still on the books punish defamation of the president and insults to the memory of Atatürk or any other person living or dead. Other penal code articles prohibit "making propaganda for an organization and its objectives," "breaching the confidentiality of an investigation," and "influencing a fair trial." Perhaps the most absurd of all is a statute that criminalizes aiding the goals of the terrorist organization "without being a member." As the Human Rights Watch Turkey researcher Emma Sinclair-Webb noted, the law could be interpreted to mean that "If the PKK says brush your teeth and you brush your teeth, then you're obviously operating on behalf of the PKK."

Such sweeping and vague provisions have been used to round up dozens of Kurdish journalists, including those from *Özgür Gündem* who were arrested in the December 2011 raid on the newspaper. In the indictments the government alleged that the journalists from the newspaper were either directly integrated into the PKK's organizational structure or were seeking to advance the organization's agenda without being members.

While the government's case lacks legal merit, many Kurdish journalists privately express support for the PKK and its jailed leader, Abdullah Öcalan. One young Kurdish reporter in Istanbul who had seen many colleagues arrested told me she never saw herself as a neutral observer. "All journalists have a side, and we have a side," she told me. "We don't think journalism is a mechanical process. We express our feelings."

When I asked if she felt her job was to report the truth or support the Kurdish political struggle, she answered, "Both." And when I followed up by asking what she would do if the two came into conflict, she told me, "Sometimes you have to sacrifice one for the other."

"We have discussions here all the time and ask ourselves, are we journalists or we part of the Kurdish struggle?" said the journalist. "There is a huge press army against us, and we need a voice of our own."

My own sense of the Kurdish prosecutions is that the government is so convinced of the direct ties between the Kurdish media and the

PKK leadership that it is acting like a rogue cop, doing whatever it takes to achieve convictions without paying too much attention to the law or the evidence. But this is what distinguishes a country governed by the rule of law from one in which the state interest prevails. Turkey has still not made the transition. Yes, Turkey is growing and has made strides. But the weakness of independent institutions and ongoing government repression creates an environment in which the information that should fuel both domestic politics and global decision making is deficient and manipulated. The same is largely true in so many other countries dominated by the new autocrats—not just Russia and Venezuela, but Ethiopia, Ecuador, Hungary, and Rwanda, to name a few others.

Following the release of CPJ's press freedom report in October 2012, I paid another visit to *Özgür Gündem* to brief the editors on the report's findings. While making a commitment to defend the newspaper's right to freedom of expression, I also wanted to make clear that it should not be construed as an endorsement of their political goals. "We have a radical democratic vision, and as a newspaper we are engaged in a militant struggle for democracy," the editor Bayram Balcı explained. "It is obvious that those who oppose us accuse us of being the same as the PKK and Abdullah Öcalan. But this is not a crime." In late 2012, Erdoğan began a dialogue with the PKK that led to a ceasefire and raised hopes for a political solution to the Kurdish conflict. As of CPJ's December 2013 prison census, most of the journalists rounded up in the 2011 sweep, including the reporters for *Özgür Gündem*, remained in jail. Erdoğan, meanwhile, continued to lash out at the media. After the daily *Milliyet* published leaked documents from a meeting between Öcalan and members of parliament from a pro-Kurdish party, Erdoğan claimed, "you cannot publish such a story if you have the slightest love for this nation." A prominent columnist for the paper, Hasan Cemal, was forced to take a two-week leave after he criticized the prime minister's attitude. After editors spiked a second column critical of the government, he quit the newspaper.[13]

In May 2013, a small protest against the redevelopment of Gezi Park in the center of Istanbul mushroomed into a full-blown crisis after authorities resorted to brutal police tactics. The protests, which grew more raucous and violent as they spread to other cities in Turkey, were an expression of accumulated grievances ranging from unchecked urban redevelopment, to growing restrictions on the sale of alcohol, to Erdoğan's imperious governing style.

The battle in the streets soon morphed into a battle over information, with Turkey's mainstream media, fearful of the prime minister's wrath and seeking to protect their owner's business interests, lining up behind the government and ignoring the demonstrations. Protesters expressed their indignation by rallying in front of media outlets and even accosting reporters in Taksim Square. When young protesters turned to social media to spread the word and share information, Erdoğan lashed out, calling the protesters "bums and looters" and describing Twitter as a "menace." Erdoğan's dim view of social media did not stop Ankara's mayor Melih Gökçek from using Twitter to denounce international journalists and calling the BBC correspondent in Turkey a "traitor and a spy."[14]

Erdoğan achieved meaningful reform in his first years in office, and his legacy will ultimately be determined by the manner in which he eventually leaves power. But in the aftermath of the Gezi Park protests, it was also clear that the battle over information in Turkey had entered a dangerous new phase, one in which the repression had become more visible and more intense. The domestic media had been tamed, partisan outlets were facing sustained legal assault, and international journalists were increasingly subject to a withering campaign of public vilification. "The Gezi protests did two things," said one prominent international journalist based in Istanbul. "They exposed the authoritarian nature of the government, and they simultaneously made the government more authoritarian."[15]

Venezuela's Institutional Assault

When Hugo Chávez first assumed the presidency of Venezuela on February 2, 1999, he deviated from the standard oath of office, swearing on the "moribund constitution" that he would lead a democratic transformation and produce a new constitution "for these times." During his fourteen years in power Chávez succeeded in transforming Venezuela through the sheer force of his personality. After a long illness, Chávez died from cancer in March 2013. His handpicked successor and vice president Nicolás Maduro succeeded Chávez as president after winning a narrow victory at the April 2013 polls. Maduro, heavyset with a thick mustache, carried around on the campaign a tiny backpack filled with Chávez's "revolutionary dreams" and claimed to have been visited by the ex-president's spirit in the form of a small bird. Like his mentor, Maduro sought to rally popular support in Venezuela by lashing out at the United States, expelling two U.S. military attaches he accused of destabilizing the country, and even suggesting that the United States might have somehow caused Chávez's cancer.[16]

It's all a distant memory now, but after Chávez won a surprise victory in 1999 over an aging beauty queen he toured the United States as part of a charm offensive. He made overtures to foreign investors and the IMF, even making a well-publicized visit to Wall Street, where he banged down the closing gavel at the New York Stock Exchange. He criticized the United States but didn't go out of his way to be antagonistic; he met with President Bill Clinton and National Security Advisor Sandy Berger and even threw out the first pitch at a New York Mets baseball game before making a surprise appearance in the Spanish-language broadcast booth, where he added his own color commentary.

Back in Venezuela, however, Chávez was focused less on disarming his critics and more on dismantling the country's traditional political order. From the outset he saw mass mobilization as the key tool to achieve this end. True to his commitment on inauguration day, he held a national referendum in April 1999 in which he asked the public to support the drafting of a new constitution. The referendum passed with 88 percent of the vote, albeit with a 60 percent rate of abstention. The Constitutional Assembly assumed nearly all legislative and judicial functions, raising howls of protest in Congress and prompting the chief justice of the Supreme Court to resign. The assembly worked feverishly over the next few months to draft a new magna carta. The document included some progressive elements—Venezuela's indigenous population was accorded special legal protections—but its primary effect was to strengthen Chávez's political hand. It extended the presidential term from five to six years and allowed for a second consecutive term. It gave members of the military the right to vote, a move that benefitted Chávez, who was widely popular with the military rank and file. It also abolished the Senate, creating a unicameral National Assembly. The new constitution was ratified in a referendum, and the following July Venezuelans went back to the polls in "megaelections" to choose not only the president and new representatives but also mayors, governors, and local delegates across the land. Chávez supporters, already highly mobilized by the referendum process, turned out in force and delivered a significant victory, with Chávez-allied parties dominating the legislature and sweeping aside the old guard in many local races.[17]

But there was one institution that the Constitutional Assembly did not address: the media. As an institution independent of government, this was clearly outside its purview. In fact, the private media, controlled by large business interests opposed to Chávez's political project, was vociferous and relentless in its criticism. With the political opposition discredited and divided and with the institutions of independent government now firmly under Chávez's control, the media became the opposition and the primary check on Chávez's power.

Chávez recognized the danger posed by a critical independent media. In formulating a response to the challenge, he also benefitted tremendously from the efforts of other governments in the region that had sought to develop their own strategies for managing information in the post–Cold War era. In the decade since the return to democracy across Latin America, the media had become an ascendant political force, demanding accountability for the abuses committed by military governments, exposing government malfeasance in the new civilian-led administrations, and earning public support. In Brazil, aggressive reporting on the elaborate kickback and corruption schemes of President Fernando Affonso Collor de Mello led to his resignation in 1992. In Argentina, the journalist Horacio Verbitsky's 1995 groundbreaking book *The Flight* told the story of the navy officer Alfredo Scilingo, who confessed to participating in the junta's death squads by pushing political prisoners from airplanes. In polls taken in the 1990s in much of Latin America, the press was consistently named the most trusted institution, ahead of the Catholic Church.[18]

The media also played a key role in challenging the autocratic government of Alberto Fujimori in Peru, which eventually collapsed under the glare of public scrutiny. Fujimori, whose parents emigrated from Japan and who spoke Spanish with a slight accent, was elected president in 1990 after campaigning as the quintessential outsider. He pledged to sweep aside the old political order, impose the rule of law, and improve security at a time when the terror tactics employed by the Maoist guerrillas of Sendero Luminoso had spread fear from the countryside into the heart of the capital, Lima. Fujimori initially delivered on some of these commitments. His signature achievements were taming runaway inflation and capturing the Sendero leader Abimael Guzmán.

In 1992, in what was dubbed the "self-coup," Fujimori dissolved the obstructionist and dysfunctional Congress and took absolute control of the government. While Fujimori's actions appeared to have had the broad support of the Peruvian public—he handily won reelection to a second term in 1995—they clearly lacked the legitimacy of Chávez's use of referendums and mass mobilization to achieve the same political goals.

As in Venezuela, the media emerged as the primary opposition force following Fujimori's consolidation of power. And as in Venezuela, the media in Peru were dominated by owners with diverse commercial interests and ties to the traditional establishment. As part of their concerted campaign against Fujimori, Peruvian media outlets hired Peru's most talented investigative reporters and provided them with the resources to investigate the government. The leading example was television channel 2—Frecuencia Latina, owned by an Israeli immigrant named Baruch Ivcher who had made a fortune in the mattress business. The station's weekly *60 Minutes*–style public affairs program produced devastating investigative pieces on the murder and torture of former intelligence agents, links between army officers and drug traffickers, and efforts by the National Intelligence Service (known by its Spanish acronym SIN) to bribe journalists.

In July 1997 the Peruvian government began a counterattack. Alleging irregularities in his application for citizenship, authorities stripped Ivcher of his Peruvian nationality, then maneuvered successfully to have Fujimori loyalists take over the station. The investigative reporters who had broken so many stories were dismissed. Journalists were bribed, threatened, attacked, wiretapped, and placed under surveillance. The SIN, under its notorious leader Vladimiro Montesinos, also launched an insidious and highly effective effort to use Lima's popular tabloids to smear government critics, including journalists. Screaming headlines—prominently displayed at every news kiosk in Lima—accused critical journalists of being communists, traitors, and "prophets of the devil."[19]

While Fujimori's strategy of targeting the media through administrative sanctions, legal harassment, and smear campaigns all took a toll, they also undermined his domestic legitimacy and ate away at his international support, notably when he withdrew from the Inter-American human rights system rather than abide by a court ruling favoring Ivcher.

With his international reputation in tatters and his domestic support collapsing, Fujimori resorted to fraud to steal the 2000 runoff election. Amid mounting public protests and ongoing corruption scandals, Fujimori flew to Japan and faxed his letter of resignation from a Tokyo hotel room. He was later arrested while visiting Chile and extradited back to Peru, where he was convicted of corruption and gross human rights violations committed under his administration. He is currently serving a twenty-five-year prison sentence.

Chávez came to power just as the Fujimori government was collapsing. Although Chávez was on the other end of the ideological spectrum from Fujimori, he clearly learned from his mistakes. Chávez was able to achieve many of Fujimori's political goals—mobilizing supporters, taking over institutions perceived loyal to the previous political order, and marginalizing the media—without resorting to the excesses of the previous era, like coups and electoral fraud.

Chávez refined and adapted the emerging strategies of media control and added his own innovations.[20] The most striking was initially to avoid confronting the media directly and instead do an end run. It all started in May 1999 with a Sunday morning radio talk show called *Alo Presidente*, in which Chávez ruminated about everything from the evils of capitalism to the beauty of Venezuelan women. The show sometimes went on for as long as eight hours. Chávez soon migrated to television and by February 2000 his lengthy discourses had become a nightly affair, with tirades against the "rancid oligarchy" cutting into prime-time programming, including the highly popular and profitable soap operas. Under Article 192 of the Telecommunications Act, introduced in 2000, broadcasters were compelled to transmit in full the president's speeches along with any other political messages. Chávez's relationship with the private media became increasingly antagonistic and adversarial as he amassed power. But he tolerated the strident criticism because he did not see the media as an existential threat. That analysis changed dramatically in the aftermath of the failed April 2002 coup. Beginning in 2001, unions, business groups, and others opposed to the Chávez government joined forces to organize massive street protests and general strikes that crippled the country. The protesters had the explicit support of the country's leading broadcasters, which presented a decidedly distorted picture of the unfolding events. Instead of moderating the public debate in an increasingly polarized society, the media took sides, airing public service announcements for the opposition and urging people to get out in the street and protest.

There was also an international component to the campaign. The Venezuelan media owners used their contacts in the international business community, the U.S. government, and the NGO community to mobilize international opposition to Chávez's power grab, and international press groups were courted and urged to act aggressively. A report presented at the March 2002 meeting of the Inter-American Press Association, a highly influential organization of media owners and executives from throughout the hemisphere, declared that press freedom no longer existed in the country.

Chávez later alleged that the media owners actively participated in the coup against him. While that has never been proven, it is unquestionable that the lopsided coverage of the coup itself—including allegations, later called into question, that Chávez supporters had opened fire on unarmed demonstrators—deeply compromised the media's credibility.

While the broadcast media had actively covered the street protests and violent clashes that preceded the coup, after Chávez was deposed and the business leader Pedro Carmona was installed by the military, television screens across the country showed old movies and cartoons. Some analysts have alleged that the news blackout was imposed on the orders of Carmona himself, a claim denied by the media owners who said the situation was too volatile to send their reporters into the street—something they had been doing without apparent regard for their reporters' safety in the preceding weeks as they provided wall-to-wall coverage of the anti- Chávez mobilization.

"The reports coming into the station were about violence, death, and looting," said Alberto Federico Ravell, the general director of the twenty-four-hour news channel Globovisión, in a televised address after Chávez was briefly deposed. "We sacrificed our ratings, our credibility with viewers, our freedom of expression by deciding not to broadcast images of violence and looting."

As the coup was unfolding on April 11, 2002, Chávez took to the airwaves to insist that he was in charge and that the situation was under control. While the television networks technically complied with the law, which required that they preempt regular broadcasting to show the president's address, they used split screen to contrast the president's assurances with the pandemonium in the streets. Chávez was furious, and after military officials who opposed the coup restored him to power, he launched a systematic campaign to tame the media, particularly the leading broadcasters, whom he denounced as the "Four Horsemen of the Apocalypse."

Chief among them was Venevisión, a broadcast network led by the businessman Gustavo Cisneros, who had supported the opposition and who the government alleged was involved in the coup. In June 2002, Cisneros met privately with President Chávez along with the former U.S. president Jimmy Carter, who brokered the meeting. Cisneros claimed that no formal deal was reached, but observers noted that the station soon dismissed many of its critical reporters and began focusing exclusively on entertainment. The government, meanwhile, began describing Venevisión as a "model broadcaster." Another critical station, Televen, took a similar approach, cutting news coverage and staying below the government's radar.

In 2004, Venezuela's National Assembly passed the Law on Social Responsibility in Radio and Television, providing a legal framework for the government regulation of news content. The law banned content that could "incite or promote hatred or intolerance" or "disobedience to the current legal order." Under the law, violent or sexual content cannot be broadcast before 11 p.m., an innocuous-sounding provision ostensibly intended to protect children but that in fact served to curtail reporting on Venezuela's shocking crime wave. Violators faced suspension or even revocation of their broadcast licenses and enforcement was left in the hands of the state broadcasting authority, CONATEL, which reports directly to the president.

In December 2006, weeks after being reelected in a landslide victory for a second six-year term as president, Chávez singled out the critical broadcaster RCTV in an address to Venezuelan troops. "There won't be any new concession for that coup-mongering channel that was known as Radio Caracas Televisión," Chávez pledged. "Venezuela must be respected." The station's twenty-year concession was due to expire in April 2007. The government made a show of following regulatory procedure, but the outcome was a foregone conclusion. While the government accused RCTV of "sensational" coverage of a well-known murder case and of showing alcohol consumption during a baseball game, a 2007 CPJ report found "the government held no hearings, followed no discernible application process, and provided RCTV no opportunity to respond to assertions made by top officials in press conferences, speeches, and interviews." The station was stripped of its frequency the following month, and its broadcast equipment was confiscated and turned over to a new public broadcaster dubbed TVES, a progovernment station that has attracted a limited audience. RCTV migrated to cable, but by 2012 ongoing legal and bureaucratic harassment forced the station to abandon news coverage all together.

In April 2013, about a month after Chávez's death, Globovisión's owner Guillermo Zuloaga announced plans to sell the station to the businessman Juan Domingo Cordero and two other partners. The sale took place under duress. The station, available only in Caracas and Valencia, had been hit with millions of dollars in fines for its allegedly sensational coverage of a prison riot and for using U.S. seismological data to report on a major earthquake in Venezuela. Zuloaga, facing a variety of legal charges including illegal importation of cars, was living in exile in the United States. Globovisión reporters were routinely denied access to public events and hounded and harassed by Chávez supporters. Regulators had accused the station of "inciting rebellion" and creating "panic and anxiety in the population." The station's license was up for renewal in 2015.

Not long after the sale was completed, President Maduro received Cordero at Miraflores Palace. The new station owner, who was rumored to have close ties to the government, promised that Globovisión would present balanced reporting and would "promote peace." Several critical anchors quit or were let go.[21] The stations that Chávez had identified as the "Four Horsemen of the Apocalypse" had all been reined in.

With his death, Chávez left behind a media landscape utterly transformed. Once dominated by privately owned outlets, today the Venezuelan state operates six publicly financed broadcast outlets and hundreds of community radio stations that spread the government's message. In July 2005, the government launched its most ambitious initiative: Telesur, a twenty-four-hour news network that carries no commercial advertising and is available free-to-air and via satellite in Latin America and the world.

Journalists face an array of legal restrictions, including prosecutions for defamation of public officials and incitement to violence. While the print media—which reaches a relatively modest audience, mostly in Caracas—remains highly critical, newspapers have been fined and subjected to punitive tax audits and advertising boycotts. Another of Chávez's insights was to recognize that the Internet—once limited to the elites with access to computers—is becoming a form of mass communication because of the availability of mobile devices. In 2010, the Law on Social Responsibility was expanded to include online speech. Chávez himself was active on Twitter and had over four million followers at the time of his death.

The effect that these restrictions have on freedom of expression was obvious in the coverage of Chávez's losing battle with cancer. Even before the president announced in June 2011 that he had had an operation in Cuba to remove "a baseball-sized tumor" from his pelvic region, rumors swirled about his health. But Chávez was never forthcoming about the disease, his treatment, or his prognosis. By undergoing treatment in Havana he was able to keep the media at bay. But he could not contain the leaks—some true, others exaggerated or false. Rather than being a straightforward news story, Chávez's declining health became a battleground in which rumors were exploited by his political enemies and pertinent details withheld by a government that sought to manipulate public opinion. Throughout his fourteen years in power, Chávez sought to "democratize" a media unquestionably dominated by large corporate interests. He justified his more aggressive interventions by citing the media's role in the aborted 2002 coup. But rather than seeking to create a pluralistic, independent media, Chávez created a structure in which the state's perspective is amplified, critical voices are marginalized, and the government has the legal authority to limit free expression. In doing so he successfully refined the initial, crude attempts at media control employed by Fujimori.

Both Chávez and Fujimori used popular support to consolidate control over independent institutions. But while Fujimori took the clearly illegal step of dissolving Congress and assuming legislative authority, Chávez used his initial electoral victory to mobilize his supporters in a "super election" that allowed him to gain control of the legislature, eliminate institutional constraints on power, and eventually pack the judiciary with supporters. While Fujimori's crude effort to strip a critical media owner of his Peruvian citizenship was easily exposed, the Chávez government largely succeeded in using regulatory authority to neutralize or shut down critical broadcasters. Whereas Fujimori got into an unwinnable fight with the print media—using his intelligence agenda to smear and entrap his critics—Chávez recognized that the power and reach of the print media is limited, and while he attacked and mocked his critics in the print media he did not move against them directly. Instead, he focused his energy on building an alternative media network loyal to the government. Finally, while Fujimori's international legitimacy was compromised by adverse rulings from the Inter-American Human Rights Commission, Chávez neutralized the threat by building a network of regional allies who emulated his policies domestically and backed him internationally.

In 2006, Evo Morales, an Aymara Indian and former coca farmer, was elected president of Bolivia with the overwhelming support of that country's marginalized indigenous majority. Morales argued that the country's private media, which had fiercely opposed him—and sometimes cast its criticism in overt racial terms—represented the interests of the country's European-descended elite. His government responded aggressively to the media criticism with threats of legal action and ongoing harassment and pressure. In Ecuador, President Rafael Correa went even further, shutting down critical radio stations, passing restrictive legislation, and filing a flurry of defamation cases against critical media outlets, including the national daily *El Universo*, which was hit with a $40 million libel action after calling the president a war criminal. Correa won the suit but issued a pardon. While Nicaragua's Daniel Ortega is hardly part of a new generation, he has updated his media strategy from the outright repression of the Sandinista era and has instead constructed a progovernment media network made of state outlets and supportive private media owned by friends and family.

The leaders of these countries—with some support from Argentina and Brazil—have also banded together to undermine the regional institutions that have nurtured press freedom in Latin America since the end of the military dictatorships. In 1997 the Organization of American States created a Special Rapporteur for Freedom of Expression to advocate for the rights of journalists facing violations of their basic human rights. The rapporteur has been highly critical of tactics employed by Chávez and his allies in the region. Their response has been to go on the offensive and push essentially to defund the rapporteur's offices and limit its range of operation. While the proposal was eventually defeated, the OAS's human rights protection system was weakened by the bruising battle.

Since the return of democracy, independent media in Latin America has served as a bulwark against government abuses throughout the region. Today, that role is deeply compromised in many countries, including Venezuela. As William J. Dobson noted in his 2012 book on global democracy advocacy *The Dictator's Learning Curve*, "The net effect of Chávez's manipulations, end runs, and power grabs has been to make Venezuela a unique paradox: with each election the country loses more of its democracy."[22] This is true today not only in Venezuela but in other countries throughout the region that are adapting the Chávez model to their own reality.

Media Development, Russian Style

From the start of the Bolshevik Revolution, the communists understood the power of information. The Soviet Union was awash in media—newspapers and magazines, radio and TV blanketed the entire country—all of it under state or Party control. Mikhail Gorbachev inherited this vast media infrastructure when he came to power in 1985 and, in the guise of giving journalists (and the public) greater freedom, used it to advance his own political goals. Vladimir Putin, however, did not inherit a compliant media he could put at his disposal. Yet to a much greater extent than either Erdoğan or even Chávez, Putin has succeeded in bringing the Russian media to heel.

The transformation of Russia's information landscape began with Gorbachev, who believed the media would be a natural ally in his battle with the entrenched Soviet bureaucracy. His view was that critical coverage could help build support for Perestroika, his program of economic restructuring. "The better informed the people are," Gorbachev said at the time, "the more intelligently they act and the more actively they support the Party and its plans and programmatic goals." It didn't quite work out that way. Things began really to fall apart when the media and the public took Gorbachev's freedom talk seriously and began to explore what interested them—not just what Gorbachev thought was acceptable to cover more freely.

The public discussion of Stalin's legacy—which Gorbachev encouraged—soon evolved into an exhaustive examination of Soviet history that exposed the myths and undermined the legitimacy of the entire communist system. Reports on corruption and inefficiency became a general critique of the overall management of Soviet society. These reports, broadcast on television and radio and published in newspapers and magazines whose circulation soared, infuriated Kremlin hardliners. In August 1991, they deposed Gorbachev in a bloodless coup while he was on holiday in the Crimea.

One of the first acts of the coup leaders was to take control of the main broadcast facilities and ban all but a handful of newspapers. But the media had grown larger and more diverse in the Gorbachev years, making it much harder to manage. Some newspapers defied the order, printing photocopied editions that made their way back onto the street. At a press conference broadcast live on Soviet television on the evening of the coup, its leaders were bombarded with questions, including one from a bold young Russian newspaper correspondent who asked, "Could you please say whether or not you understand that last night you carried out a coup d'état?" Later that night, an extraordinary broadcast showed barricades being erected around the Russian White House as Boris Yeltsin stood atop a tank and issued his famous appeal defying the hard-line coup. The media coverage helped mobilize public demonstrations that seemed to unnerve the coup plotters, who abandoned their effort. Gorbachev was restored to power, but his Soviet Union collapsed within months.

The communist collapse liberated a new breed of journalists across Russia and the former Soviet Union who took pride in the role that information played in toppling the old order. The best reporters were filled with indignation about past abuses and used their technical skills to reveal suppressed truths to the public. They also reported aggressively on long-hidden corruption and social ills as the old system disintegrated.

But these were difficult times for the Russian public, with living standards plummeting and national pride deeply wounded. With a weak and ineffectual government and virtually no civic culture, aggressive reporting on social ills like homelessness and crime fueled despair rather than encouraging solutions. The collapsing economy forced some media outlets to shut down; others struggled to make payroll, leaving journalists open to bribes and pressure.

Into the breach stepped two newly wealthy "oligarchs," Boris Berezovsky and Vladimir Gusinsky, who offered deep pockets and financial stability but also lots of political baggage that fueled cynicism about the role of the media. During the 1996 presidential elections, with Yeltsin facing Gennady Zyuganov, a strong communist challenger, Gusinsky, who owned the NTV network, and Berezovsky, who had a controlling stake in the rival ORT network, made an agreement to do whatever it took it earn Yeltsin a victory. The broadcasters ignored Yeltsin's obvious shortcomings—including his problems with alcohol—and instead aired what amounted to continuous campaign ads in the guise of news reporting. Gusinsky and Berezovsky cast their partisan coverage as necessary to defend press freedom, arguing that a communist victory would have meant an end to open media. The intervention of the two private networks in the campaign was instrumental in Yeltsin's ultimate victory, but it left a bitter taste in the mouths of a portion of the Russian public, which began to see the media not as an independent force operating in the public interest but simply as another political actor seeking to advance its own business interests.

By the end of 1999, Yeltsin, deeply discredited and hobbled by drink, handed over the reins of power to Vladimir Putin. The networks split over Putin during the 2000 presidential election, when he ran as Yeltsin's handpicked successor. While Berezovsky backed Putin, Gusinsky blatantly favored Putin's opponents. After winning the presidency, Putin was quick to take revenge, sending the tax police to raid NTV. When Berezovsky also began to criticize the new government, Putin moved against him as well, using legal prosecutions and government-backed hostile takeovers to bring both networks under Kremlin control. The Russian public was largely indifferent because it no longer perceived the media as an independent check on government power. Instead, many believed, with some justification, that the networks had picked the losing side in an ugly political battle and had gotten their comeuppance.[23] Putin meanwhile cast the successive Kremlin takeovers of critical broadcast networks as "business disputes." He even suggested in a 2005 interview with *60 Minutes* that the situation facing Russian broadcasters was no different from the criticism that had forced Dan Rather to step down in 2004 as anchor of the *CBS Evening News.* "We understood that he was forced to resign by his bosses at CBS," Putin explained to his interviewer, Mike Wallace. "This is a problem of your democracy, not ours."

Having made the determination to rein in media freedom, Putin constantly recalibrated the level of repression based on internal and external events. One area that has been consistently off limits throughout his decade in power both as president and prime minister is independent reporting on the military conflict in the North Caucasus, including the brutal counterinsurgency carried out in the breakaway republic of Chechnya. Putin sent a clear message regarding his intentions soon after taking office, when he made an example of a journalist, Andrei Babitsky, who had reported critically on the Chechen conflict for the U.S. government–funded Radio Liberty. Babitsky was detained on January 16, 2000, by Russian forces operating outside Grozny, Chechnya's besieged capital. He was beaten, and his guards tortured him by tossing tear gas canisters into his cell. In a stage-managed sequence of events intended to humiliate and discredit him, Babitsky was turned over to "Chechen militants" in exchange for Russian prisoners of war. The alleged militants, who eventually released him, were actually members of a pro-Kremlin militia.[24]

Just as Chávez refined and adapted the political model developed by Alberto Fujimori in Peru, Putin learned from the excesses of Serbia's President Slobodan Milošević. Milošević, who died of a heart attack in 2006 while facing prosecution for war crimes in The Hague, focused his energy on controlling mass media, notably state television. Relentless coverage of ethnic divisions both fueled the military conflict in the Balkans while also building political support for Milošević among the Serb population. RTS—Radio Television Serbia—broadcast crude propaganda, blaming Croats and Muslims for the massacres carried out by Serb forces, spawning shocking racial theories of Serb superiority, and vilifying the West. Meanwhile, Milošević had the wherewithal and savvy to engage the international media and tolerate a certain amount of criticism from Belgrade-based print media and the independent radio station B92, which he saw as having limited influence among the general population.[25]

In Russia, Putin has drawn a similar distinction between mass media and elite media. The takeover of the NTV and ORT television companies left the Kremlin firmly in control of national broadcast networks through which the vast majority of Russians get their news and information. The effects of this policy were made dramatically clear in September 2004, when Russian security forces stormed a school in the provincial town of Beslan, where Chechen separatists were holding hundreds hostage. In the ensuing chaos, more than three hundred people were killed, half of them children. Previous national calamities—including the Kursk submarine disaster in 2000 and the botched 2002 raid on a Moscow theater also occupied by Chechen militants —generated a flurry of critical television coverage. But Putin faced little criticism in the aftermath of the Beslan incident. "As soon as the storming of the school was over, so was television coverage," noted the Russia analyst Masha Lipman. "There were no survivors' accounts, no stories of desperate people who lost loved ones, no independent experts' analysis, and no public discussion whatsoever."[26]

Since the takeover of the national broadcast networks, the Kremlin has relied on weekly meetings and periodic talking points issued to editors to dictate television coverage. Rather than using television to mobilize his supporters—as Milošević had—Putin sees it as a means to placate and distract the population, thereby fueling the culture of complacency. Russian television is nothing if not entertaining, with a daily diet of outrageous game shows, steamy soap operas, sports, and movies. As John Kampfer noted in his 2010 book *Freedom for Sale*, Russian television helps reinforce Putin's implicit pact with the Russian public, in which the president delivers economic growth and security in exchange for political quiescence.[27]

Today the Russian media landscape is complex, with the television networks beholden to the Kremlin, an independent but cautious national print media concentrated in Moscow, and a handful of scrappy outlets probing the limits and suffering the consequences. The greatest consequences by far have befallen *Novaya Gazeta*, the fiercely independent Moscow newspaper that has seen five of its reporters murdered. The government's cynical indifference to the record of violence against the Russian media—which is explored more thoroughly in chapter 7—is a critical backdrop to the documented record of direct repression. While the government is not necessarily implicated in such crimes, it clearly benefits from an environment in which the country's relative handful of investigative reporters work in a climate of fear and intimidation. This may explain why Russia's record of impunity in the killing of journalists is one of the worst in the world. Russia ranked ninth on 2012 CPJ's Impunity Index, with sixteen unsolved journalists' murder since 2002.[28]

But the rules are not the same for everyone. The most prominent and successful independent media outlet is the Moscow-based radio station Ekho Moskvy. Each day the station reports the news as it sees fit: it criticizes the political leadership, it airs debate and dissent, and it challenges authority.[29] And it has been doing the same thing more or less since its founding in 1990 at the height of Perestroika. No one from its staff has been killed; it has never been shut down, although it is not immune to government pressure and threats. In 2009, the station's director, Alexei Venediktov, came home to find an ax embedded in the door of his Moscow apartment. The primary shareholder of Ekho Moskvy is Gazprom, the Kremlin-backed oil conglomerate that controls NTV. The removal by Gazprom of two of the station's independent directors just weeks before the March 2012 presidential elections was a not-so-subtle reminder of who calls the shots.[30]

How does Ehko Moskvy survive in Putin's Russia? One of the great shortcomings of a traditional totalitarian system is that widespread media censorship meant that the leadership had no way of assessing the public mood (in the Soviet system, this was one of the functions of the KGB, which obviously failed to deliver when it mattered). The critical reporting, the call-in shows, and the moderated public debates that are Ekho Moskvy's daily grist allow Russia's leaders to hear what people are thinking, at least the elite in Moscow. It also provides this same critical constituency some opportunity to air their grievances publicly and to feel informed and engaged. Finally, it mollifies foreign critics, by giving the superficial impression of an open society and obscuring the broader policy of legal repression and control.

In creating distinct policies toward mass media that operate under de facto government control and elite media that are given some latitude for critical expression Putin confronts a dilemma. In which category does the Internet fall? Throughout his time in power, Putin has treated the Internet the way he has treated Ekho Moskvy—a relatively harmless way for Russians to blow off steam. This made sense because Internet penetration in Russia is relatively low for an industrialized country—officially around 46 percent—and the Internet is generally available to the same segment of the population that already reads *Novaya Gazeta* and listens to Ekho Moskvy. But rising living standards in Russia and cheaper technology are threatening to turn the Internet into a form of mass communication. As he has done successfully in the past, Putin is reassessing the threat and taking action.[31]

Perversely the first indication that the Internet was beginning to have a significant influence on national political life was the November 2010 attack on an outspoken blogger, Oleg Kashin. While Kashin had a column with the business daily *Kommersant*, he was very much a member of the emerging online community, a prolific Tweeter and social media user who offered scathing commentary on a variety of issues, from environmental depredations to the rise of Kremlin-backed nationalist groups. His attackers waited for him outside his home in central Moscow with metal rods hidden in bouquets of flowers. A gruesome video captured by a security camera shows them delivering a blizzard of blows, making a special point of destroying Kashin's hands.[32]

Kashin's beating fueled an outpouring of indignation from Moscow's online community, which helped fuel popular mobilization around the December 2011 parliamentary elections and the March 2012 presidential polls in which Putin, after a four-year hiatus as prime minister, was returned to office in the Kremlin. The antifraud protests were concentrated in Moscow and featured tech-savvy youth who organized online and shared critical posts and links. This was the first time the Internet was a factor in Russian political life. An independent blogging platform, livejournal.ru, became a vital source of critical commentary, and the leading opposition figure, Alexsei Navalny, hosted a wildly popular anticorruption blog.

But the Moscow protests, which drew tens of thousands of animated Putin opponents into the streets in the weeks after Putin was returned to the presidency with 60 percent of the vote, fizzled quickly after Putin was inaugurated in May 2012. Putin made clear he now saw the Internet as a political threat that he was determined to control, an effort that responded to his fears of a Color Revolution. This is the kind of rapidly escalating mass movement that filled the streets and toppled governments in Georgia and Ukraine. Putin does not see such street protests as spontaneous expressions of popular will; rather, he views them as carefully orchestrated political movements carried out by determined political opponents and financed by Western governments. He recognizes the role of mass media in generating support for street protests, which is one reason he has kept a tight lid on the national broadcasters. Now, online journalists, bloggers, and activists were in his sights.

Once in office Putin wasted no time in launching a broad crackdown on civil society and the media. Critical bloggers and other dissidents were rounded up and harassed. Navalny was arrested and convicted on trumped-up corruption charges then freed on appeal and allowed to compete in Moscow's mayoral elections in September 2013, finishing a strong second with 27 percent of the vote. He was subsequently given a five-year suspended sentence, a verdict that could legally block his participation in electoral politics. Even more alarming was the emerging effort to restrict the Internet. Under the guise of blocking child pornography, the state Duma passed sweeping legislation granting authorities broad discretion to ban websites without adequate due process or review. In March 2013, the Duma member Aleksey Mitrofanov, who heads the Parliamentary Committee on Information Policy, warned that "an era of absolutely free Internet in Russia has ended." "When there were around two million users, the Internet was not a political or economic factor; it was not a factor at all," Mitrofanov explained. "But when it became a factor then they [the authorities] are going to deal with it."[33]

Putin's unique contribution to the democratator model has been to construct a system that is ruthlessly efficient in using the law to squelch political challenges and utterly incapable of using the law to bring to justice those who perpetrate violence against his critics, including a number of leading journalists. In most of the countries around the world, journalists confront either the threat of violence or the threat of state repression. But in Russia they confront both. The Russian government exercises too much control—and, by its own design, too little.

Democratators confront a paradox in that they must win popular elections in order to carry out the repressive policies that keep them in power. Once in office they claim to be fulfilling the popular mandate and acting within the framework of international norms.

In Venezuela, Chávez's popular mandate derived from his connection to his country's downtrodden majority to whom he has directed considerable state resources. In Russia, the Putin narrative is that untrammeled democracy leads to chaos, at least in the Russian context, and that his disciplined, rational approach has delivered a higher standard of living and greater personal liberties (but not political freedom) for all Russians. Erdoğan, meanwhile, has brought stability and steady growth to Turkey while challenging the power of the entrenched elite, including the military. He casts the steps he has taken to counter terrorist and security threats as necessary and consistent with the practices of democratic governments.

For human rights and press freedom groups, the key to challenging the power of these new autocrats is to disrupt their narrative of progress by exposing and publicizing the mechanisms of repression. How this can be accomplished is discussed in the final chapter of this book, but it should be noted that human rights groups and press freedom groups have achieved some success, and widespread international campaigns have led to a reduction in violence against the press in Russia and a reduction in the number of journalists jailed in Turkey.

At the same time, the durability of the democratator model in Russia, Venezuela, and Turkey shows that governments are growing more sophisticated and more effective at managing repression and that despite new information technologies they are able to control the media and selectively censor information they deem harmful to their political interests. Democratators are spreading—in Latin America among the leftist bloc that allied itself with the late president Chávez; in Europe, in states like Hungary, that are backsliding on their democratic commitments; and even for a time in the Middle East, where the Egyptian president Mohamed Morsi drew inspiration from the Turkish example. These governments do not see independent media as a bulwark against government abuse; rather, they perceive it as a competing political interest like so many others that must be managed and controlled. The sad reality is that the majority of voters seem to agree.

THREE

~~The Terror Dynamic~~

On February 4, 2005, the Italian journalist Giuliana Sgrena left the relative safety of her Baghdad hotel and traveled to a mosque near Baghdad University. Refugees from Fallujah—where the U.S. Marines had waged a brutal campaign to oust al-Qaeda-aligned militants— had taken shelter there, and Sgrena wanted to document their experience. But the Fallujah refugees were having none of it. "We don't want anybody," one of their leaders told Sgrena. "Why don't you stay at home? What can this interview do for us?"

Not getting the story was a bitter disappointment for the fifty-six-year-old veteran from the leftist *Il Manifesto*, who had covered conflicts around the world. But it was just the beginning of what would turn out to be a terrible ordeal. As Sgrena was leaving the interview, several men in a minibus cut her off and abducted her and her driver. Sgrena managed to dial out on her cell phone while she was being taken away, and a colleague in Rome said he heard "pistol shots and people running, but I did not hear her speak."

Two weeks later, Sgrena appeared on one of the most wrenching hostage videos to emerge from the Iraq war. Looking frail and bereft, she pressed her hands together while beseeching the Italian government to save her life by withdrawing its forces from Iraq, as her captors had demanded. "I beg you to help me," she said between sobs. "I beg my family to help me and those who stood with me to oppose the war and the occupation." A banner identified her captors as a previously unknown group, "Mujahedeen Without Borders."

Moved by Sgrena's ordeal—and angered by Italy's involvement in a deeply unpopular war—tens of thousands of people took to the streets in Rome to demand her release. Banners with her photo were hung from Rome's city hall. Under tremendous pressure to resolve the hostage crisis, Prime Minister Silvio Berlusconi dispatched to Baghdad his personal friend Nicola Calipari, a veteran Italian security agent and hostage negotiator.

On March 4, exactly a month after she was first abducted, Sgrena's captors put her in a car, covered her eyes with cotton and dark sunglasses, and drove her through the streets of Baghdad. Then they got out, leaving her alone. Ten minutes later, she heard a friendly voice. "Giuliana, Giuliana, I am Nicola. Relax, You're free." There were widespread reports that the Italian government had paid a ransom of between $6 and $8 million to secure Sgrena's release.

Sgrena's relief was short lived. Less than a mile from the safety of Baghdad International Airport, her car came under fire from U.S. soldiers manning an improvised checkpoint. Calipari threw himself on top of Sgrena and tried to protect her from the hail of bullets. He died after being shot through the head. Sgrena was injured by shrapnel in the shoulder. She was transported to a hospital in Baghdad, then flown home to Italy to recover.[1]

U.S. forces claimed that Sgrena's car had approached the checkpoint at a high rate of speed and had not responded to the flashing lights and warning shots. Sgrena denied it all; the car was not speeding, and no warning of any kind was issued. An internal investigation carried out by the U.S. military faulted Calipari for "not coordinating with U.S. personnel," noting that this was "a conscious decision on the part of the Italians as they considered the hostage recovery an Intelligence mission and a national issue."[2] A separate investigation, carried out by the Italian government, noted that the Italians had alerted U.S. authorities to the Sgrena rescue operation but saw no reason to keep them informed about its movements inside Iraq since the rescue team was on the road prior to the 11 p.m. curfew.[3]

Sgrena's ordeal encapsulated the challenges reporters faced in Iraq, squeezed between militants who targeted them and U.S. forces who either viewed them with extreme suspicion or failed to implement policies to mitigate risk. The deadly consequence of this twin threat was an unprecedented media death toll in Iraq, with more than two hundred journalists and media workers killed over the course of the war.[4] But the violence emanating from Iraq was part of a larger global trend, which saw journalists' killings spike worldwide. Between 2002 and 2012, 506 journalists were killed, according to CPJ data, compared to 390 in the previous decade.[5] One factor contributing to the increase was that during this period journalists became regular victims of terrorist violence, including murders and kidnappings.

The tactics employed by terror groups—including the proliferation of suicide attacks—inevitably fueled aggressive antiterror tactics, which further jeopardized the safety of journalists. In fact, journalists working in Baghdad at the time of Sgrena's abduction described checkpoints as exceedingly perilous, and many reported being menaced and having warning shots fired at them. Two journalists from the Saudi-backed Pan-Arab network al-Arabiya were killed in March 2004 by U.S. forces, and in January 2005 the NPR correspondent Anne Garrels came under fire from Iraqi soldiers helping man a U.S. checkpoint. In the aftermath of the Sgrena shooting, CPJ and Human Rights Watch sent a joint letter to Defense Secretary Donald Rumsfeld calling for improved procedures.[6] Military forces in both Iraq and Afghanistan also viewed the press with increased hostility because someone walking around the battlefield with a camera might not be a journalist at all but rather a propagandist for the insurgents. Iraqi and Afghan reporters—including those working for established international news agencies—were regularly detained, abused, or interrogated based on this suspicion.

The terror threat has transformed the way large media organizations operate around the world. Journalists, wary of kidnappings and bombings, sometimes had to report from fortified bunkers and were more reluctant to meet with sensitive sources for fear they might be set up for abduction. Military forces honed their communications strategies as well, often providing full support and access to embedded reporters and treating independent journalists with disdain. As a result, critical stories have gone largely unreported. Journalists working in Iraq at the height of the conflict struggled to report effectively on the opinions of average Iraqis or to provide a coherent picture of the insurgency or its political demands. The lack of information hindered policy makers and undermined global understanding. Similar dynamics have played out wherever al-Qaeda exerts influence, from Afghanistan, to Yemen, to Mali and Syria.

The Pearl Killing

The new wave of terror attacks on the media began with the murder of the *Wall Street Journal* correspondent Daniel Pearl, killed in Pakistan in February 2002. Pearl was not the first high-profile Western journalist to be kidnapped. Among the many journalists who have suffered such a fate were the AP correspondent Terry Anderson, kidnapped in Lebanon in 1985, and Charles Glass of ABC News, kidnapped there in 1987. The CBS News correspondent Bob Simon and NPR reporter Neal Conan were both held by Revolutionary Guards in Iraq in 1991. But these journalists were eventually released (Glass escaped his captors), often after intensive international campaigns. The motive for the kidnappings was also clear. In most cases, journalists were kidnapped either to influence coverage or to extract a political advantage.

What was particularly unsettling about the Pearl abduction was not only the terrible way it ended. It was also the murkiness of the motive. Why precisely had Pearl been kidnapped, and what advantage did his abductors seek to extract? The question has never been adequately answered, perhaps because Pearl's kidnappers and executioners never fully considered the reasons for their actions. While the Pearl abduction is widely perceived as the culmination of an elaborate plot, it was much more of crime of opportunity.[7]

The events that would lead to Pearl's kidnapping and murder were set in motion on September 11, 2001. The next day, Pearl, the *Journal*'s South Asian bureau chief, traveled from his base in Mumbai, India, to Karachi, Pakistan, to investigate the 9/11 attacks, then stayed on reporting from Pakistan. He was working in Islamabad on a story about Richard Reid, the so-called shoe bomber, after his December 22, 2001, attempted attack. Pearl believed that Reid had links to a reclusive radical cleric named Sheik Mubarak Ali Shah Gilani. As word spread in Islamist circles that Pearl was looking to interview Gilani, a British

Pakistani militant named Omar Sheikh saw an opportunity to lure the reporter into a trap.

Sheikh, who grew up in Britain and attended the London School of Economics, had an ease and sophistication that made him seem familiar and trustworthy to Westerners. Yet Sheikh, only twenty-eight years old, was a committed Islamic militant who had organized the kidnapping of Western tourists in India in 1994. He was arrested for that crime but freed in 1999 in exchange for passengers on an Indian Airlines flight hijacked by Pakistani militants.

Sheikh was able to convince Pearl that he could arrange a meeting with Gilani in Karachi, the lawless port city where Islamic militants have a strong presence. (As it turned out, Gilani, who was not involved with Richard Reid, was laying low in Lahore.) Immediately following his meeting with Pearl near Islamabad, Sheikh flew to Karachi to assemble the kidnapping team. The entire operation was thrown together in two days, and many of the planning meetings were held in restaurants and other public places, including a McDonald's.

On January 22, 2002, Pearl and his pregnant wife Mariane flew to Karachi, where the *Wall Street Journal* reporter expected to meet with Gilani. The next evening, at around 7 p.m., a taxi driver dropped Pearl at the popular Village Restaurant, from where Pearl left voluntarily, climbing into a red Suzuki Alto that he expected would take him to the Gilani interview. Instead, he was driven to a safe house provided by a local businessman and militant leader that was located in an isolated neighborhood on the outskirts of the city and surrounded by a high wall. Later, Pearl was stripped of his clothes, given a tracksuit, and chained to a car engine in a cinderblock outbuilding.

At the time of the kidnapping, Omar Sheikh had already left Karachi in an apparent attempt to create deniability. But he continued to communicate with the kidnappers, whom he instructed to send photos to the media accompanied by demands for the release of prisoners held by the U.S. military in Guantánamo Bay, Cuba. Sheikh did not plan to kill Pearl when he kidnapped him and in fact did not participate in his execution.

Khaled Sheikh Mohammed, the al-Qaeda operations chief who had planned the September 11 attacks, had fled Afghanistan after the

U.S.-led invasion and settled in Karachi. Mohammed initially learned of Pearl's kidnapping through newspaper accounts. Mohammed—who is referred to by U.S. officials as KSM—only become involved in the Pearl operation after receiving a call from another senior al-Qaeda official. Money may have changed hands, or Mohammed may have simply muscled his way in on the kidnapping operation. In late January or early February, Mohammed showed up at the safe house where Pearl was being held with two men, possibly his cousins, and a shopping bag holding knives and a video camera.

The decision by Mohammed to murder Pearl was apparently based on several factors, none of which appear to have been considered carefully. First, Pearl's murder was a way of demonstrating ruthlessness and resolve in the face of the U.S.-led invasion of Afghanistan that had toppled the Taliban government, devastated al-Qaeda's terrorist infrastructure, and taken a considerable toll on the organization's leadership. Mohammed later told interrogators at Guantánamo, where he is now being held after being captured in Pakistan in March 1, 2003, that Pearl's Jewishness was "convenient" but was not the motive for his abduction or murder.

Based on the gruesome video made of Pearl's killing—which was actually a reenactment because the video camera failed on the first take—Mohammed clearly saw the murder as a recruiting tool that he hoped would inspire al-Qaeda followers. It certainly sent a message of contempt for Western public opinion and to the journalists who helped shape it.

But there were deep divisions within al-Qaeda about whether the Pearl killing advanced the organization's interests, according to Morris Davis, the former chief prosecutor for the Guantánamo Bay military commissions. Morris claimed that "Osama bin Laden was angry that KSM had slaughtered Pearl so publicly and brutally, arguing that the murder brought unnecessary attention on the network," according to a report from the Pearl Project, a team of journalists that investigated the journalist's killing.[8]

Bin Laden himself was obsessed with his image and had a sophisticated understanding of the international media. He granted interviews to a number of Western journalists prior to the 9/11 attacks. Peter

Bergen, who produced a 1997 CNN interview of bin Laden with Peter Arnett, noted that as a journalist "once you came into bin Laden's inner circle you never felt threatened. He did fairly active outreach with media and threatening journalists would have been counterproductive."[9] Indeed, bin Laden used the 1997 interview with Arnett to reiterate his declaration of jihad against the United States, and when asked about his future plans noted, "You'll see them and hear about them in the media, God willing." In May 26, 1998, bin Laden arranged for a large group of Pakistani journalists to interview him, and two days after that he sat down with John Miller from ABC News. "Publicity was the currency that bin Laden was spending, replacing his wealth with fame, and it repaid him with recruits and donations," wrote Lawrence Wright in *The Looming Tower*, his history of al-Qaeda.[10]

Indeed, one of the most disturbing aspects of the Pearl murder was the role that the international media played in amplifying the message of terror. After he was kidnapped, Pearl's family and colleagues came to the conclusion that the best way to win his release was to create the most sympathetic possible rendering in the global media. This was in accordance with the prevailing thinking at the time, which held that humanizing a kidnapping victim like Pearl and generating global sympathy and support would raise the political cost of killing him. It was a strategy that had worked reasonably well in previous high-profile kidnappings of journalists, such as Terry Anderson, who was released at the end of a seven-year campaign.

At CPJ—where all of us were deeply moved by his ordeal and where some of our staff knew Pearl personally—we shared this view and did all we could to generate additional awareness and sympathy, particularly in Pakistan, where we had good contacts in the media. We were in regular touch with the *Wall Street Journal* to coordinate strategy and tried to take some of the burden off of editors at the paper by responding to the relentless demand for media interviews, particularly from cable news stations. We organized an open letter from leading journalists in the Arab world demanding Pearl's release, and we provided moment-by-moment updates on our website. Publicly, we made the argument that journalists covering conflict have always made when they get in a jam, calling on the kidnappers to release Pearl so that he could "tell their story."

Pearl's pregnant wife, Mariane, while initially reluctant to do media interviews, was eventually persuaded that this was the best hope for saving her husband's life. With her French and Cuban background, she presented a worldly, optimistic, and compassionate outlook and was a compelling figure. Prominent Muslims—from the boxer Muhammad Ali to the singer Youssef Islam, formerly Cat Stevens—urged the kidnappers to release Pearl in the name of Islam.

While no one could have known it at the time, this strategy played into KSM's hands, allowing him to maximize the emotional pain inflicted through Pearl's murder. Through intensive media coverage many people developed such a close identification with the reporter that when he was killed they reacted as if they had lost a friend.

For al-Qaeda's followers Pearl's murder sent a different message: International journalists were legitimate targets of terror operations, and the goal should be to maximize media attention of such abductions. The fact that the Pearl murder may have stemmed from the impulsive actions of KSM rather than official al-Qaeda policy no longer mattered. Targeted attacks on the media carried out by militants either linked to or inspired by al-Qaeda multiplied, and this in turn had a profound effect on the ability of journalists to report the news from parts of the world where the group maintains a presence. In many instances, the implied sanction conferred by Pearl's murder provided a modicum of a religious justification for what was essentially a criminal enterprise, kidnapping for ransom. Meanwhile, the snuff video became such an effective tool for generating media coverage that it was eventually adapted and put to entirely different purposes by criminal organizations in Mexico.

Pearl's murder deeply unsettled the relatively tight community of international correspondents and had a significant effect on the way media organizations went about their business. From Cuban revolutionaries to PLO fighters, militant and revolutionary groups had historically sought to cultivate journalists because they offered the sole conduit to communicate with the broad global public. Historically, journalists had found that their inherent usefulness was their best insurance policy. But the Pearl killing "changed the rules of the road," according to Peter Bergen, who said prior to the murder he would "not have given a second thought to wandering around Karachi or wandering around Afghanistan."

Al-Qaeda's rise as a militant network resulted in good measure from the organization's ability to exploit inexpensive and ubiquitous Internet technology to coordinate terrorist actions, including the 9/11 attacks. They also relied on the Internet to communicate with their following and with the global public, "obviating the need to talk to journalists," according to Bergen. It is of course ironic that the same information technologies that have allowed people around the world to become more connected and more informed have increased the risk to professional journalists working in conflict zones. The proliferation of new forms of communications has undermined the single most important factor that kept journalists safe—the de facto information monopoly that made them useful to all sides.

While the al-Qaeda leadership may not have made an active decision to murder Pearl, his killing did send a clear message that in the Internet era there were other ways to communicate and that traditional journalists were dispensable, useful primarily as hostages and props in elaborately staged videos designed to convey a message of terror to the world.

Terror in Iraq

The threat to the media implied by the Pearl murder became the reality in Iraq where journalists in large numbers became victims of terrorist violence. The Iraq war was the most deadly conflict for the press in history, but most journalists were not killed in combat situations. Murder was far and away the leading cause of death, comprising 62 percent of those killed. International journalists faced extraordinary risk, like all foreigners operating in Iraq at the time. But the vast majority of the journalists killed—83 percent—were Iraqis.[11] They were singled out for a variety of reasons—in reprisal for their coverage, because of the affiliation with Western news organizations, and as a means of undermining the formation of Iraqi civil society. It is important to note that the strategy was largely successful. While the postinvasion period saw a brief flourishing of indigenous media, independent voices were quickly snuffed out as the civil conflict intensified. By late 2004, Iraqi media outlets had split along sectarian lines, and those seeking to report in some semblance of neutrality were routinely targeted.

Perhaps the low-water mark was the 2006 murder of the television reporter Atwar Bhajat, who began her journalism career as an on-air correspondent for an Iraqi national network before joining al-Jazeera and, shortly before her death, al-Arabiya.[12] Born to a Shiite mother and Sunni father, Bhajat was arguably the country's best-known journalist, recognized for her fearless coverage of the conflict and her efforts to use her reporting to overcome the emerging sectarian divide. She refused to identify Iraqis in her reports as Sunni and Shiites—telling her editors that such identification only fueled divisions—and wore a gold pendant in the shape of her splintering country. Bhajat, only thirty years old, was murdered along with her two-person crew when she rushed to cover the fighting in her hometown of Samarra, which erupted in violence after Sunni militants blew up a Shiite shrine. A witness later reported that men driving a white van were searching for Bhajat, demanding to know the whereabouts of the "correspondent." Their precise motives have never been determined, although one of the kidnappers of the *Christian Science Monitor* reporter Jill Carroll boasted that he had killed Bhajat because "she said the Mujahedeen are bad."[13]

Kidnapping journalists also became a favored strategy of militant groups, and the tactic was used both to generate ransom and apply political pressure. Between 2004 and 2009, fifty-seven journalists were kidnapped in Iraq.[14] Seven of them were Americans, nineteen were Europeans, twenty-three were Iraqis, and eight more came from other countries. Many of the kidnapped Iraqis were employees of international news organizations, and seventeen of these fifty-seven journalists were murdered in captivity.

The first documented kidnappings of journalists in Iraq took place in early 2004, during a period of intensifying sectarian violence. These initial cases appear to have been motivated by the desire of the emerging militias to assert authority over physical territory. The ostensible justification for the detention and interrogation was to verify the journalists' credentials and determine if they were spies. The kidnapped journalists were generally released after a few hours. Among those detained were Stephen Farrell, then with the *Times* (London); John Burns from the *New York Times*; and journalists from Japan, the Czech Republic, and France. In at least some instances the kidnappers simply Googled the reporters' articles to confirm that they were in fact members of the press.

The stakes changed dramatically as al-Qaeda began to increase its presence in Iraq throughout 2005 and to integrate its operations with the emerging Sunni militias. Al-Qaeda's media strategy in Iraq was never fully articulated and reflected the networked nature of the organization. But there was no question that in the aftermath of the Daniel Pearl killing al-Qaeda-aligned and -inspired groups both inside and outside Iraq considered journalists, particularly Western journalists, legitimate targets.

Many of the foreign fighters who poured into Iraq to support the insurgency had trained in al-Qaeda camps in Afghanistan, and some had fought in the wars in Bosnia or Chechnya. The most prominent among the foreign militants—thanks in part to the U.S. government media campaign to paint him as the face of Islamic terrorism in Iraq—was a Jordanian who went by the name Abu Musa'b al-Zarqawi.[15] In May 2004, Zarqawi's group earned global attention with a grizzly execution video of an American businessman named Nicolas Berg. The video showed Berg sitting in an orange jumpsuit—a reference to Guantánamo prisoners—surrounded by five heavily armed men clad in black military attire with their faces covered. After reading a proclamation, the executioner, reputed to be Zarqawi himself, grabs Berg by his hair and uses a knife to sever his head from his body.[16] The execution borrows heavily from the iconography of the Pearl video. A month later—and for good measure—Zarqawi's group decapitated a South Korean contractor also clad in an orange jumpsuit. On August 19, another al-Qaeda-linked militant group managed to get its hands on a journalist, the Italian freelancer Enzo Baldoni. After releasing a video threatening to kill Baldoni if Italian forces did not withdraw from Iraq within forty-eight hours, the kidnappers carried out their threat.

The same militant group that kidnapped Baldoni also nabbed two French journalists, Christian Chesnot and Georges Malbrunot, along with their Syrian driver.[17] The fate of the two French journalists inspired protests in Paris and a massive media campaign. While there is no evidence this had any effect on the kidnappers, it undoubtedly put additional pressure on the French government to resolve the case. The *Times* (London) reported that the French government paid $15 million dollars for the release of the two journalists. The French government maintains it did not pay ransom. On January 5, 2005, another French reporter, Florence Aubenas, a correspondent for *Libération*, was abducted outside her Baghdad hotel along with her Iraqi translator, Hussein al-Saadi. The French government reportedly paid $10 million for her release.

The payment of ransom was a hugely complex and emotional issue for international journalists covering Iraq.[18] The U.S. government did not pay ransom but sometimes would stand aside and let families or employers make their own arrangements. The U.S. military was also more likely to launch a military rescue operation, making it more difficult and expensive for the kidnappers to keep American hostages for long periods. European governments, including the French and Italians, were widely reported to pay significant ransoms but officially always denied it. "We all believed that ransom was being paid in the European cases," noted Rajiv Chandrasekaran, who served as Baghdad bureau chief for the *Washington Post* between 2003 and 2004. "Privately I sure hoped that if I were picked up someone would pay a ransom for me. I do wonder if some of the militant groups would pick up the Americans for the propaganda value and pick up the Europeans to pay the bills."[19]

At the time that Western journalists were becoming an increasing target, al-Qaeda was expanding its media operations, intended both to inform and inspire its followers. "Jihad Media," as it was termed, ranged from al-Qaeda's official website, As Sahab, to the informal, unaffiliated bloggers and social media users who supported the cause.[20] Jihadi chat rooms were active forums to exchange information, debate tactics, and discuss matters of ideology and doctrine. Video was the primary form of communication for militant groups, and insurgent groups in Iraq, notably Zarqawi's forces, often incorporated videographers to record their operations. Their videos were sent out of the country to pro-al-Qaeda media production houses that turned them into minidocumentaries, often slickly produced, and then pushed them out to sympathetic websites. Media operations were compartmentalized, with al-Qaeda militants involved in military and terrorist operations in Iraq, Afghanistan, Pakistan, Somalia, Morocco, and Gaza using their own video production teams to document their activities.

Videos and other messages from the al-Qaeda leadership were often sent to al-Jazeera, and those deemed newsworthy were aired regularly on the network, a controversial practice harshly criticized by the U.S. government but also by journalists who covered the Iraqi conflict. The station defended the practice, noting that videos provided by the U.S. military were routinely aired on American networks.

These videos were both popular and effective, although numbers are hard to come by. However, it should be noted that kidnapped journalists who were held for extended periods in Iraq and Afghanistan describe their captors watching the videos for hours, cheering successful attacks on the U.S. military and engrossed by the beheadings. Al-Qaeda also began to develop media operations, specifically targeting Western audiences, including Muslims in the United States. They dressed up their propaganda in journalistic idioms with the English-language al-Qaeda magazine *Inspire*, famously featuring a how-to article entitled "Make a Bomb in the Kitchen of Your Mom" that reportedly served as the recipe for the pressure cooker explosives used by the Boston Marathon bombers. The founder of *Inspire*, the al-Qaeda propagandist Anwar al-Awaki, and his cousin Samir Khan, who edited the magazine, were killed in a September 30, 2011, drone strike in Yemen. Both were targeted despite the fact that they were American citizens.[21]

The al-Qaeda strategy of developing its own communications system while targeting independent and international media operating in Iraq transformed the media landscape in Iraq at the height of the conflict. From late 2004 until 2007, international reporters took their lives into their hands every time they left their fortified compounds, and armed security advisors, many of them ex-military, were integrated into newsgathering operations. The astronomical security costs ate up a huge percentage of the shrinking international news budgets, forcing news operations to cut back on coverage of other parts of the world and accelerating a process of consolidation that was already underway. The risks forced many international news organizations to rely on local stringers to do street reporting. These local journalists were less visible but more vulnerable. Militants particularly targeted Iraqi journalists working for the "Americans." Iraqi employees of the *New York Times*, AP Television News, and the American network ABC were all murdered.

The terror tactics also thwarted the development of an independent Iraqi media; this was part of a deliberate strategy to undermine civil society and institutions of the functioning state. While Iraqi media proliferated—with the establishment of dozens of broadcasters, newspapers, and websites—these outlets, like the rest of the society, became increasingly partisan and shrill. Rather than helping forge a common experience, media amplified the grievances of the different factions and groups, heightening the sense of victimhood and betrayal and fueling the divisions that sustained the civil war.

"We Don't Target Journalists"

On April 8, 2003, as U.S forces pushed into the heart of Baghdad, a unit assigned to Army's Third Infantry Division came under sustained enemy fire. A tank commander scanning the rooftops located on the upper floor of a tall building a person he believed to be an Iraqi spotter observing troop movements through binoculars and possibly calling in mortar strikes. He requested and received permission to engage the target and fired a single incendiary round into what turned out to be the Palestine Hotel, the center of international media operations in Baghdad. Two journalists, Taras Protsyuk from Reuters and José Couso from the Spanish broadcaster Telecinco, were killed in the attack, and several other journalists were injured. Earlier that same morning, amid an intense street battle, a U.S. missile struck a generator on the roof of the al-Jazeera bureau in Baghdad, killing the correspondent Tareq Ayyoub and injuring another staff member. The al-Jazeera office in Kabul had been bombed in November 2001 during the U.S.-led invasion of Afghanistan. No one had been killed in that strike.

A CPJ investigation determined that the shelling of the Palestine Hotel and the deaths of the two journalists were avoidable because senior U.S. military commanders were aware that the hotel was a center for the international media but failed to communicate the information to forces on the ground.[22] U.S. officials also failed to respond appropriately to the incident. Senior military officials asserted, falsely, that U.S. forces had come under fire from the Palestine Hotel and offered platitudes like "war is dangerous" and "we don't target journalists deliberately—not now, not ever."[23] A Pentagon investigation cleared all involved of wrongdoing.

While the U.S. military was open to embedding journalists in its military operations, it was callously indifferent to the presence of independent or "unilateral" journalists. Over the course of the conflict at least sixteen journalists were killed by U.S. forces' fire.[24] The killings were the inevitable consequence of the deployment of overwhelming firepower and the failure to take into account the possible presence of journalists in the combat environment. In August 2003, the Reuters correspondent Mazen Dana was shot and killed while filming outside the Abu Ghraib prison by a U.S. tank gunner who mistook his camera for an RPG. In July 2007, the Reuters photographer Namir Noor-Eldeen and his assistant were killed by U.S. forces firing on suspected militants from a helicopter gunship. Noor-Eldeen's killing was the focus of the infamous "Collateral Murder" video released by Wikileaks. While far more journalists in Iraq were targeted for murders by militant groups, the killings by the U.S. military helped fuel the perception encapsulated in the Sgrena incident that journalists were caught between the opposing forces. Moreover, they set a global precedent that resonated far beyond Iraq—in conflict and nonconflict zones around the world.

In many ways more troubling than the killings were the large number of journalists detained by U.S. military forces, because these were deliberate acts. Dozens of journalists were held in Iraq and also in Afghanistan, accused of everything from collaborating with militant groups to compromising operation security. Al-Jazeera reporters were a particular target and were detained on numerous occasions while covering operations. Pentagon officials often alleged that they had prior knowledge of the planned attacks. U.S. journalists working for large international media organizations were not immune. The situation was so acute that in November 2004 representatives of thirty U.S. and international media organizations sent a letter to the Pentagon spokesman Larry DiRita stating that they had "documented numerous examples of U.S. troops physically harassing journalists and, in some cases, confiscating or ruining equipment, digital camera discs, and videotapes."

Most detained journalists were questioned and released, but at least fourteen were held in Iraq, Afghanistan, and Guantánamo for extended periods without due process because of suspicion of involvement with insurgent or militant groups. Some were subjected to horrific abuse. Three Iraqi journalists working for Reuters near Fallujah in January 2004 were held for three days and, according to Reuters, "two of the three said they had been forced to insert a finger into their anus and then lick it, and were forced to put shoes in their mouths." Reuters also reported that "All three said they were forced to make demeaning gestures as soldiers laughed, taunted them and took photographs." Soldiers threatened to take them to Guantánamo Bay, "deprived them of sleep, placed bags over their heads, kicked and hit them and forced them to remain in stress positions for long periods."[25] In April 2006, U.S. forces in Iraq detained the AP photographer Bilal Hussein, whose photographs of insurgents firing on U.S. forces during the siege of Fallujah were part of a package awarded the Pulitzer Prize. Bilal was accused of having ties to insurgents but was never charged with a crime. He was held for two years and released in April 2008.[26]

When I met with officials at the Pentagon in summer of 2009 to discuss the issue of open-ended detentions of journalists, they actively defended their policies, arguing that they were engaged in an information war with al-Qaeda and that militants used journalists to further their propaganda goals. "Just because you are carrying a camera does not make you a journalist," argued Defense Department General Counsel Jeh Johnson during our meeting. "And how do you know that every journalist is innocent?"

It is understandable that al-Qaeda's media strategy of using videographers to document attacks fueled suspicion and made it harder for the U.S. military to differentiate between journalists and militant propagandists.[27] But the Pentagon's lack of due process in such cases set an extremely troubling precedent. None of the sixteen killings of journalists was ever adequately investigated, and most were not investigated at all. And none of the journalists detained by the U.S. military—including the al-Jazeera cameraman Sami Al-Haj, who spent six years as a prisoner in Guantánamo Bay—was ever subjected to any meaningful legal process much less convicted of a crime. For most international journalists in Iraq, the nightmare was of being kidnapped by al-Qaeda and imagining your family watching the videotape of your executions. But for Iraqi journalists in particular, the prospect of being mistaken for a militant by the U.S. military and shot while out gathering the news or being detained was also a considerable concern.

Public pressure and negotiations with the U.S. military and other allied forces did lead to some changes in policies. Checkpoint procedures were improved, leading to a decline in incidents involving journalists; the army field manual was revised to include training on the possible presence of journalists on the battlefield; and the U.S. military agreed to undertake prompt, high-level reviews and to notify media organizations within thirty-six hours whenever one of their employees were detained (although this procedure was not always followed). At the same time, the actions taken by the U.S. military in Iraq legitimated the notion that aggressive management and control over information is a key component of counterterrorism operations, and that example reverberated around the world.

During its December 2012 military operation in Gaza, the Israel Defense Forces targeted Palestinian media outlets that it designated as terrorist operations, justifying its measures by citing U.S. military attacks on al-Qaeda's information network. And when French troops carried out operations in Mali in early 2013 to drive out Islamic militants who had taken over the north of the country, they took pains to restrict media access, producing what one veteran reporter described as a "war without images or facts."

The antiterror rhetoric more broadly framed helped legitimate repressive actions in countries like Turkey, where, as noted in the previous chapter, Prime Minister Erdoğan denounced the PKK's "terror" media and called on Turkish journalists not to cover the Kurdish conflict, noting (falsely) that the U.S. and British journalists had declined to cover military operations in Iraq and Afghanistan. When Ethiopian government forces overran the positions of the separatist Ogaden National Liberation Front in June 2011, they detained two Swedish journalists who were embedded with the organization. The journalists, Martin Schibbye and Johan Persson, were subjected to mock executions, forced at gunpoint to participate in a crude propaganda video, and publicly condemned by Prime Minister Meles Zenawi as "messenger boys of a terrorist organization." They were convicted under Ethiopia's antiterrorism law and held for more than a year before being pardoned and expelled from the country. As troubling as that treatment is, it is not terribly different from the way that U.S. forces treated journalists they suspected of having ties to terrorism, including the two Reuters correspondents subjected to vile abuse by U.S. soldiers and the AP correspondent Bilal Hussein, detained for a year in Iraq without charge.

The terror/antiterror dynamic has played out differently in different conflicts and in different circumstances, but in every single instance it has had a devastating effect on the work of the media, transforming the coverage of war over the last decade. "When I covered the war in Bosnia in the mid-1990s for the *Christian Science Monitor*, foreign journalists were seen by both sides in the conflict as people to manipulate," recalled the veteran war correspondent David Rohde, speaking at a UN event on the safety of journalists. "Most local people did not like foreign journalists, but they tolerated us and generally viewed us as civilian observers, not parties to the conflict. Their basic goal was to get journalists to present their side's narrative of the conflict to the outside world."

"A decade later, when I covered Afghanistan and Pakistan for the *New York Times*, foreign journalists were no longer seen as civilian observers," Rohde continued. "They were seen by insurgents as a vehicle to vast fame among their fellow Taliban and vast wealth. This became clear to me five years ago when I was abducted by the Taliban while reporting in Afghanistan and taken to Pakistan's tribal areas. My captors' initial demands for my release were $25 million in cash and the release of fifteen prisoners from Guantánamo Bay, Cuba." After seven months in captivity, Rohde and a colleague escaped, using a rope to climb out a bathroom window and then finding refuge on a Pakistani military base. His case is discussed in greater detail in the next chapter.[28]

The situation in Syria at the end of 2013 was even more dramatic and volatile. When the conflict first exploded in early 2012, the more secular-minded rebels fighting the Assad regime welcomed the international media and protected journalists traveling with them on the front lines. The primary risk was from proregime forces that deliberately targeted the media, in one notorious incident in February 2012 shelling the improvised media center in Homs and killing the veteran foreign correspondent Marie Colvin and the French photographer Rémi Ochlik.

But as the al-Qaeda-aligned faction of the Syrian rebels gained the upper hand, the risk shifted. Journalists become specific targets of the Islamists, reportedly on the orders of Ayman al-Zawahiri himself, who had replaced bin Laden as the head of al-Qaeda. Once captured, the journalists were simply held. No ransom was demanded. No videos were made. Because of the fear that a media campaign would increase the emotional value of the kidnapped journalists, as had occurred in the case of Daniel Pearl, their friends and colleagues asked that there be no media coverage at all. At the end of 2013, more than thirty journalists, both international and local, were missing in Syria, believed to be held by the rebels. While their friends and families agonized, to the general public most of these journalists were unknown, nameless, and forgotten.

FOUR

~~Hostage to the News~~

Within the terror dynamic, there was one, specific, horrifying risk that emerged with Daniel Pearl in Pakistan, spread to Iraq, then to Afghanistan as that conflict intensified, then to Syria, once the jihadi rebels gained the upper hand, with flare-ups in other hot spots like Somalia, Yemen, and Mali. That risk is the institutionalized and now ritualized kidnapping, featuring hostage videos to exert political influence and secure ransom—and, if things went badly, the grisly execution. The actual number of journalist kidnappings is relatively small, although this is impossible to calculate precisely since many are kept secret. But their effect has been profound. Kidnappings have served in some instances as a vital source of revenue for militant organizations, helping sustain conflict. They have garnered significant publicity and attention for militant causes. And like all effective terror operations, they have had a profound emotional and psychological effect, changing the way that journalists operate.

As noted in the last chapter, journalist kidnappings are not a new phenomenon. Up to and including the Pearl case, the standard response was to use the power of the media itself to put pressure on the perpetrators to release their hostage. That strategy worked so long as those holding the journalist were affected by the negative publicity. But this logic was subverted by the Pearl case, in which publicity had no effect on the outcome and only served to draw attention to the kidnappers' message. In other instances, intensive publicity drove up ransom demands. In recent years, the pendulum has swung to the other extreme. Now, many cases of journalists' kidnappings are not reported at all. The controversial practice is known as a media blackout.

The media strategy for responding to journalists' kidnappings developed over years through trial and error without ever being formalized. The discussion among media organizations about how best to respond to kidnappings began in the summer of 2004 following the abduction of the filmmaker Micah Garen.[1] Garen was captured in the southern Iraqi city of Nasiriyah along with his translator Amir Doshi. The two were working on a documentary about the looting of archaeological sites and were accosted while filming gun dealers in the Nasiriyah market. They were trundled into a car and driven to the local office of the Mahdi Army, a militia that had formed in the Shiite slums of Baghdad in the aftermath of the U.S. invasion and grown into a formidable military organization with ties to the criminal underworld.

At the time of the Garen kidnapping, the Mahdi Army was engaged in a fierce confrontation with U.S. forces in the holy city of Najaf, and its leader Muqtada al-Sadr was pinned down with his fighters inside the Iman Ali Shrine. Perhaps because of the ongoing fighting, the Mahdi Army representative in Nasiriyah refused to take custody of the journalists. Angered at being rebuffed by Sadr's representative after delivering a person they believed to be an "American spy," the kidnappers drove Garen and Doshi to a remote hiding place they had fashioned in a cluster of date palms. As they rode in the car a young man wearing rectangular glasses reassured Garen in English: "Don't worry, we are not Zarqawi. If you are innocent, everything will be OK."

Garen's family, friends, and colleagues who had gathered in New York knew none of these details and were haunted by the specter of the Pearl killing. In fact, they reached out to Pearl's mother Ruth in California, who told them she was praying for Micah. "You need to keep positive," she counseled. Garen's girlfriend, Marie-Hélène Carleton, was besieged by the media and tormented over the decision of whether to launch the kind of public campaign that had been attempted in the Pearl case.

Soon word spread through Nasiriyah, eventually reaching Doshi's family, that the abduction was linked to the Mahdi Army. The information was reassuring because Sadr and the Shiite religious leaders in

Nasiriyah did not have a history of kidnapping journalists and might be vulnerable to public pressure.

But then things took a bizarre and unsettling turn. On August 18, the kidnappers released a video of Garen surrounded by four masked men holding automatic weapons and rocket-propelled grenade launchers. As Garen looked straight into the camera, one of his kidnappers read a statement saying that Garen would be executed if the U.S. forces did not pull out of Najaf within forty-eight hours. The group identified itself as the Martyr's Brigade, and the video iconography was borrowed from the al-Qaeda playbook. But the fact that the kidnappers were calling for a U.S. pullout from the Shiite religious city of Najaf seemed to confirm that, as Garen's kidnappers had told him earlier, this was not an al-Qaeda operation.

The challenge was to figure out how to convince Sadr and the Mahdi Army leadership that harming Garen and Doshi would undermine their political goals. The media became a key component of this strategy. At a time when Sadr himself was under siege in Najaf, the murder of a Western journalist would have helped the United States further vilify him and rally support for the military assault. Making a humanitarian gesture, on the other hand, could undermine that effort, allowing Sadr to demonstrate that while he was willing to fight to protect the interest of the Shiite population of Iraq, his struggle was principled.

On August 19, Garen's family gave an interview to Arabic-language satellite channels, making clear that while they did not hold Sadr responsible for the kidnapping, they were asking for his help in ending it. The following day, Sadr himself, still in hiding in Najaf, released his own written statement on his letterhead. It read, "From the lips of Sheik Muqtada himself, let him go within forty-eight hours and do not harm him." Garen and Doshi were soon brought to the Sadr office in Nasiriyah, where they were formally released. A week later, on August 27, the U.S. military agreed to a ceasefire, allowing Sadr and his men to vacate the Imam Ali Shrine in Najaf peacefully.

In early November 2004, Garen and his then-fiancée Carleton visited CPJ's offices to discuss their ordeal. Garen agreed that the use of the media was crucial to the successful outcome in his case and that in principle publicly affirming that a kidnapping victim is in fact a journalist can help dispel suspicion that he is a spy. He pointed out that his kidnappers had access to high-speed Internet and satellite television, which they monitored constantly. He was wary of emotional public appeals, which he believed were unlikely to have much of an effect on the kidnappers.

The Birth of the Blackout

While the media strategies became more sophisticated following the Garen case, the first attempt to impose a media blackout did not come until more than a year later, when the *Christian Science Monitor* correspondent Jill Carroll was abducted in Baghdad. Gunmen commandeered Carroll's car while she was on her way to interview a Sunni politician and executed her translator on the spot. Word of Carroll's kidnapping spread quickly among journalists in Baghdad, but her editors at the *Monitor* asked that media organizations withhold any coverage of the abduction. Their argument was that Carroll might be lying, denying to her kidnappers that she was a journalist for example, and media coverage might blow her cover. *Monitor* editors were also hoping that a blackout might somehow facilitate a quick negotiation for Carroll's release. After a few days, journalists grew uncomfortable withholding vital news, and the *Monitor* agreed to release a statement acknowledging Carroll's abduction.

In the end Carroll spent eighty-two days in captivity.[2] She was forced to make about a dozen videos, but only four of them were made public by the kidnappers. Meanwhile, the *Monitor* organized a media campaign calling for Carroll's release. While taking a relatively low-key approach in the United States, they sought to use local Iraqi media to paint Carroll as a friend of Iraq. It is not clear what role, if any, the media campaign played in the eventual decision to release Carroll. One of her captors' key demands was the release of Iraqi women held at the Abu Ghraib prison, of which there were only a handful. On January 26, the U.S. military released five female detainees, along with some 450 male prisoners. While the U.S. military insisted this was not done in response to Carroll's kidnapping, it did, as Carroll herself later noted, make it "harder to justify killing me."

In the aftermath of the Carroll kidnapping, international news bureaus in Iraq once again beefed up their security, and journalists limited their movements. To give one example, the *New York Times* bureau in Baghdad in 2006 consisted of "two houses with blast walls on all sides with crosshatched machine guns on the roof, forty-five armed guards, and three armored cars at a cost of about $250,000 each," according to the correspondent Dexter Filkins.[3] Describing conditions at the time, he noted: "We have at least one security advisor there all the time, and he's about $1,000 a day. Sometimes we have two. We haven't been able to, for some time really, go anywhere outside of Baghdad, and most of Baghdad is increasingly off limits to us, and increasingly off limits to our Iraqi staff, who would ordinarily be able to go out there. And so your circle just gets smaller and smaller every day."

Captive in Afghanistan

As a result of this kind of increased security, kidnappings of journalists declined in Iraq. The cost to newsgathering was high, but under the circumstances media organizations had few options. However, in Afghanistan, the situation was different. There, a relatively freewheeling media culture came up against a dramatically deteriorating security environment, resulting in a spate of new abductions. Journalists and other Westerners were targeted by both the Taliban and criminal organizations seeking to extract ransom.

One of the most devastating kidnappings took place in March 2007, when Taliban fighters nabbed the Italian journalist Daniele Mastrogiacomo and his assistant Ajmal Naqshbandi. The two had traveled to Helmand province for a prearranged interview with a legendary Taliban leader named Mullah Dadullah, who had lost a leg in the fight against the Soviets. While Naqshbandi had successfully arranged numerous Taliban interviews, there was always a risk, and this time things went terribly wrong. The entire interview was a trap. Mastrogiacomo later realized that Mullah Dadullah had orchestrated his abduction.

Throughout the five-week kidnapping, the Taliban used the media and the threat of violence masterfully to achieve their objectives and inflict the maximum amount of political damage on the government of President Hamid Karzai. Several days after snatching Mastrogiacomo and Naqshbandi, the kidnappers beheaded their driver Sayed Agha. The videotaped murder—replete with fighters gloating as the executioner wiped the bloody knife on his tunic—was aired on Italian television and also featured Mastrogiacomo pleading for his life. It so shocked and terrified the Italian public that Prime Minister Romano Prodi, his governing coalition shaky, put tremendous pressure on Karzai to capitulate to the captors' demands and release Taliban prisoners including Mullah Dadullah's brother. Prodi knew that an execution video featuring Mastrogiacomo could have easily led to the collapse of his government, and Karzai knew such a scenario could lead in turn to the withdrawal of the 1,800 Italian troops stationed in Afghanistan at the time. This was no doubt a factor in Karzai's calculations.

Mastrogiacomo was released on March 19 in exchange for five Taliban prisoners, but the Taliban captors held on to Naqshbandi, demanding the release of two more. On April 6, President Karzai went on television to declare he would not negotiate and described the deal for Mastrociacomo's release as "an extraordinary situation that won't be repeated again." Two days later, the Taliban announced that they had beheaded Naqshbandi. Anger at Naqshbandi's execution was directed at Karzai rather than the Taliban, and Afghan journalists took to the street to protest what they saw as a standard that placed a higher value on the life of a Westerner. In the documentary *The Fixer*, a former Taliban militant asserted that the order to execute Naqshbandi came from the Taliban's Pakistani backers, who saw an opportunity to weaken Karzai and advance their own strategic interests.[4]

In the aftermath of the Mastrogiacomo kidnapping, requests for media blackouts became more or less routine. There were exceptions. For example, when the BBC correspondent Alan Johnston was kidnapped in Gaza in March 2007, the British broadcasting network launched a highly effective global campaign that put pressure on the Hamas government to secure his release. Johnston was freed after 114 days in captivity. But there was also a clear consensus that if the kidnapping were carried out by an al-Qaeda-inspired group or even a criminal organization, then publicity was unhelpful. In the worst-case scenario, publicity increased the emotional toll the kidnappers could inflict through a videotaped execution, as had occurred in the Pearl case. Media coverage was also likely to fuel street protests and rallies calling for the journalists' release, which had no effect on the kidnappers but put pressure on governments to resolve the case, which in the European context generally meant paying ransom.

As someone who was in regular touch with media organizations to provide counsel when journalists were kidnapped, I also observed that they were increasingly relying on professional security companies. These companies systematized the response—setting up command centers, rotating staffing, keeping families informed, liaising with governments, and in some cases carrying out ransom negotiations with the kidnappers. While media organizations were conflicted about media blackouts because they sought to balance their essential responsibility to report the news with a desire to help their colleagues, security contractors experienced no such conflict. Their only obligation was to their client. Media coverage, they believed, could complicate sensitive negotiations and increase ransom demands. They also believed that managing media and responding to journalists' queries was a tremendous distraction during a period of crisis. Unless there was a specific objective to be achieved through the media, they believed, it was better to keep things quiet.

This was the dynamic that played out during the October 2008 kidnapping of the Canadian reporter Mellissa Fung, who was abducted while traveling to a refugee camp just outside Kabul. Her employer, the CBC, immediately requested there be no media coverage, a request that was honored for the twenty-eight days of her captivity. Fung was held in deplorable conditions, kept in a dank hole, denied adequate food, and sexually abused. Her kidnappers, led by two brothers, were not insurgents but rather common criminals who wanted a ransom payment; they did not have explicit political demands, nor did they make a video. In fact, Fung later reported, they did not even have a video camera. Fung was released after Afghan officials identified the kidnappers and detained their relatives, essentially orchestrating a hostage exchange that won the reporter her freedom.[5]

One of the most sustained and sophisticated media blackouts involved the *New York Times* journalist David Rohde, who was abducted in Afghanistan in November 2008 along with his fixer Tahir Ludin and their driver Asadullah Mangal.[6] Rohde, who had taken a leave from the newspaper to work on a book project, had arranged an interview with a Taliban leader he knew as Abu Tayyeb. Again, the interview was a trap. After being captured, Rohde, Ludin, and Mangal were marched across the border to Pakistan, where they were held for seven months, mostly in the town of Miranshah in North Waziristan.

The *Times*, in consultation with Rohde's wife Kirsten Mulvihill and the Rohde family, immediately requested a complete news blackout, which they actively enforced during the entire seven months of the captivity. The original motivation for the blackout was an early request from the kidnappers that there be no media attention. At some point, the kidnappers had a change of heart, producing a series of videos of Rohde that they hoped to get on al-Jazeera. In fact, according to Mulvihill in the book she coauthored with Rohde called *A Rope and a Prayer*, al-Jazeera purchased the tape for an "undisclosed amount" and even aired a short teaser. Al-Jazeera agreed not to air the tape only after the *Times*'s executive editor Bill Keller called the station's top brass in Doha to make a personal appeal.[7] Al-Jazeera's failure to put the video on the air apparently frustrated the Taliban captors, who, according to Rohde, saw the media as a tool they could use to demonstrate their brutality, raise their political demands, and increase the value of their hostages. It also frustrated Rohde's colleagues Ludin and Mangal, who had hoped media attention would stimulate ransom negotiations.

In June 2009, as those negotiations dragged on, Rohde and Ludin escaped, using a rope to climb out a window. They then made their way to safety at a nearby Pakistani army base. Mangal was eventually released from captivity and reunited with his family in Kabul.

Rethinking the Blackout

After Rohde was back in New York, I spent some time meeting with him and Mulvihill, talking to them about their own experience and considering how CPJ could be helpful the next time a journalist was kidnapped. While the media blackout obviously had nothing to do with Rohde's escape, he believed it was vital in making a complex and volatile situation easier to manage. I supported the blackout of Rohde's case and believed it was the right decision at the time. But after much consideration and reflection, I am no longer sure that blackouts are advisable except in the rarest of circumstances.

First, there is the question of their effectiveness. Certainly widespread media attention, including the broadcast of emotional appeals from family members and hostage tapes from the kidnappers, can drive up ransom demands or make it easier for the kidnappers to achieve their political objectives. But I'm hard pressed to come up with a case where the complete suppression of news was essential to a positive outcome in a kidnapping.

Second, requests for blackouts are difficult for media organizations to evaluate and can be confusing and contradictory. When they come from media organizations, such requests are generally honored, but when the requests came from governments they give pause. In December 2009, two journalists from the national broadcaster France 3 were kidnapped along with their Afghan colleagues by the Taliban while reporting on a road construction project outside Kabul. The French government called for a media boycott, but the families and press freedom organizations pushed back, holding public rallies and events to keep the case in the public spotlight. The two journalists were released in June 2011 after 547 days in captivity.

I have also seen cases in which family members and employers disagree on the need for a blackout and make contradictory requests. There was even a situation in Syria in early 2013 in which two journalists disappeared while working together, and the family of one asked for coverage while the family of the second asked for a blackout. Media organizations did their best to comply.

That kind of selective coverage—even with the best of intentions—damages the media's credibility since for the most part it is international journalists working for major international media outlets that receive the consideration. This is not a question of policy. As Bill Keller noted in defending the blackout in the Rohde case, the *Times* considers requests to suppress news of kidnappings not just for journalists but for others as well.

But in reality it is usually editors with large media organizations that are in the best position to make the request because they know whom to call in the critical first minutes and hours before the news becomes public. Moreover, the web of mutual obligations that have been created after repeated blackouts makes it hard for individual media outlets to deny requests even if they believe that the news value outweighs the potential risk for the kidnapped journalist. After aggressively enforcing the media blackout in the Rohde case, is the *New York Times* in a position to reject a blackout request?

The use of blackouts in journalists' kidnappings is also uncomfortable because media organizations routinely publish information that is embarrassing, damaging, and even dangerous to individuals for a variety of reasons. They do this because their primary mission is to inform the public, and they justify all sorts of intrusions on that basis. The issue of blackouts and media credibility arose again in December 2012 when the NBC correspondent Richard Engel was kidnapped while reporting in Syria. The media gossip website Gawker learned of the abduction and refused to honor a request from NBC to withhold coverage, incurring the wrath of many frontline journalists.[8] By late 2013, over thirty journalists were missing in Syria, many believed kidnapped by the Islamist factions of the Syrian rebels. Some of these cases were public, but about a dozen were not. The decision to black out coverage may have made sense in each individual instance, but collectively the large number of blackouts obscured the scope of the problem and reduced media coverage of the troubling shift in the security environment in Syria. In order to draw attention to the risk, CPJ decided to make public the total number of kidnapped journalists in Syria without providing names or details of specific cases.[9]

Going forward, however, I believe the best course of action would be for media organizations routinely to report the news of a journalist's kidnapping in a straightforward unemotional way, omitting, for example, demands from the kidnappers and indicating in clear language that they are withholding certain information at the request of family members or editors. Of course in the Internet age it would be a simple matter for the kidnappers to record their demands on a hostage video and post it online, and those who are interested in the information will find it. But if the mainstream media does not actively report on it, it is less likely to generate the kind of public pressure and visibility that complicate hostage negotiations. This is a compromise solution and one that poses significant challenges in a highly competitive environment in which news organizations no longer exercise a media monopoly. Nevertheless, if media organizations all over the world can agree among themselves *not* to cover journalists' kidnappings, then surely they can also agree on how to cover them.

~~FIVE~~

~~Web Wars~~

Founded in 1984 in the midst of the first wave of media reforms in China, the Guangdong-based *Southern Weekly* was launched with a modest goal. According to the original editor Zuo Fang, the newspaper would not necessarily print the whole truth. But it would not publish lies.[1] Over the course of its existence, its ambitions have grown. Today *Southern Weekly* is regarded as one the boldest and most innovative publications in China, renowned for its probing investigative reports on official corruption from every corner of the country.

The newspaper periodically publishes "special editions" pegged to major events or holidays. As 2012 came to an end, with a change in China's leadership on the horizon, editors were finalizing the details of a New Year's edition with an editorial letter as the centerpiece. The original editorial, according to a chronology compiled by David Bandurski at the China Media Project, played on the phrase "China Dream," coined by the general secretary and soon-to-be president Xi Jinping.[2] It called for "the dream of constitutionalism" to be realized in China.

When the newspaper hit the streets in early January, reporters and editors were appalled. The editorial had been completely rewritten by Guangdong's propaganda chief Tuo Zhen, who recast it as an innocuous and unchallenging bromide proclaiming, "We are now closer to our dreams than at any time before." That phrase was taken directly from an editorial in the official *People's Daily*. The magazine had been experiencing increased censorship of its news coverage, but the rewritten editorial crossed a line. By directly substituting official propaganda for independent editorial content, it undermined the integrity of the publication and the relationship of trust with readers. Journalists immediately denounced the unprecedented interference on the social media website Sina Weibo. As a firestorm spread online, dozens of journalists from the magazine launched a strike. Hundreds of supporters rallied outside the Southern Media Group headquarters in Guangzhou. The outpouring in defense of *Southern Weekly* and in support of press freedom attracted attention from the international news media. After a few days, central authorities stepped in to cut a deal. The government promised not to punish the journalists who had gone out on strike and also committed to easing up on censorship. The journalists agreed to go back to work.[3]

The protests, however, made an impression and led to one of the periodic flare-ups of what could be termed "Internet optimism" in China. This is a view that spreading online communication is empowering China's citizens and weakening the authority of the Communist Party. Another documented outbreak had occurred a few months earlier, in April 2012, when the artist and activist Ai Weiwei published an op-ed in the *Guardian* with a dramatic prediction. "It still hasn't come to the moment that it will collapse," he wrote about China's one-party system. "That makes a lot of other states admire its technology and methods. But in the long run, [Chinese] leaders must understand it's not possible for them to control the Internet unless they shut it off—and they can't live with the consequences of that. The Internet is uncontrollable. And if the Internet is uncontrollable, freedom will win. It's as simple as that."[4]

Ai—who has exploited virtually every communications medium from plastic art to documentaries to blogs to challenge the Chinese system of information control—has legitimate street cred and can't be dismissed as an Internet utopian. And he is hardly the first to make the prediction. The *New York Times* columnist Nicolas Kristof noted in a 2005 column that the Chinese leadership was "digging its own grave" by giving the Chinese people broadband.[5]

Many informed observers, activists, academics, and technologists not just in China but around the world share Ai's vision of the Internet as a liberating force. They believe that controlling the flow of information in the digital age is ultimately futile because governments—including the Chinese government—understand that they cannot deliver prosperity without embracing connectivity. In this vision, the peer-to-peer nature of online communication, the constant drumbeat of bottom-up technological innovation, and the overriding desire of people everywhere to inform and be informed overcome resistance from repressive governments that seek to control online speech. The view was summed up by the Egyptian democracy activist and former Google employee Wael Ghonim, who in a moment of wild exuberance following the fall of Egypt's President Hosni Mubarak in 2011 told CNN, "If you want to liberate a government, give them the Internet."

Some countries, such as North Korea, Cuba, and Eritrea, clearly believe this to be so and simply do not allow their citizens to access the global Web. Many more take the approach championed by the democratators, expressing rhetorical support for an open Internet and either seeking to hide their restrictive actions or engaging in more targeted censorship. Examples are Thailand, which blocks online criticism of King Bhumibol Adulyadej, and Turkey, which has shut down YouTube because of videos that insult Atatürk. (In March 2014, in the midst of a corruption scandal in which incriminating personal conversations were posted online, Prime Minister Erdoğan called for a complete ban on YouTube and Facebook in Turkey.)

China's approach is unique. The country's leaders embrace the Internet but argue that it is one of many tools that must be managed by the state to ensure economic development and social harmony. They directly challenge the notion that it cannot be controlled. This argument has obvious appeal in many countries that see the Internet as essential for economic development but want to limit its destabilizing and disruptive aspects. What distinguishes China is that it has the technological means and resources to make its vision a reality.

The preceding chapters have described some of the myriad ways in which technology has transformed international journalism. This chapter looks at the sustainability of the Internet itself as the primary vehicle through which news and information is disseminated globally. Based on my own experience, there are two essential questions that directly concern journalists and advocates for open societies. The first is whether the political environment that has allowed the Internet to flourish as a global system of largely unfettered information sharing is sustainable. This chapter explores the Chinese-led effort to recast fundamentally the nature of the Internet and use the United Nations to embed its authoritarian conception in its governance structure. The second question, covered in the next chapter, is whether the ability of governments to use Internet technology for the surveillance of journalists and their activities will chill global free expression.

The Chinese Way of Censorship

The Chinese government's Internet policy is most fully articulated in an April 2010 presentation from Wang Chen, the deputy director of the Chinese Communist Party's Propaganda Department. Wang's speech to the Standing Committee of the National People's Congress was posted online in early May of that year, then almost immediately taken down. It was later replaced with an edited and redacted version. But the original speech was captured and preserved by activists and translated by the U.S.-based organization Human Rights in China.[6] What's notable about the document is the comprehensive vision of the Internet as an indispensible component of national infrastructure, comparable to roads or high-speed rail. As Wang explained, "The Internet has now become a new tool for production in modern society, a new method for scientific and technological innovations, a new vehicle for trade and commerce, a new platform for social and public services, a new channel for mass culture dissemination, a new space for activity and entertainment, and a tremendous force in promoting economic development and social progress."

The Chinese government has invested heavily in Internet development, spending more than $600 billion to build more than eight million kilometers of fiber-optic cable. Today, there are well over 500 million Internet users in China (as many as 700 million in some estimates), more than any other country in the world. Most are quite satisfied with their online experience, which they find wildly entertaining. They can watch movies, download music, play games, use social networking sites, share photos, maintain blogs, and engage in nearly the full range of activities available to online users in the West. Most Internet users in China don't even realize that the Internet is censored—or if they do realize it, they don't care.

For Wang, one of the great benefits of this Internet revolution in China is that it allows people to raise their concerns directly with the government. "The Internet has increased the government's capabilities in social management and provision of public services," Wang noted. "It has opened up and broadened the channels that connect the Party and our government with the masses." But Wang also argues that people must be shielded from certain kinds of harmful information, including information about "security emergencies." While the Internet is a place to share information, it is certainly *not* a place to organize politically. Wang proposes strengthening Chinese law to ensure that this does not take place.

First, Wang asserts, China must retain control of the domestic Internet. Second, it must manage connectivity to ensure that China is able to exercise full sovereignty over what it perceives as an essential component of its national infrastructure. Third, China must harness the power of the Internet to combat negative perceptions of China internationally. He proposes establishing a "national web television station" and news websites in order to create "an international public opinion environment that is objective, beneficial, and friendly to us." Finally, Wang argues that China must push for a new system of global Internet governance and control that is more centralized and accountable to the demands of sovereign states.

Rather than imposing broad restrictions on Internet access, China practices "just-in-time" censorship that in most cases is narrowly targeted. Officials tolerate a broad range of expression, including criticism of government policies, and recognize that in a media environment as large and complex as China's it has to pick its battles. Criticism of the Communist Party, support for Tibetan or Uighur autonomy, or mentions of Falun Gong invite an immediate and firm reaction. But then there is a large gray area in which it is hard to predict the government response, for example reporting on corruption or abuse of power. In her 2012 book *Consent of the Networked*, the former CNN China Beijing correspondent and Internet freedom pioneer Rebecca MacKinnon describes this new system as "networked authoritarianism." She writes: "The key to the system's success is that the regime does not try to control everybody all the time; its controls on political information are nonetheless effective *enough* that most Chinese—including educated elites—are unaware, or have a distorted view, of many issues and events in their own country, let alone in the rest of the world."[7]

The best-known feature of China's system of Internet control is what has been termed the "Great Firewall of China," a complex and evolving system of Internet filtering that allows the government to block hundreds of thousands of undesirable websites. The Chinese system is based on the private network firewalls that prevent people from accessing prohibited websites from their work computers and was built with the same technology, purchased from the U.S. technology giant Cisco. The system works because all Internet traffic in and out of China passes through only eight gateways. It is true that for those with an interest and even a modicum of technological prowess the censorship system can be breached using circumvention tools like proxy servers. But only the most engaged Internet users in China make the effort.

The next layer of Internet control is indirect and involves what takes place within the virtual space already contained by the Great Firewall. Domestically, the Chinese government largely delegates censorship to private companies. This is known as "intermediary liability," and what it means is that every company operating in China—whether Chinese or foreign—is liable for everything that appears on its search engines, blogging platforms, or social networking sites. Companies receive directives on what to censor, but they are also expected to use their judgment and anticipate what might be objectionable to the authorities. Failure to censor aggressively can result in legal sanction up to and including loss of a business license. While Chinese companies—including the leading search engine Baidu—readily comply with these demands, international companies have not always been so enthusiastic. Google's discomfort with this policy was one of the reasons it shut down its domestic Chinese search engine in March 2010. (Google also came under a concerted state-sponsored cyber attack targeting the Gmail accounts of human rights activists based not only in China but in the United States and Europe.) Today, Google China operates out of Hong Kong, meaning the Chinese government can block it entirely. But it can't compel Google to censor its search results.[8]

If blocking and filtering don't work, China employs more direct methods. Dissident bloggers are often shouted down by government-employed commenters who troll the Web and post comments denouncing critics and supporting the official position. Nicknamed the "50 cent party" for the fee they are paid per post, progovernment commenters reportedly account for 20 percent of all posts in China.

In the aftermath of the successful uprising in Tunisia, Chinese authorities took preemptive action to block discussion of what was briefly termed the "Jasmine Revolution." In February 2011, a number of online activists called for those supporting reform in China to gather at an appointed hour and take an inconspicuous stroll through the streets of Beijing. The protest never got off the ground: Foreign journalists and security officials easily outnumbered the estimated several dozen people who participated. But Chinese officials were not taking any chances. They blocked online searches for "jasmine," removed from the Internet videos of officials singing a popular folk song about jasmine flowers, and interrogated florists about recent purchases of the flower, which is an iconic image in Chinese culture. They also cracked down on all expressions of popular dissent, rounding up journalists, activists, and critics.[9]

In cases of regional unrest, the central authorities have been known simply to unplug the Internet. This occurred briefly in 2008 when violent protests erupted in Tibet and even more dramatically in 2009 when ethnic riots broke out in the predominantly Muslim Uighur region, in China's northwestern Xinjiang Uighur Autonomous Region. Over a ten-month period, the Internet was entirely unavailable in Xinjiang—no e-mail, no Web access, and no Skype. International and cell phone services were also disrupted, including text messaging.[10] China is hardly the only country to throw the Internet kill switch in times of crisis. Iran, Burma, and Syria have also done so, as did Egypt famously at the height of the Tahrir Square uprising.

Online critics also face legal measures, up to and including arrest. Twenty-three of the thirty-two journalists jailed in China at the end of 2012 had worked online, according to CPJ research.[11] While traditional journalists working for mainstream media outlets are routinely fired or demoted for failing to follow propaganda directives, imprisonment is increasingly reserved for nontraditional journalists who use information to advance an activist cause. Nineteen imprisoned journalists are from the minority Tibetan and Uighur ethnic groups, including, for example, the documentary filmmaker Dhondup Wangchen, whose film *Leaving Fear Behind* chronicled daily life in Tibet in advance of the 2008 Beijing Olympics. He was released in June 2014 after serving a six-year sentence on state security charges.[12] Those jailed also include political dissidents who use the Internet to express ideas that in a more open environment would be published on the op-ed page of a daily newspaper. The Nobel Prize winner and democracy activist Liu Xiaobo is imprisoned not only for his political activism but for critical writing he published on overseas websites.

As Ai acknowledged, the Chinese system of Internet control has worked reasonably well. But there are enough tensions and flaws to give hope to the Internet believers. The 2008 Sichuan earthquake is generally regarded as a media milestone in China. When the quake hit on May 12—only twelve weeks before the Beijing Olympics were set to begin that August—Chinese and international journalists poured into the region, providing unprecedented firsthand accounts of the devastation. Chinese authorities may have been simply overwhelmed, but in the end they did not the make usual efforts to restrict coverage. Reporters provided gripping evidence of the human toll, incredible stories of survival, and portraits of officials struggling to deal with the emergency and provide relief. These reports were tolerated and indeed helped garner widespread sympathy and support for the victims both within China and around the world. But the government's response changed dramatically once reporting shifted to stories on government shortcomings, including the substandard school construction that led to the deaths of thousands of children who were crushed in the collapsed buildings. International journalists seeking to cover the story were manhandled, and at least two Chinese journalists were jailed. Independent reporting from the quake zone dried up.[13]

The government was also unable fully to control the narrative in the aftermath of the high-speed train crash that took place in Wenzhou in July 2011 and left more than forty people dead. Once again

journalists swarmed the scene and provided detailed accounts contra-
dicting the official version that attributed the accident to a lightning
strike. Popular suspicion was aroused by government efforts to bury
the damaged rail cars quickly rather than carry out a systematic investigation. When skeptical journalists demanded an explanation, the
Ministry of Railways spokesman Wang Yongping said that it was necessary to bury the train to support the rescue effort, then blurted out,
"Whether you believe it or not, I believe it anyway." The cynical comment raised further hackles, and netizens used Chinese social media
to vent their frustration.[14] A year later, when heavy flooding inundated
Beijing, Chinese journalists at a press conference openly challenged
public officials who refused to provide adequate information. However, officials limited the fallout by ensuring that critical stories were
removed from the Web.[15]

Chinese officials acknowledge shortcomings in their effort to manage the Internet. "As long as our country's Internet is linked to the
global Internet, there will be channels and means for all sorts of harmful foreign information to appear on our domestic Internet," Wang
conceded. A key strategy to address this problem is to encourage
the development of alternative Chinese technology that can be more
easily censored and controlled. Facebook and Twitter are blocked in
China but Sina Weibo—the Chinese Twitter equivalent—is flourishing. It has many appealing features not found on Twitter, such as the
ability to comment on posts. Renren and Kaixin are Facebook-like
social media sites. The Chinese video sharing site is called YouKu.
TomSkype is a joint venture with Skype, and WeChat is a popular
chat application particularly for mobile devices. All told there are estimated 590 million social media users active on such sites.[16] The government uses monitoring and filtering to make sure the conversation
does not get out of hand. According to the California-based *China
Digital Times*, posts containing certain keywords are banned from
publication, others are flagged for editorial review, and others can be
published but are unsearchable. The prohibited terms are constantly
changing, but almost two thousand were documented in a one-year
period beginning in April 2011. In December 2011, the Beijing municipal government issued a directive requiring Weibo users to register
their real names.

One issue that has played out repeatedly on social media is protests over land grabs. The Chinese authorities refer to public protests as "mass incidents," and of the estimated ninety thousand that take place each year, a third reportedly involve land disputes. The most dramatic recent example took place in Wukan, a fishing village in Guangdong, where residents rose up to protest land seizures by local officials and essentially drove out the local authorities after a series of violent clashes that took place in the fall of 2011.

"At the height of the Wukan incident, none of the Chinese media could get in to report, but villagers in Wukan and netizens kept updating their blogs until it drew the attention of the foreign press," recalled the investigative reporter Liu Jianfeng, who covered the Wukan uprising for *China Economic Times*. "A lot of foreign press got into Wukan after they saw it on Weibo. After that, the domestic media covered the story."[17]

The Wukan uprising became a parable about the ways in which social media and the Internet in China could empower local villagers and the media itself. But by the spring of 2013, the leaders of the protest movement had split, authorities had reasserted control, and none of the confiscated land has been returned. Meanwhile, one of the first media directives issued by the incoming government of President Xi Jinping seemed aimed specifically at controlling the particular kind of news cycle described by Liu, in which social media fuels international media attention, which is in turn picked up by the Chinese press. The directive banned Chinese media from citing international news reports without permission and required news organizations to keep records of all their activities on Weibo. While questions were raised about the enforceability of new directives, they sent a clear message that the new government had identified an emerging information threat and was determined to eliminate it.[18]

"A Big Country on the Internet"

While all of these measures help China manage online dissent, they do not address the leadership's more fundamental concern, which is the structure of the global Internet. As the *Peoples Daily* put it in an

August 2012 editorial, "Ultimate control over the Internet has been an important tool for the United States to promote its power politics and hegemony worldwide, and any other country may fall victim to this. As a big country on the Internet, China opposes the U.S.'s unreasonable and unilateral management of the Internet, and seeks to work with the international community to build a new international Internet governance system."[19]

In their groundbreaking 2006 book *Who Controls the Internet? Illusions of a Borderless World,* Jack Goldsmith and Tim Wu argued that governments have effectively asserted control over much of the Internet's infrastructure and use it to set national standards, something China has clearly done. But when it comes to the global system, which is much less regulated, the United States has a distinct advantage. The Internet was largely developed in the United States, and so the country retains disproportionate influence over the institutions that manage its infrastructure. Meanwhile, under the "code is law" maxim of Lawrence Lessig, global information companies like Google and Microsoft that are also based primarily in the United States set standards for the world. From a freedom-of-expression perspective, the outsized role of the United States has benefits. But recent U.S. actions have undermined the open-society values on which the Internet was built and have played into China's arguments for structural reform to enable greater state control.

The ability to use the Internet to communicate freely across borders is not an accident. The original developers of the Internet espoused a libertarian ethos and sought to build a system resistant to censorship, and it is this feature that has made it a unique platform for critical expression, including journalism. "The First Amendment is hardwired into the Internet," notes Danny O'Brien, who heads up global strategy at the Electronic Frontier Foundation, a San Francisco–based group that advocates for online freedom.[20] For the most part, the United States has defended the decentralized Internet and promoted it as a tool for free expression.

But the U.S. government has also used its privileged position to develop an unprecedented system of global surveillance. The contours of the U.S. online spying program are coming into focus as documents leaked by the former NSA contractor Edward J. Snowden are made public and analyzed. But what is already clear is that the United States has used control over the Internet's infrastructure—for example, the fact that much of the world's Internet traffic passes through servers in the United States—to vacuum up vast troves of information. The U.S. government has also used its legal authority over the U.S.-based Internet giants like Google, Yahoo!, and Facebook to compel compliance with demands for information.

For freedom of expression advocates, the U.S. efforts to use the Internet to spy on the world while simultaneously promoting freedom of expression online are contradictory. But China believes that a free and open Internet *and* massive U.S. surveillance are equally threatening to its national interests.

This is why China is desperately seeking to assert control over the global Internet's structure and pushing for an international framework recognizing what it calls "cyber sovereignty," the principle that within a state's territory the Internet should be under the jurisdiction of that country.[21] China is also advocating for a "multilateral and democratic management mechanism under a UN framework" to replace the current Internet governance system, which is commonly referred to the as the "multistakeholder model." In the current system governments, private institutions, civil society groups, and individuals all contribute to the management of the Internet.

From the Chinese perspective, the decentralized system of Internet governance poses significant security risks. Most immediately the loose coordination and global dispersion of stakeholders allows what Chinese officials deem to be "harmful" information from the global Internet to jump the firewall. It also inhibits China's efforts to control its image in the rest of the world. Chinese officials are concerned because the global Internet accessible *outside* China does not adequately reflect their perspective on key issues, like Tibetan autonomy. Particularly galling is the fact that a key piece of Internet infrastructure—the Root Name Servers—are administered by the Los Angeles–based Internet Corporation for Assigned Names and Numbers, or ICANN. While ICANN is a private corporation, it operates under license from the U.S. Commerce Department, which maintains oversight of critical functions. ICANN's main role is to serve as the Internet's traffic cop, making sure that information goes where it is directed. While

ICANN has opened itself up to public review in recent years and is formally committed to the multistakeholder process of broad consultation around policies, the reality is that input at its open meetings is largely limited to well-funded NGOs clustered in the United States and Western Europe. China has no particular influence.

The fact that the Obama administration has made the promotion of Internet freedom a central goal of U.S. foreign policy—a position hailed by U.S. Internet companies and many Internet freedom advocates—only reinforces the Chinese government's view that Internet freedom is really a cover to advance U.S. interests. In a landmark speech in January 2010, U.S. Secretary of State Hillary Clinton proclaimed, "On their own, new technologies do not take sides in the struggle for freedom and progress, but the United States does. We stand for a single Internet where all of humanity has equal access to knowledge and ideas."[22] Endorsing the "freedom to connect"—which Clinton likened to freedom of assembly online—she described how the United States is supporting online social movements and investing in the development of circumvention tools to allow people in repressive countries to overcome politically motivated censorship. A letter sent to NGOs on May 24, 2011, from the top State Department human rights official Michael Posner outlined U.S. government efforts not only to support new circumvention tools but to invest in the development of secure communications strategies for mobile phones, push banned content through domestic firewalls, train activists in cyber security, and provide direct support to online dissidents. From the perspective of the Chinese Communist Party, these activities do not spread freedom; they undermine its grip on power.

Of course, the United States increasingly has a credibility problem when it comes to advocating for Internet freedom, one that the Chinese government seeks to exploit. The U.S response to the WikiLeaks scandal—discussed in chapter 8—fueled charges of hypocrisy from critics who noted that U.S. support for Internet freedom seemed to soften when its own interests were threatened. The Obama administration's aggressive stance against online piracy is seen by many activists as an effort to protect U.S. commercial interests at the expense of online free expression. And of course the Snowden revelations have highlighted the strategic advantage derived from having so much of the Internet infrastructure physically located in the United States. At a UN-sponsored Internet Governance Forum that took place in Bali, Indonesia, in October 2013, a U.S. official who defended the NSA surveillance program as serving a "limited purpose" like "identifying terrorist threats and criminal activities" was booed by the delegates and publically admonished by a Chinese official who suggested that the United States look in the mirror.[23] "The role that the United States has been trying to play as the protector of freedom and openness, not too many people take that seriously any more," noted Rebecca MacKinnon.[24]

Using its growing diplomatic clout and soft power, China is building a global coalition to counter U.S. dominance on the Internet. The coalition includes major regional powers like Iran and Russia and myriad countries throughout Africa and the Middle East. They are fighting on two fronts. First, they seek to internationalize Internet governance by putting it under UN control. Second, they seek to challenge international legal standards, which define freedom of expression as a transnational right that is guaranteed "regardless of frontiers." In a report presented to the Geneva-based Human Rights Council in 2011, Frank La Rue, the UN's Special Rapporteur for Freedom of Expression, argued that in order to conform to international law, restrictions on online speech must be narrowly tailored to protect national security, public order, health or morals, and the rights and reputations of others.[25] China and its Internet-censoring allies do not agree.

"Freedom of expression was extended with the spread of democracy in the latter half of the twentieth century," observed the historian Timothy Garton Ash, who has written widely on the issue. "Today we have an emerging superpower, China, which has a nineteenth-century norm regarding state power. For many countries this view is attractive. They are very interested in China's example. Postcolonial countries across the board are able to say, 'Yes, you do have to pay regard to our frontier.'"[26]

Nowhere has China's influence on media and the Internet been more ambitious—and more pernicious—than in Africa, a region where aid and trade are forging new relations. In Ethiopia—which has a burgeoning online community operating mostly outside the country and working to break the government's stranglehold on information—the Chinese government has provided $1.5 billion in loans for training and technology to block objectionable websites and television and radio transmissions.[27] The investment in censorship technology is being coupled with a massive expansion of the Chinese media presence throughout the region. While much attention has been focused on the glittering facility that China has built in Times Square for its English-language international broadcaster CCTV, the more important investment has been in Africa. In Nairobi, Kenya, the Chinese government has built lavish studios that serve as a regional media hub, and CCTV has established fourteen correspondents throughout the region. "Many media do not give Africans a correct image of China, its culture and its plans in the continent," Liu Guangyuan, China's ambassador to Kenya, said in a speech marking the station's launch in January 2012. Kenya's vice president agreed. Kalonzo Musyoka praised the Chinese approach, which he claimed links media to development and offers nuance and depth in contrast to Western coverage, which portrays Africa as "the continent of endless calamities."[28]

Xinhua, the Chinese state wire service, which maintains twenty bureaus in Africa, provides dispatches free of charge to struggling African newspapers and is seeking to raise its profile as an alternative to Western media companies that both China and Africa insist have an inherent bias. China is also investing heavily in training, which includes not only journalists but also government press officers. Rodney Sieh, a Liberian journalist who participated in a three-week-long seminar in Beijing in August 2011, said the curriculum featured not only tutorials on independent journalism but "propaganda for the Chinese model of media," according to a March 2013 CPJ report on China.[29] That model holds that mass media is not a forum through which individuals can realize their right to freedom of expression; rather it is the means through which societies can advance their collective interest as determined by the country's leadership.

This is the same argument that China makes in international forums on Internet governance. China believes that the current Internet structure allows the U.S. government to "unilaterally close the Internet of another country." As an example, it noted that at the request of the U.S. government ICANN shut down the .iq top-level domain name during the Iraq War, crippling the Iraqi Internet.[30] The Chinese long alleged that because most of the Internet's root servers are physically located in the United States, American authorities can monitor global Internet traffic, "gaining access to all information transmitted online," a fear borne out by the Snowden revelations.

China's hope is that it can bring Internet governance under the control of the International Telecommunications Union, a body created 150 years ago to regulate global communications networks. Today it operates under the auspices of the United Nations and helps create regulatory standards that ensure that wired and wireless communications operate seamlessly across borders, that communications satellites don't smash into each other while whizzing through space, and that television and radio frequencies don't overlap. At various times and under various circumstances, the ITU has been proposed as a forum for Internet administration. But the United States has adamantly opposed the idea. At an ITU-sponsored conference that took place in Dubai in December 2012, a furor erupted when China, Russia, Sudan, Egypt, and host nation the United Arab Emirates introduced a last-minute proposal to bring a broad spectrum of Internet governance, including the Domain Names Registration system, under ITU control. Eighty-nine countries signed the document, including nearly all of the African countries participating. The United States and European nations worked feverishly against the proposal, and in the end more than fifty countries, including all eligible EU members, refused to support it, effectively blocking it from moving forward.[31] Despite this, ITU Secretary General Hamadoun I. Touré claimed victory, noting, "History will show that this conference has achieved something extremely important. It has succeeded in bringing unprecedented public attention to the different and important perspectives that govern global communications."[32]

At the time, the ITU resolution was merely unsettling, because China and other countries that want to hand Internet governance to the United Nations clearly lacked the diplomatic and political support to achieve their goal. But the equation has changed in the aftermath of the NSA spying revelations, which put a deep strain on the U.S.-EU Internet alliance. Europeans, who place a high value on privacy, were outraged that their personal communications may have been accessed by the NSA, and European leaders reacted with fury at the scope of the surveillance, with German officials calling the spying "reminiscent of the Cold War" and the French Foreign Ministry summoning the U.S. ambassador to offer a formal rebuke. Marietje Schaake, a member of the European Parliament and leading expert on Internet freedom issues, drove the point home. "The negative impact of the exposure of the NSA activities is not limited to the United States' foreign policy objectives but could also harm the global open Internet," she noted. [33]

Germany, along with Brazil, whose president Dilma Rousseff was also subject to intrusive spying by the NSA, is pushing for a UN resolution on Internet privacy. Even ICANN seems to be growing increasingly uncomfortable with the United States' dominant role in Internet governance. At an October 2013 conference in Montevideo, Uruguay, the leaders of the organizations that coordinate the Internet's technical structure called for the "globalization" of ICANN functions. The signatories included the head of ICANN, Fadi Chehadé.[34] (The United States later announced that it would cede control of ICANN to an international group beginning in 2015.)[35]

The threat to the global Internet is not imminent, but it is growing and multifaceted. While the possibility of China and other Internet-restricting countries handing Internet governance to the United Nations is still remote, its effect would be "catastrophic," says MacKinnon, who believes UN governance would represent the end of the Internet as a shared global resource. The fact that more and more people around the world are accessing the Web through mobile devices rather than broadband already gives governments more direct control, since wireless networks are more easily monitored and censored.

A more immediate concern is that China's international advocacy is helping advance its argument that the restrictions governments impose on the domestic Internet are legitimate in an international context. Experts are expressing increased alarm about the possible emergence of a "Splinternet," with divergent national systems that are not fully connected. "Around the world countries are increasingly restricting the Internet and seeking to bring it under state control," notes Dan Gillmor, an author and Internet expert.[36]

China's ability to construct a domestic Internet with its own norms has global security implications that go beyond its leadership of the antilibertarian movement and its example to authoritarian regimes. This is because as China becomes more adept at managing information domestically, it also disrupts the flow of information across borders. China's economic and political health, of course, is central to the world economy, yet the government suppresses information on everything from major political developments to mundane economic data. In August 2012, the *New York Times* reported that as exports had slowed and domestic demand slackened, many industries were accumulating a massive backlog of unsold inventory. Yet the Chinese government sought to obscure the extent of the problem by, for example, halting the release of data about new car registration.[37]

Basic information about a variety of issues with a global impact—from environmental degradation to food safety—is censored online. The government routinely withholds data about air quality in Beijing and actively suppresses information—including on microblogs—about popular demonstrations against pollution, like the 2011 mass demonstrations against a chemical plant in Dalian. Food safety issues—from tainted milk, to exploding watermelons treated with growth hormones, to waste oil resold to restaurants for cooking—are routinely censored or covered up.[38] Even more alarmingly is that there is some evidence that Chinese government censorship is undermining the integrity of the global Internet, according to the blogger and technologist Isaac Mao. Internet users from Chile to California who carry out searches in Chinese can be routed through servers inside China—and thus caught in the country's censorship web. "People living in New York City who try to study Chinese would hit the wall when websites include some 'sensitive words,'" Mao explained.[39]

Even as the overheated Chinese economy begins to cool, China continues to provide a powerful alternative vision of the role of information and media. It's a vision that has an obvious resonance in many parts of the world. While Ai Weiwei's dream may yet come true, there is also a nightmare scenario in which governments around the world continue both to strengthen their ability to manage and control the Internet and to build the international support to do so. The result could be that information would be managed and manipulated not only for citizens of repressive regimes but at least hypothetically for Internet users everywhere. This is obviously a grave threat to the current system of global news and information upon which people around the world depend.

SIX

~~Under Surveillance~~

While governments around the world have very different perspectives on freedom of expression online and the nature of Internet governance, they are in fundamental agreement on the use of online surveillance for domestic law enforcement and international espionage. The indignation expressed by countries like Germany and Brazil in the aftermath of the NSA-spying revelations stem from the magnitude of the surveillance, not its existence. China, meanwhile, expressed no particular qualms. Its criticism is all about the U.S. double standard and the fact that it has used its control of Internet infrastructure to secure an unfair advantage in the online surveillance arms race.

The irony is that China may be the country least affected by the NSA spying program, at least based on what had been revealed by late 2013. U.S. Internet companies have a limited presence in China. The most popular search engine in the country is not Google but Baidu, a Chinese company partially owned by the government. While documents released by Edward Snowden have made clear that the NSA had access to the data stored by U.S. companies like Facebook and Google, presumably they had less reach into Baidu, which is not subject to U.S. jurisdiction or oversight.

The fact is that governments on all continents have found the Internet to be an incredibly valuable tool for monitoring the activities of their citizens and for carrying out global information-gathering operations. That is not going to change. Journalists are ideal targets for state surveillance. Their job is to communicate with politicians, critics, dissidents—and even terrorists. They rely heavily on their mobile devices, which are extremely easy to monitor and intercept, and in general they are not particularly tech savvy or security conscious. Many journalists I speak with about information security tell me they just assume their communications are monitored and behave accordingly. Their sources, however, may not be operating with the same assumption.

It's obviously difficult to discern the level of surveillance of journalistic communication, but recent examples suggest that snooping is extremely widespread. A clandestine Chinese cyber security operation widely linked to the government hacked the personal e-mail accounts of individual journalists and also infiltrated international media organizations like the *New York Times*, Bloomberg, and the *Washington Post*. At CPJ we've had e-mails with journalists in Ethiopia and Colombia intercepted by government intelligence agencies in those countries.[1] The NSA hacked into the internal communications of al-Jazeera in 2006, according to documents leaked by Edward Snowden and cited in *Der Spiegel*.[2]

In a report issued in April 2013, UN Special Rapporteur for Freedom of Expression Frank La Rue described growing government surveillance efforts as a fundamental threat to global freedom of expression. La Rue noted,

> States cannot ensure that individuals are able to freely seek and receive information or express themselves without respecting, protecting, and promoting their right to privacy. Privacy and freedom of expression are interlinked and mutually dependent; an infringement upon one can be both the cause and consequence of an infringement upon the other. Without adequate legislation and legal standards to ensure the privacy, security, and anonymity of communications, journalists, human rights defenders, and whistleblowers, for example, cannot be assured that their communications will not be subject to States' scrutiny.[3]

The NSA spying program, though, did real damage to La Rue's proposition by making it more difficult to argue that massive state surveillance—including the hacking operations carried out by China—

violates international norms. While there is of course a real difference between the hacking of the accounts of international journalists carried out by Chinese authorities and the use of metadata by the NSA to analyze patterns of communication, the Chinese operation looks less aberrant today and more like an effort to level the playing field.[4]

Obviously journalists can—and should—make a greater effort to ensure that communication is secure. But there is a broader and unresolved question as to whether online surveillance has become so pervasive and effective that it is having a chilling effect on the global media. In other words, is surveillance a new form of censorship? Already, some of the more sophisticated media organizations have changed the way they do business. Many reporters now limit electronic communication with sensitive sources and even with their editors. Even more fundamentally, "You can no longer guarantee anonymity to a source," said Janine Gibson, the U.S. editor of the *Guardian* who oversaw Glenn Greenwald's coverage of the Snowden leaks. "That's a terrifying thing for the journalists we work with."

I first began to appreciate how online surveillance and monitoring can be used not only to undermine the work of the press but also to dismantle information networks when I met the Iranian journalist Maziar Bahari, who was imprisoned for three months following the disputed 2009 presidential elections in Iran. While the common perception is that online information is gleaned through hacking, spyware, or government surveillance, these are not the only methods. In Bahari's case the sensitive online information was extracted through torture.

I had become deeply involved in Bahari's case after he was arrested at his mother's home in Tehran in June 2009. Agents from the Revolutionary Guards turned the apartment upside down, confiscated his video collection, and hauled him off to Evin prison, where for three months he was interrogated about his reporting for *Newsweek* and his documentary work for British Channel 4. Soon after his arrest, I got a call from Bahari's editor at *Newsweek*, Nisid Hajari, who was seeking advice on how to garner international attention and put pressure on Iran to release him. Those efforts, eventually successful, included an online petition campaign, a media strategy, and direct interventions with Iranian officials.

After Bahari was released, he came to New York, and we spoke about his interrogation. We discussed the kinds of questions he had been asked. Bahari's interrogator, whom he nicknamed Rosewater in reference to his powerful cologne, berated, manipulated, and at times brutalized him. Rosewater immediately demanded access to the password for Bahari's e-mails and Facebook page and began poring over all of the information they contained—his friends, his posts, his likes. Bahari, who had been educated in Montreal and lived in London, had sophisticated and sometimes ironic cultural interests. He "liked" the Russian playwright Anton Chekhov and the American comedian and B-movie actor Pauly Shore. This made Rosewater suspicious—he assumed Chekhov was a Zionist and Shore a spy. He also went through Bahari's Facebook friends one by one, aggressively accusing Bahari of having sexual relationships with all the women he had friended, including the Nobel Prize–winner Shirin Ebadi. He even tried to use Facebook to establish that Bahari was having an extramarital affair in an apparent effort to blackmail him into cooperating. Bahari's British wife Paola was in London at the time of the incarceration, pregnant with their first child.

Later, Rosewater discovered an incriminating video online. It featured Bahari being interviewed by the *Daily Show* correspondent Jason Jones, who was pretending to be a spy. The skit, which was intended to highlight U.S. ignorance about Iran, was hilarious, but Rosewater was not amused and could not be convinced that the segment was intended as a joke. After his release, Bahari developed a close relationship with Jones and with the *Daily Show*'s host, Jon Stewart, who in the summer of 2013 took a hiatus from his television show to direct a movie based on Bahari's experience. The film is tentatively titled *Rosewater*.

While Bahari's interrogation was at times bizarre—even comical—it highlights what a treasure trove of information can be obtained through a Facebook page and how that can be used to dismantle networks. In the first giddy weeks following the June 2009 elections, as protesters took to the streets of Tehran and other cities to express their outrage at the manipulated results that extended the term of President Mahmoud Ahmadinejad for four more years, new technologies were widely seen as helping fuel Iran's Green Movement. Social media and new information technologies facilitated communication between the protesters, allowing them to stay informed and coordinate action. After international reporters were expelled or confined to their offices in Tehran, their most crucial source of information became tweets, blogs, images, and videos provided by the protesters themselves. The most iconic image of the uprising was the death of the protester Neda Agha-Soltan, captured not by a professional photographer but by fellow demonstrators.

But subsequent reports made clear that the Iranian twitterati were a tiny portion of population, concentrated in the affluent sections of Tehran. Social media helped shape elite opinion and action inside Iran and had a profound effect on the international media trying to cover the protests from outside the country. But its importance as a tool of mass organization was greatly overstated.

Moreover, the Iranian government was able to launch an effective counterattack combining old-fashioned brutality and new technologies to reassert control over the information sphere and stamp out the protest movement. During the 2009 postelection crackdown in Iran, the security services routinely tortured journalists and activists like Bahari to obtain their social media and e-mail passwords and then used the information to reverse engineer the protests' networks, hauling in friends and torturing them and so on. Iranian security officials populated Facebook, surreptitiously friending journalists, activists, and others and then accessing their networks. Iranians exiles returning home were made to log into their Facebook accounts when they arrived at the airport. Security forces used social media to crowdsource photos of protesters, posting pictures and asking for help identifying individuals. At times, the government slowed the Internet to a crawl, blocked critical sites, and used a technique known as deep packet inspection to monitor Web traffic. Dozens of reporters were rounded up. Some were released after undergoing interrogations, but many were jailed for extended periods.[5]

Iran's Green Movement was supposed to be the first Twitter revolution. In fact, it should be viewed as a cautionary tale about the limitations of new technologies as a tool to confront autocratic regimes and the competing power of surveillance. Two years after Iran's 2009 elections, the revolutions in Tunisia and Egypt prompted a similarly optimistic response about the power of social media. But on closer examination Twitter and Facebook played a comparable role during the Arab revolts. Initially, they mobilized the elite, made it more difficult for the authorities to contain news and information, and fueled global awareness about the abuses. These are not insignificant contributions. But it is also important to recognize that most of the people who participated in uprisings in Tunisia and Egypt were not even online, and satellite networks, notably al-Jazeera, were a more important source of independent information than Facebook. More importantly, the use of Facebook and other social media platforms by governments to dismantle political networks has become a standard practice. The Syrian government used Trojan horse viruses—attachments and links that appear legitimate—to install spyware on the computers of activists and journalists.[6] As in Iran, those arrested by Syrian state security forces were immediately compelled to surrender their passwords under the threat of torture. Clearly, while activists took one lesson from the Arab Spring, Iranian authorities and other repressive leaders took another. They determined to put more resources into ensuring control of online information. Online and real-world repression has accelerated as a result.

Under President Ahmadinejad, the Iranian government sought to develop what could be termed a permanent solution to its Internet problem: Building a national Web featuring only approved content. In announcing in April 2011 that Iran planned to use filtering and monitoring to create a "Halal Internet," Iranian officials praised China's efforts, describing the country as a global model for online censorship. Evidence suggests that China may have offered more than just inspiration. Two Chinese companies, Huawei and ZTE, provided surveillance and censorship technology to Iran. In many ways the Iranian project is even more ambitious and draconian than the Chinese model. Iranian officials have described a project whereby the "approved" Iranian Internet would exist alongside a filtered version of the global Internet for a period, but at some point Iran would opt out of the global system, limiting access to the "halal" version. The hope of officials is that the new system would replace the Web not only in Iran but in other Muslim countries.[7]

During the 2009 elections, Iran thought it could gain legitimacy by having a more open media, but by 2013 it had given up on that approach. While authorities arrested dozens of journalists during the postelection crackdown in 2009, in 2013 they arrested them *before* the vote took place. By March 2013, as Iranians prepared to go to the polls to elect a new president, forty-five journalists were in jail, and dozens more were under threat of reincarceration after having been released on furlough.[8] For a brief period following the 2009 election, the Internet was seen as a safe space where activists could associate and share information. By 2013 that perception had changed. While there was considerable online activity, it was more circumspect and more cautious. The concern was understandable, as the Iranian government repeatedly demonstrated new ways of exploiting technology for repression. In one incident in January 2013, Iranian security officials picked up in Tehran the sister of a BBC reporter based in London, forced her to give up her Facebook password, and took over her account. The interrogators used the Facebook chat feature to menace and threaten the reporter in London, essentially using her sister as hostage. It may have been the first-ever state security interrogation carried out via Facebook.

Standing up Against Secrecy

What can we do to counter the threat of online surveillance? While it's important to keep the pressure on governments, authoritarian and democratic alike, it's unrealistic to expect them to change their behavior, at least in the short term. So journalists and information activists must first work to improve their own online security while simultaneously putting pressure on technology companies to provide support to vulnerable users.

One challenge is that journalists have become so utterly dependent on insecure communications technologies to do their work. Cell phones, BlackBerrys, and iPhones have become essential reporting tools for both professional journalists and amateurs. But these devices are also repositories of vast amounts of personal information that governments crave as keenly as any advertiser. Internet communication via e-mail, Skype, or chat is never totally secure, and using SMS is "like sending a postcard through the mail," according to Katrin Verclas, a cofounder of MobileActive, an organization that supports activists using mobile technology to create social change. In an October 2011 *New York Times* op-ed, the technologist and privacy activist Christopher Soghoian took journalists to task for their general cluelessness about digital security. "Government officials often attempt to get journalists to reveal their sources by obtaining subpoenas and compelling testimony and the required telecommunications records," he wrote. "But sometimes that's not even necessary, because sources have already been exposed by their own lax communications."[9]

The risks, varied and evolving, have been brought into high relief by the Snowden revelations. E-mail, for example, is never secure. Using encryption technology can make e-mail safer, but reports by ProPublica based on the Snowden leaks indicate that the NSA cracked many of the codes "using supercomputers, technical trickery, court orders and behind-the-scenes persuasion to undermine the major tools protecting the privacy of everyday communications in the Internet age."[10]

Meanwhile, smart phones can be converted to tracking and monitoring devices that record movements and conversations. The only way to make sure you are not being tracked from a GPS-enabled phone is to remove the battery completely at sensitive times, something that is not even possible with an iPhone. BlackBerrys are generally considered more secure, which is why the company has come under tremendous pressure from countries like the United Arab Emirates, Saudi Arabia, and India to provide security forces and law enforcement with backdoors to monitor communication.

Much of the technology used to carry out this kind of cyberspying is developed by U.S. and other international companies. For example, FinFisher software, which allows a remote user to take control of a smart phone or computer, is marketed to law enforcement but sometimes used by repressive governments to monitor the political activities of their own people. Bahraini activists received an e-mail that seemed to come from an international journalist but when clicked open installed FinFisher on their devices. "Everything a regime would need to build an incredibly intimidating digital police state is commercially available now, and export restrictions are currently insufficiently monitored and enforced," note Google's Eric Schmidt and Jared Cohen in *The New Digital Age*.[11] The ability of governments to track their citizens will likely increase as voice and facial recognition software come online.

One strategy that activists and journalists use to mitigate risk is to disable e-mail and Facebook accounts when their colleagues are detained. They have at times enlisted support from technology providers. When a wave of journalists was detained in Iran prior to the 2013 elections, Google was contacted by an Iranian journalist outside the country and agreed to disable the Gmail accounts of those in custody.

But activists and journalists believe the companies can do more. At a meeting organized by CPJ in Silicon Valley, Rami Nakhle, an activist and blogger who helped provide video footage to international journalists covering the Syrian conflict, explained the risk to a group of engineers and technologists who helped build and maintain the modern Internet. "People I know lost their lives or were tortured for months as a result of security bugs. I am not saying this to blame you, because they know the risks they are taking, and they're brave enough to take risks. If you really can help them here with just a small investment in their security, you may save many people's lives."[12]

On occasion, companies have been called to task. The son of an Iranian journalist imprisoned in Iran filed a lawsuit in the United States against Nokia Siemens, alleging that the company had provided technology used by the Iranian government to intercept cell phone communication and round up dissidents. The Finnish company said it had provided off-the-shelf software, but it did eventually announce it would not do business with Iran.[13]

In 2007, Yahoo! chief executive Jerry Yang was raked over the coals at a congressional hearing for providing to Chinese authorities access to the personal e-mail account of the Chinese journalist Shi Tao. One e-mail, which Shi had forwarded to sources outside of China, contained the propaganda directives sent to Chinese journalists for their coverage of the fifteenth anniversary of the Tiananmen uprising. Shi was convicted and sentenced to ten years in jail for "leaking state secrets abroad." A chastened Yang offered a personal apology to the journalist's mother, who attended and sat in the first row.[14]

Facing the threat of legislation that would have regulated information and technology companies operating in repressive countries, Google, Yahoo!, and Microsoft began discussions with human rights groups and socially responsible investors to develop a set of principles and standards around freedom of expression. Those discussions eventually led to the formation of a nonprofit organization called the Global Network Initiative, or GNI. Working together, the GNI developed a set of principles around freedom of expression and privacy grounded in international human rights standards. The adoption of these principles gave the companies additional leverage to push back against intrusive demands from governments. The GNI has succeeded in creating greater accountability and transparency within the participating companies, although the enforcement mechanism remains weak. More importantly, it has created dialogue and trust that have made it easier for human rights groups to engage with the tech companies around their concerns.

While participation in the GNI has not grown as rapidly as once hoped, the organization got a big boost in early 2013 when Facebook became an official member. Another significant development, while not a formal GNI initiative, took place in October 2013 when GNI members Google, Facebook, Yahoo!, and Microsoft, along with Apple and AOL, sent a joint letter to members of the U.S. Senate registering their objections to the scope of the NSA spying program. The letter noted, "Our companies believe that government practices should be reformed to include substantial enhancements to privacy protections and appropriate accountability mechanisms for those programs."[15]

Generally, the way that tech companies respond to public pressure to improve the security of vulnerable users is based on their corporate culture and business model. Suppliers of software and hardware used for monitoring and surveillance have been the least responsive. Their position is that they are selling a legal product that has a legitimate purpose and that they can't be responsible if it is misused. Google's business model, on the other hand, depends on maintaining the confidence of individual users. Their unspoken commitment is, "We might know everything about you, but you can totally trust us." When events occur that cause people to lose trust—such as the state-sponsored attack on Chinese dissidents' e-mail accounts—the company takes action to protect its brand. Google's decision to pull out of China and its aggressive response to the NSA surveillance revelations are highly rational from a business perspective. Google was also one of the first e-mail providers to implement across-the-board encryption, and activists believe that e-mailing between Gmail accounts is still one of the more secure ways of communicating, although the assumption at this point is that the NSA can gain access to such communication.

Facebook takes a very different approach. The company believes that since the platform is all about sharing information, users should understand that posting on Facebook is essentially a public activity. Facebook has taken some steps in response to user demands for greater privacy and control over information, but the company ethos—and the default setting—is to encourage users to be as public as possible. In the view of Rebecca MacKinnon, Facebook has become a quasi-public space with its own rules about privacy and free expression. These rules change constantly and are enforced by a company with limited accountability and oversight. In acknowledgment of the arbitrary and capricious standards, MacKinnon has dubbed this space "Facebookistan."[16] Like other Silicon Valley–based social media companies, Facebook relies on a team of "deciders" to screen content and remove postings that violate its terms of service. For example, Facebook removes posts that attack individuals based on "race, ethnicity, national origin, religion, sex, gender, sexual orientation, disability, or medical condition."

One of the key battles with activists is centered on Facebook's real-name policy. Facebook does not permit pseudonyms, anonymous users, or multiple profiles. It actively enforces this policy and deletes accounts that are in violation. The company argues that the real-names policy ensures more civil discourse—since you can't hide behind a pseudonym—and protects activists by making it more difficult for government supporters or even state security agents to use the network to harass and monitor their opponents. This makes a certain amount of sense until you realize it's exactly the same argument made by the Chinese government to justify its real-names policy. It's also unenforceable since already more than one billion people are on Facebook, and the company can't possibly check every name. The policy is actually prejudicial to political activists, since they are likely to come to the attention of authorities who can turn to Facebook and request that their accounts be removed. Finally, these policies are unlikely to stop a security agency with the resources to create a fake online identity.

Activists using social media to disseminate news and information find Facebook's position deeply frustrating. In fact, Facebook's real-names policy nearly killed off Wael Ghonim's We Are All Khaled Said page, which would eventually grow to a million followers and serve as a hugely important source of information during the Tahrir Square protests in Egypt. Because Ghonim—who feared detection and arrest in Egypt—was administering the page anonymously, Facebook shut down the page for violation of its terms of service. A colleague of Ghonim's in the United States got in touch directly with Facebook and informed them she would serve as the administrator for the group under her real name. The group was restored in less than twenty-four hours.[17]

Esraa Abdel Fattah, one of the founders of the April 6 movement in Egypt that also played a critical role mobilizing online support for the Tahrir Square uprising, told me during a visit to Cairo in March 2013 that she was scandalized by Facebook's indifference. She described a visit to Facebook's Washington, D.C., office earlier that year during which she made the case that the company should adapt its product to better meet the security needs of activists working in dangerous environments. "I said, 'don't you realize that people are using your tools to spread democracy and human rights?' You have to take responsibility. You have developed a very important tool that is changing the whole world. You have to find ways to help people use it safely. You can't just stand by and let people be killed for their beliefs." Abdel Fattah said she got sympathy from the company representatives but no commitment.

While continuing to rally against government policies that undermine the free circulation of information online, journalists and activists need to improve the security of their own communications, recognizing that they are likely targets of surveillance. They also need to apply systematic pressure on companies like Google, Yahoo!, Twitter, and Facebook, whose services provide the backbone of the social aspect of the Internet. In the current environment, these companies have become convinced that pervasive government surveillance undermines their business interests, as customers around the world want to be able to communicate securely. Making them explicit allies in the struggle for press freedom is the most immediate challenge.

SEVEN

Murder Central

On July 17, 2013, the UN Security Council met to discuss the "protection of journalists in armed conflict" and, for the first time in its history, invited journalists themselves to provide testimony. Among those who spoke was Mustafa Haji Abdinur, a reporter from Somalia. "They call me a dead man walking," he told the council's members. "Day after day, I tell stories to the world of the people of Somalia, the troubles they face and their hopes for the future. But today I sit here having carried with me the stories of my comrades and colleagues, my fellow journalists who paid the ultimate price for reporting from those same streets."[1]

Somalia is one of the most deadly countries for the media in the entire world, with fifty-one journalists killed since 1992, including a dozen in 2012. Haji's cell phone is filled with the numbers of murdered colleagues. He refuses to delete them. "In such a terrible situation, it is fair to ask: 'Why become a journalist?'" he continued. "There is no doubt that without a free press there can be no freedom for a country. I tell the council that we have a higher objective for good and that by doing our jobs we feel that we are saving lives."

Country after country—including representatives from Pakistan and Colombia, both places where journalists have faced systematic violence—pledged to defend press freedom and to combat impunity. "It is clear that all attacks on journalists are unacceptable," said the Russian ambassador, Vitaly Churkin. Member states also expressed their support for the "UN Plan of Action on the Safety of Journalists and the Issue of Impunity," a global strategy to reduce violence against the press.[2] The plan is being tested in several key countries, including Iraq, Nepal, South Sudan, and Pakistan, where a March 2013 conference brought together press groups, international donors, human rights organizations, and UN officials.

The UN Security Council session was a milestone. It demonstrated that the world had taken notice of the threat posed by the unchecked killings of journalists and had recognized the link between the ongoing violence and the failure to achieve justice. The murder of journalists represents a threat to global peace and security because it suppresses the flow of information from countries undergoing conflict. As Haji told the council, "When a journalist is killed, the news dies too. A whole society can be forgotten simply because there is no one left to tell its stories."

The UN action was also a victory for journalists and press freedom advocates around the world, who for years had pushed for greater international attention to stem the tide of violence. Murder, after all, is the ultimate form of censorship. Killing journalists not only suppresses coverage; it produces fear and self-censorship, which ripple through the press corps. Statistics compiled by press freedom organizations including CPJ suggest that the number of journalists murdered has skyrocketed in recent years.[3] Murders in conflict zones carried out by terror groups are one reason, and those causes and consequences were discussed in chapter 3. But many killings are tied to criminal organizations, military forces, and political factions that operate with government support or protection. Journalists targeted are primarily local reporters covering crime, corruption, and human rights. Government officials are directly implicated in nearly a quarter of all journalists killed worldwide since 1992. In around 90 percent of all cases, the murders are carried out with impunity, meaning no one is ever convicted of a crime.[4]

Based on data of journalists killed since 1992, CPJ publishes an annual "Impunity Index," which ranks the countries around the world where journalists are systematically murdered and the killers routinely go free. Topping the list are conflict-ravaged countries like Iraq and Somalia. But most of the other countries on the list are nominal democracies that are not at war. The Philippines, for example, has the third-highest rate of impunity for journalist killings in the world. Mexico is seventh on the list; Russia is ninth.[5] Fighting against impunity in countries like Syria, Somalia, and Iraq is necessary, but prospects for justice are low. In other countries it is possible to make progress by exposing the crimes, rallying the public, and then pressuring the authorities to take specific, concrete steps to achieve justice. The goal is to create a dynamic in which failure to solve the crime results in a direct political cost for the government in power, at least in terms of its international reputation.

In 1995 the Inter-American Press Association, a publishers' group that fights for press freedom in the Americas, began a regional anti-impunity campaign. IAPA's effort, launched with support from the Miami-based John S. and James L. Knight Foundation, sought to investigate journalist murders, track progress, mobilize public support through a hemisphere-wide media campaign, pressure public officials, and push for legal action.[6] While these efforts helped achieve a notable number of convictions, journalist killings remain an acute problem in a number of Latin American countries including Mexico, Brazil, and Honduras. Other groups, including CPJ, Reporters Without Borders, the International Press Institute, and the International Federation of Journalists, have all made impunity a key focus of their advocacy over the last decade. In 2011, international, regional, and domestic press freedom organizations joined forces in a global anti-impunity campaign coordinated by the International Freedom of Expression Exchange, or IFEX, a global network of freedom of expression organizations headquartered in Toronto, Canada.[7]

It is notable that governments and international institutions like the United Nations have now publically recognized the scope of the problem. There have also been declines in the level of violence against the press in a number countries, including Colombia, where overall security has increased as the civil war has ebbed. But globally levels of violence against journalists remain exceedingly high and convictions remain exceedingly rare.

This chapter looks at two very different countries where journalists have been targeted with murder and violence: Russia and the Philippines. In each, some combination of international and domestic pressure has forced the government to take action. In each, there has been some measure of progress, and in Russia the rate of violence has slowed. Yet fear and self-censorship have become deeply embedded in the press corps in both countries. In this environment, the flow of information to the world depends almost entirely on the willingness of journalists to risk their lives to report the news. "All of my colleagues who have been killed had one thing in common: they were committed to telling the story of their country to the rest of the world," Mustafa Haji told the UN Security Council, pledging to continue his own work despite the risk. "They may call me a dead man walking, but I report the news."

No Justice in Russia

Three days after the journalist Anna Politkovskaya was gunned down in the elevator of her Moscow apartment building, Russian president Vladimir Putin finally stepped forward to condemn her murder. Tellingly, he did so not in Russia but in Germany, where Putin was meeting with Chancellor Angela Merkel. Putin described Politkovskaya's killing as an "unacceptable crime that cannot be allowed to go unpunished." But he also felt compelled to note that Politkovskaya's "influence on political life in the country was extremely insignificant in scale. She was known in journalist and human rights circles, but her influence on political life in Russia was minimal." Putin's description was undoubtedly accurate, but his effort to minimize the importance of Russia's most courageous investigative journalist so soon after her murder was deeply hurtful. What Putin didn't say was that Politkovskaya's influence was limited in Russia because she had been banned from appearing on the country's private television networks, all beholden to the Kremlin.

Politkovskaya was forty-eight at the time of her death. She had spent seven years of the previous decade as an investigative reporter with the fiercely independent Moscow newspaper *Novaya Gazeta*. She was murdered on October 7, 2006, while returning from grocery shopping. Her killer shot her three times in the chest and shoulder before delivering the coup de grace as she lay on the ground. He casually tossed his silencer-equipped gun to the ground before fleeing the scene. For days following the killing, flowers piled up outside Polit-kovskaya's building, and there were small rallies to demand justice. But there was no mass outcry.

Outside of Russia, however, the response was very different. Polit-kovskaya had been repeatedly honored internationally for her coura-geous human rights reporting. I had a chance to meet her when she visited New York to receive an award and was inspired by her physical courage and intellectual fearlessness, which at times bordered on the reckless. Her books on the war on Chechnya—which featured detailed descriptions of depravities committed by the Russian forces, chroni-cles of civilian suffering, and unstinting denunciations of the Russian leadership, including Putin himself—had been widely translated.[8]

After her killing, there were demonstrations in cities throughout Europe, condemnations from governments around the world, and a flurry of letters and protests from press freedom and human rights groups. As international pressure on Russia mounted, the Russian government shifted its approach, at times adopting a defiant posture, at other times seeking to show progress in bringing the killers to jus-tice. Through repeated engagement with Russian officials over many years I saw the positive influence of international advocacy—and also its clear limitations.

The Politkovskaya killing was not an isolated incident. In fact, Politkovskaya was the thirteenth journalist to be murdered since Pu-tin became president in 2000. Among the other prominent victims was the American journalist Paul Klebnikov, an investigative reporter who founded *Forbes Russia*. He was killed while leaving his Moscow office on July 9, 2004, by a gunman who fired nine times from a mov-ing car. Klebnikov had covered a variety of topics, from crony capital-ism to political scandals, and had made many powerful enemies in the process. Like Politkovskaya he had closely investigated the web of cor-ruption and kickbacks tying the Kremlin to the massive state-funded program in Chechnya that had transformed the capital Grozny from a rubble-strewn ruin into a gleaming showcase of the reconstruction effort.[9] Politkovskaya, for one, was not fooled. Her reporting often fo-cused on exposing Chechnya's president, Ramzan Kadyrov, whom she accused of crimes ranging from skimming reconstruction funds to personally overseeing torture sessions. Ramzan, who had succeeded his father Akhmad, a former separatist rebel who was assassinated in 2004 after he abandoned their cause and switched to the Russian side, was not pleased. He was reported to have condemned Politkovskaya to death during a meeting with his advisors.[10]

Three months after Politkovskaya's murder, in January 2007, I traveled to Moscow along with CPJ's chairman Paul Steiger, board member Norman Pearlstine, and Europe and Central Asia Program Coordinator Nina Ognianova. We had come to deliver hundreds of petitions addressed to Putin and collected at CPJ's International Press Freedom Awards dinner the previous November. Ognianova pushed relentlessly for a high-level meeting, and Russian authorities seemed unsure of how to respond. While they didn't want to confer legitimacy on our concerns, they couldn't simply ignore us given our visibility and the level of international concern. We were eventually able to secure a meeting with Ella Pamfilova, the chairwoman of the Russian Human Rights Council, a quasi-independent body created by Putin to advise him on human rights issues. Over tea and cookies, Pamfilova expressed sympathy for our cause. When we handed her the four hundred petitions, she offered to deliver them personally to President Putin.

We also met with a second-tier foreign ministry official named Boris Malakhov, who had served as a Soviet diplomat in the United States. The meeting got off to an unpromising start, with Malakhov mounting a potted defense of Russia's human rights record. But he then dropped a bombshell. The Prosecutor General's office had informed him that morning that it was investigating the possible involvement of Chechen police in the Politkovskaya killing. The Chechen police, who report directly to Kadyrov, may have killed Politkovskaya, Malakhov told us, because she was about to publish an investigation alleging their involvement in torture. Malakhov had clearly wanted to demonstrate to our visiting delegation that Russian investigators were making progress. But he had not been authorized to provide to us a detailed update on the investigation, and when we announced the results of our meeting at a press conference held on January 23 we set off a firestorm.[11]

Malakhov, under pressure from the Prosecutor General, denied that he made the statement.[12] But there was no possibility of misunderstanding. The meeting had been conducted in English and attended by two renowned editors, Steiger and Pearlstine, who confirmed Malakhov's comments. The revelation of possible official involvement in the Politkovskaya killing implicated Kadyrov, who issued a vaguely menacing statement calling our announcement a "carefully planned provocation."[13] Kadyrov was widely perceived as untouchable thanks to his role in restoring some semblance of stability in Chechnya. He was also widely suspected of involvement in corruption and kickback schemes involving reconstruction funds that implicated senior Kremlin officials, schemes uncovered by Politkovskaya herself. Kadyrov's statement appeared as a warning to the Russian media that had covered our press conference not to pursue the story further.

The Malakhov meeting had clearly been a disaster from the perspective of the Russian government. It generated media headlines around the world quoting a Russian official as suggesting possible state involvement in the Politkovskaya killing. It exposed rifts in the Russian leadership, highlighting the division between the Foreign Ministry and the Prosecutor General's office. It also alienated Kadyrov, a critical if highly problematic Kremlin ally.

By the middle of 2007 the Russian government was taking a new tack. Instead of minimizing the Politkovskaya murder and dismissing international criticism, the Putin government had decided to engage. "For our country . . . the issue of journalist persecution is one of the most pressing," Putin said during his annual press conference on February 1, 2007. "And we realize our degree of responsibility in this."[14] In an apparent breakthrough in August of that year, Russian prosecutors announced the arrest of ten suspects in the Politkovskaya murder (an eleventh suspect was arrested soon after). That same month, five members of a criminal gang in the republic of Tatarstan were convicted of carrying out the 2000 murder of the *Novaya Gazeta* reporter Igor Domnikov. These were the first convictions in a journalist's killing since Vladimir Putin had come to office.[15]

But the effort to demonstrate a commitment to justice in the Politkovskaya murder was subverted by the incompetence of prosecutors and the clear deficiencies in Russia's criminal justice system. By the time the trial got under way in November 2008, only four of the original eleven suspects were still in custody. In the dock were two brothers, Dzhabrail and Ibragim Makhmudov, accused of serving as lookouts, and a former policeman accused of organizing the killing. The trial was marred from the outset by a hamfisted effort to bar the media. The prosecution's case was based almost entirely on circumstantial evidence, which the defense lawyer demolished. The jury took less than two hours to render its verdict, and on February 19, 2009, the defendants were acquitted. Politkovskaya's family and colleagues blamed the prosecutor's office for failing to present sufficient evidence but more broadly for focusing on minor figures in the conspiracy at the expense of the masterminds. Citing procedural violations, the Supreme Court overturned the acquittals a few months later and ordered a new trial.

Meanwhile, in an alarming setback in the larger battle against impunity, two more journalists were murdered in 2009, both from *Novaya Gazeta.* In January, gunmen brazenly executed the prominent human rights lawyer Stanislav Markelov and the twenty-five-year-old reporter Anastasia Baburova on a Moscow street corner. In July, four men forced the renowned human rights advocate and contributor to *Novaya Gazeta* and other publications Natalya Estemirova into a car in Grozny, Chechnya, executed her, and dumped her body. Estemirova was a close friend of Politkovskaya and had been personally threatened by Kadyrov at a meeting a month before her killing, according to a statement by Memorial, the Russian human rights group for which she worked.[16] Dmitry Medvedev, who by then had replaced Putin as president while Russia's maximum leader endured a hiatus in the prime minister's office, condemned both murders and even took the unprecedented step of meeting with *Novaya Gazeta*'s editor, Dmitry Muratov.

In September 2009 CPJ released a seventy-two-page report on the failure of Russian authorities to achieve justice in the killing of (by then) seventeen journalists since Putin first assumed the presidency 2000. *Anatomy of Injustice: The Unsolved Killings of Journalists in Russia* featured contributions from a variety of Russian and international experts and identified incompetence, secrecy, conflicts of interest, corruption, and political interference as the primary impediments to successful prosecutions. The CPJ delegation that traveled to Moscow to release the report was led by the board member

Kati Marton and included Ognianova and a senior adviser, Jean-Paul Marthoz. During their visit, they had the opportunity to meet with a team of eleven investigators looking into the various journalist murders. The meeting was contentious at times, but the mere fact that the Russian government was willing to give CPJ direct access to the investigators was encouraging. Two weeks earlier the Russian Supreme Court returned the Politkovskaya case to the prosecutor's office for further investigation and ordered that separate cases against the triggermen and organizers be merged. Marton and Ognianova were able to secure a commitment from the Investigative Committee to meet again in a year's time to provide a progress report.

In September 2010 Marton, Steiger, Ognianova, Marthoz, and I returned to Moscow for the update.[17] This time, the officials were extremely well prepared. The day we arrived the Russian government announced the reorganization of the office of the Investigative Committee that carries out criminal probes and gathers evidence for prosecutors. Since the founding of the new Russian state, the Investigative Committee had reported to the Prosecutor General, who in turn reported to the presidency. Under the reorganization, the Investigative Committee would operate independently, and its head, Aleksandr Bastrykin, would report directly to President Medvedev. Bastrykin told us the reorganization was an effort to professionalize the Investigative Committee, turning it into the Russian version of the FBI. "I want to be Russia's J. Edgar Hoover," Bastrykin told us. Given Hoover's reputation for running roughshod over civil liberties, his pronouncement was not necessarily reassuring. But the meeting was extremely positive. The breakthrough came when we handed Bastrykin a list of (now) nineteen journalists murdered in the line of duty since 2000, when Putin first became president. Instead of quibbling with our findings, as Russian officials had sometimes done previously, Bastrykin asked a team of about a dozen investigators arrayed around the large conference table to provide detailed briefings on the status of each of the cases.

The lead investigator on the Politkovskaya murder Petros Garibyan told us that the killers were motivated by a desire to ingratiate themselves with President Kadyrov. This was different from what Malakhov had told us two years earlier, and the new legal theory did not implicate the Chechen police or Kadyrov directly. Nevertheless, his statement seemed to be a signal to Kadyrov that he should not get too comfortable. Bastrykin added that the suspected triggerman in the Politkovskaya murder, Rustam Makhmudov, had been identified and was in hiding in Belgium. He also acknowledged that prosecutors had "rushed" the earlier case against two accomplices to court, a mistake he was determined not to repeat.

At our behest, the Investigative Committee agreed to reopen five murder investigations, including the 2003 death of *Novaya Gazeta*'s deputy editor Yuri Shchekochikhin, whose colleagues believe he was poisoned. Shchekochikhin was a legendary (if unconventional) figure in the Russian journalism world. He used his status as a member of the state Duma to report on classified government activities, including a scandal involving a chain of furniture stores that he alleged were being used by the FSB—the successor to the KGB—to launder money through the Bank of New York. A friend to both radical activists and FSB colonels, he died after succumbing to a never-diagnosed "allergy" that killed him within days as his organs failed one by one and his skin flaked off his body. Some compared his symptoms to those exhibited by Alexander Litvinenko, the exiled FSB agent and Putin critic who died in a London hospital after being poisoned with polonium. Suspicions of possible state involvement in the crime were heightened by the fact that Shchekochikhin's clinical test results were classified as a "medical secret."

Investigators also told us they were optimistic about obtaining convictions in the murder of the *Novaya Gazeta* freelancer Anastasiya Baburova and the human rights lawyer Stanislav Markelov. The two were shot down on a busy Moscow street corner on January 19, 2009, after Markelov held a press conference to denounce the early release of a Russian army colonel, Yuri Budanov, who had been convicted of kidnapping and killing an eighteen-year-old Chechen girl. Baburova, a twenty-five-year-old reporter specializing in the coverage of neo-Nazi groups, was walking with Markelov after the press conference when they were approached by a masked gunman who shot Markelov in the head with a silencer-equipped pistol and then gunned down Baburova when she tried to intercede. A few months after our meeting, a jury in Moscow convicted the radical nationalists Nikita

Tikhonov and his common-law wife Yevgeniya Khasis in the killings. Tikhonov was sentenced to life in prison and Khasis to eighteen years. On May 31, 2011, Rustam Makhmudov was arrested in Chechnya. He had returned from Belgium to escape the Belgian police, who had intensified their search. He went on trial in July 2013 with his brothers Dzhabrail and Ibragim, who were alleged to have served as lookouts and accomplices. Lom-Ali Gaitukayev, their uncle, also went on trial for having organized the hit on behalf of an unidentified mastermind. A former police officer is accused of being the organizer. All were originally acquitted in the 2009 verdict overturned by Russia's Supreme Court.[18] They were sentenced to long prison terms in June 2014. Anna Politkovskaya's children, Ilya and Vera, boycotted the legal process, which they described as illegitimate. They accused investigators of failing to pursue the masterminds and were particularly disappointed by the December 2012 plea arrangement with the former police official Lt. Col Dmitry Pavlyuchenkov, who is serving eleven years in prison for his role in coordinating the hit team. Under the terms of his agreement Pavlyuchenkov was required to help identify the mastermind of the crime. But Politkovskaya family representatives and editors at *Novaya Gazeta* said that he failed to cooperate. Large portions of his trial were held in secret and closed to the press.[19]

Who is the mastermind? In his remarks immediately following the murder, Putin suggested that the murder was organized "outside the country," implicitly pointing the finger at Boris Berezovsky, the exiled oligarch and sworn Putin enemy who committed suicide in his London home in March 2013. Berezovsky's name, however, has never surfaced in any of my meetings with Russian investigators. The name I kept hearing was Kadyrov. Kadyrov certainly has a motive. Politkovskaya's reporting had not only exposed his role in torture and other gross human rights violations but also chronicled the widespread corruption associated with the reconstruction effort. Kadyrov has also been linked to many other political killings in Chechnya, including the Estemirova killing.

More than a decade after Putin first came to power and seven years after the brutal murder that shocked the conscience of the world, what have been the benefits and limitations of the strategy of engagement around impunity? While justice is at best partial, low-level perpetrators have been convicted in three journalists' murders, including in the Politkovskaya case. Violence against journalists in Russia continues, but at significantly lower levels than seen earlier in the decade. More recent media killings have taken place in the conflict-ravaged North Caucasus, not on Moscow street corners. In Russia investigators are extremely capable, undoubtedly a Soviet-era legacy. After years of working there, I have come to the conclusion that the investigations are generally able to "solve" the crimes and that the leadership knows who carried out the killings. However, they have blocked or limited prosecutions because those identified as the likely perpetrators operate with some level of official protection. During an extended visit to Moscow in the summer of 2011, Ognianova met with a senior official in the office of the Investigative Committee to push for more aggressive action in the Estemirova and Politkovskaya cases. Frustrated and exasperated by the relentless pressure, the investigator finally laid it on the table. "Russia would rather have five human rights activists killed than arrest Kadyrov," he said, his voice rising. "If you want to start another war in the North Caucasus, go ahead and arrest Kadyrov." In Russia justice is nothing more than a crude political calculation.

Putin, back in the presidency since 2012 after completing a six-year switch with Dmitry Medvedev, has recognized the damage to the country's international reputation caused by the murders of journalists that have received so much attention. In recent years, Russia has become less violent and more repressive. The "democratator" strategy described in chapter 2 today takes precedence over the policy of official tolerance for the criminal mafias that left too many bodies on the street. Some have noted that Politkovskaya was murdered on Putin's birthday, suggesting that her killers may have wanted to give Putin a present. Today, murder is a gift he does not want.

Murder in Mindanao

In Russia, which under Putin has experienced a decade of political stability and economic growth, the media is tightly controlled. In the Philippines, which has stagnated economically, the political culture is freewheeling, volatile, competitive, and deeply corrupt. The media is largely open and vibrant. What Russia and the Philippines share is a history of violence against journalists that has landed them both squarely on CPJ's Impunity Index.

In the Philippines, the press is both a check on power and an enabler of corruption. In the provinces, many journalists are under the sway of local political bosses who pay them to provide positive stories about them and negative coverage of their political rivals. This form of journalism had become so pervasive that it even has a name: AC/DC, for Attack Collect/Defend Collect. The victims of these paid smear campaigns have not always taken the criticism in stride. With guns rampant in the provinces, disputes are often settled with violence. Murders are almost never solved.

The Philippines also has a strong tradition of crusading reporting and a small but vital cadre of investigative journalists. The pervasive culture of impunity makes these journalists equally vulnerable to violent attack. Among the best-known journalists to be killed was Marlene Garcia-Esperat, a whistleblower and columnist from the volatile island of Mindanao. Her 2005 murder convulsed the nation.

Because of her unyielding temperament and her flashy attire, Garcia-Esperat was nicknamed the Erin Brockovich of the Philippines. The daughter of a prominent politician in Tacurong, she was encouraged from a young age to fight injustice and corruption. After obtaining a degree in chemistry—a rarity for a woman in the Philippines—she took a position at the Ministry of Agriculture in Cotabato in Mindanao, testing livestock for chemical exposure. The work should have been routine, but something was deeply amiss. In 1989, less than a year before Garcia-Esperat started in her position at the Agriculture Ministry, another employee in the same department had been murdered in what was purported to be a botched robbery. There were rumors linking the killing to the department's top regional finance official, a man named Osmeña Montañer. Another Agriculture Department worker who also alleged corruption against Montañer had been shot and left in a coma. She eventually recovered.[20]

It didn't take Garcia-Esperat long in her new position for her to confirm that funds were going missing. Despite generous allocations from the federal government, her lab was woefully equipped. By 1996, after years of digging, she had uncovered evidence of a massive corruption scheme, and the following year she filed formal complaints with federal authorities. The day before auditors were to arrive from Manila to carry out an investigation, the Agriculture Department building housing the evidence was burned to the ground in a suspicious fire. Furious, Garcia-Esperat went to the press for the first time, giving an interview to a local newspaper, the *Midland Review*, and a radio station, DXKR. After being warned that her life was in danger, Garcia-Esperat fled to Manila with the documents she had salvaged from the fire and entered a witness protection program. Montañer and his driver were charged with arson, but the charges were later dropped.

Garcia-Esperat spent two years living in a rundown Manila safe house separated from her family, but the case against Montañer went nowhere. Disillusioned and furious, she returned to Mindanao and decided to pursue justice through a different means—the media. She bought time on DXKR for a radio program, and as her notoriety grew she was eventually given a weekly column in the *Midland Review*, entitled "Madam Witness." She also made arrangements to bring the story of corruption in the Agriculture Department to the national media in collaboration with a journalism nonprofit, the Philippine Center for Investigative Journalism, or PCIJ.

As Garcia-Esperat become more prominent the death threats grew. She was warned repeatedly about plots against her life. She dismissed them, telling an interviewer, "I grew up on bullets." But she was scared. In February 2005 she wrote a letter to President Gloria Macapagal-Arroyo informing her that "military intelligence operatives are allegedly out to liquidate the undersigned and silence her forever." The following month, an assassin who had been casing her home for weeks finally saw an opportunity. After Marcia-Esperat sent her bodyguard home for the Easter holiday, the gunmen slipped into her home. He greeted her with a friendly "Hello, ma'am," then shot her in the face as she sat at the table enjoying a holiday meal with her family. Her young children witnessed the horrific crime.

Unlike the Politkovskaya murder in Russia, Garcia-Esperat's killing sparked widespread outrage and indignation in the Philippines. The Philippines not only has a strong independent media but also a community of press freedom advocates including unions and human rights groups who spearheaded protests and pushed for action. International groups amplified the pressure by sending open letters to high officials in the Philippine government. Based on a careful analysis of available data, CPJ declared the Philippines the "most murderous country for journalists" in the world, more deadly than Iraq at the time.[21] While President Macapagal-Arroyo disputed that characterization, she was forced by the public pressure to take action. In May 2005, she gave a press conference flanked by Garcia-Esperat's two young sons and announced that the Justice Department was being given a "green light" to go after the masterminds of the murder. She also announced the creation of a special task force to investigate journalists' killings. Over the next year, investigators made significant progress in apprehending the organizers of the Garcia-Esperat murder, who quickly turned state's witness. The former military intelligence officer Rowie Barua affirmed that he had been hired by Montañer and his assistant Estrella Sabay to carry out the killing.

The Garcia-Esperat case appeared for a time as a fleeting opportunity to overcome the culture of impunity in the Philippines. With Nena Santos, Garcia-Esperat's lawyer and personal friend, spearheading the quest for justice, and with support from leading Philippine press groups and the international community, the legal process moved forward in fits and starts. Charges were dismissed, then reinstated. Officialdom was nominally cooperative. It was a relatively simple matter to get an appointment with the special police task force set up by President Arroyo to investigate the journalists' murders, and investigators were more than happy to meet with international visitors and give presentations outlining progress. There were also some exceptionally committed public servants like Leo Dacera, a Justice Department official who without the full support of his bosses made investigating journalists' murders a personal crusade. Nominally the head of the witness protection program, Dacera was also leading the Garcia-Esperat prosecution and, with the assistance of Nena Santos, was pushing back against efforts by Montañer and Sabay to delay the proceedings. A February 2008 conference on "Impunity and Press Freedom" attracted nearly two hundred participants, including representatives of the Philippine government. The conference's keynote speaker, Supreme Court Chief Justice Reynato Puno, declared, "Bullets fired in the direction of journalists pierce not only human flesh, but also our republican ideals." His remarks made headlines.[22]

Despite these efforts, the case against Montañer and Sabay eventually stalled. In December 2009 an appellate court quashed the outstanding arrest warrants against the officials, who reportedly returned to work at the Agriculture Department in February 2010.[23]

There were other reasons beyond the dysfunctional Philippine criminal justice system why the case did not move forward. Nena Santos told me during a visit to Manila that she had documents linking the corruption in the Agricultural Department in Mindanao directly to the president's husband, Jose Miguel Arroyo. The corruption was not just about money. According to widespread media reports, the funds were part of a widespread vote-buying scheme in Mindanao that had helped President Arroyo win reelection in 2004.

The public pressure had put the issue of impunity firmly on the national agenda, and while President Arroyo made a show of responding, her range of action was limited by her own corrupt dependence on powerful military and regional political bosses to deliver votes and maintain the system of federal government largesse that kept her in power. The regional bosses responsible for many of the killings continued to thwart justice, gumming up the legal system with endless appeals. In meetings with Philippine officials, press freedom groups insisted that that unless the impunity issue was addressed as a priority the violence would continue and might possibly grow. But we could not have imagined what came next.

On the morning of November 23, 2009, at around 9 a.m., a convoy of six cars pulled out from the home of Esmael "Toto" Mangudadatu, the vice mayor of the town of Buluan in Mindanao. Mangudadatu had decided to run for governor of Maguindanao province, and in order to launch his candidacy he needed to file papers in the provincial capital of Shariff Aguak. The problem was that Shariff Aguak was controlled by a rival family, the Ampatuans, who had long dominated political power in the region. Mangudadatu was a formidable figure in his own right and had previously been an ally of the Ampatuans. But the family patriarch Andal Ampatuan Sr. made clear that he would not tolerate a political challenge. Mangudadatu knew he was a marked man but assumed that according to Muslim tradition his female relatives would not be harmed. He dispatched his wife and sisters to file the candidacy on his behalf. To increase their security he invited local journalists to accompany them. More than thirty journalists took him up on the offer and joined the convoy.

That same morning another convoy of six or seven vehicles left the compound of Andal Ampatuan Jr. in Shariff Aguak and headed southeast. Andal Jr., the volatile and violent son of the Ampatuan patriarch, had organized a force that included one hundred men, among them elements from the local police, as well as a Hummer mounted with a .50-caliber machine gun. In a scrubby field at the end of a dirt road, Ampatuan's men had dug three massive trenches using backhoes emblazoned with the family name.

The Ampatuan clan has dominated politics in Maguindanao since the Marcos era but had consolidated their control under President Arroyo. The arrangement was fairly simple. In exchange for delivering votes on election day—the casual nature of the fraud was suggested by the fact Arroyo sometimes received more than 100 percent of the vote in towns under Ampatuan control—the family was given a free hand to run the province as its personal domain. The Ampatuans were also permitted to operate a massive private militia, ostensibly "a force multiplier" in the military's battle against separatist Muslim rebels but in reality a means to intimidate rivals and ensure unchecked political control.

Journalists in the region had long sought to navigate the volatile political environment and had learned to put aside competitive rivalries for the sake of security. They were not a particularly aggressive bunch; to the contrary, they often made alliances and cut political deals with the Ampatuans. While Mangudadatu had been correct that the presence of the media could serve as a hedge against the worst abuses, and while journalists themselves had calculated correctly that working cooperatively in a large group would increase their overall security, they had both badly miscalculated the level of brutality that Andal Ampatuan Jr. was prepared to employ.

As the convoy carrying journalists and the Mangudadatu relatives drove into the ambush, they were cut off in front and in back. The handful of cell phone calls and text messages that were sent in the

initial moments paint a terrifying picture. Mangudadatu's wife Gena-
lyn managed to get a call out to her husband in which she described
people being beaten with rifle butts. A text message sent by one of the
journalists read simply, "pray for us, our situation is critical."

All six cars were immediately commandeered; cell phones and
identity documents were apparently confiscated. The cars were driven
for approximately half an hour to the field where the killing would
take place. The women were executed first; some were reportedly
raped and sexually mutilated. They were then tossed into the previously dug graves. The backhoes were used to crush the vehicles,
which were also buried. The killers had nearly completed the job by
late afternoon when the military arrived on the scene, tipped off by a
journalist who, after receiving a cell phone message from a colleague,
had alerted the local military commander. The day before, the top
military commander had denied a request from a journalist to provide
security for the convoy, assuring him that the road was safe.

What became known as the Maguindanao Massacre was the single
most deadly day for the media in history.[24] Thirty-two journalists and
media workers were executed. According to a report prepared by the
International Crisis Group, "Some of the killers taken into custody
expressed more remorse about the killing of journalists" because they
thought they would be targeting the Mangudadutus.[25] The journalists'
murders also turned what might have been perceived as a local power
struggle into an international incident, partly because it mobilized the
domestic and international groups that had already been active in the
Garcia-Esperat case.

Within weeks of the killing, Philippine groups, including the National Union of Journalists of the Philippines (NUJP) and Center for
Media Freedom and Responsibility (CFMR), had organized street
protests in Manila, rallied the national media, and traveled to Mindanao to carry out an investigation and support the families of the victims. Two weeks later, an international delegation traveled to General
Santos City in Mindanao, where the participants held an emotional
meeting with the families, visited the graves of the slain journalists to
pay their respects, and were briefed by local officials about the status
of the investigation. Under intense international pressure the authori-

ties moved quickly to arrest Andal Ampatuan Jr., his father, and dozens of other alleged accomplices, but cracks quickly emerged in the investigation, cracks that would become fissures in the coming weeks and months.

While the trial was moved to Manila to protect against witness tampering, many key witnesses in the case were under extreme pressure. The home of an eyewitness who testified in the bail proceeding that he had seen Andal Ampatuan Jr. murder the first victim with an automatic rifle came under mortar attack, and his lawyer was shot in the neck (he survived). Another witness in the case, a member of the local militia who had acknowledged his participation and agreed to turn state's witness, was murdered as he was about to enroll in the witness protection program. Men who said they represented the Ampatuans visited the families of those killed and offered enormous sums to the widows if they would agree to sign blank papers.

In July 2010, President Benigno Aquino III succeeded Arroyo as president. The new president had an impressive political pedigree. His mother, Corazon Aquino, entered political life after her husband, Benigno Aquino Jr., was assassinated in 1983. She was sworn in as president three years later after the People Power Revolution, which she helped lead, brought down the Marcos dictatorship. The younger Aquino, known as Noynoy, had campaigned on a platform of reversing the country's record of impunity and had pledged that justice in the Maguindanao Massacre would be a priority of the new administration. His newly appointed justice minister, Leila de Lima, called it a "litmus test."

But when CPJ met with members of the Aquino administration at the Malacañan Palace in August 2010, the challenges to a successful prosecution were immense. Only nineteen of 196 suspects in the crime, including Andal Ampatuan Jr.; sixteen police officers; and two private militia members were on trial; forty-seven suspects in custody had not yet been arraigned. Another 130 suspects, including police officials and members of the Ampatuans' three-thousand-man-strong militia, were still at large. Lawyers for the Ampatuans had filed a flurry of motions that had successfully delayed the legal proceedings. Prosecutors, meanwhile, were forced to rely on the direct testimony of eyewitnesses because much of the forensic evidence had been compromised. In the most egregious example, the bodies of the victims had been extracted from the graves using a backhoe rather than shovels.

The underfunded and inept Philippine justice system was clearly overwhelmed by the complexity of the Maguindanao massacre prosecutions. There were hundreds of suspects, some in custody, some on the loose. The trial was moved to Manila for security reasons, but the change in venue created a tremendous logistical strain and complicated the testimony of eyewitnesses who were already vulnerable to bribery and threats. Overcoming these challenges would require the full focus and attention of the federal government, which was overwhelmed by the nation's other pressing challenges. The cause of justice also suffered a serious blow when Leo Dacera died of a heart attack on November 4, 2010. He was fifty-four. Dacera had recently been named lead prosecutor in the Maguindanao massacre case.[26]

The contrast between the Philippines and Russia demonstrates the challenge of fighting impunity at a global level. In Russia, there had been little domestic outcry to the killings of Anna Politkovskaya and other journalists, but the Putin government had pushed forward a handful of prosecutions in order to blunt international criticism. The level of violence against journalists had declined even as the country became more repressive. In the Philippines, meanwhile, the dynamic was exactly reversed. The massive public outpouring in response to the Marcia-Esperat murder and later the Maguindanao massacre put the issue of impunity high on the national agenda. But the government has been unable to deliver justice, both because of the overwhelming deficiencies in the criminal justice system and because of a lack of political will. Violence against journalists in the Philippines continues unabated while the stakes have grown. They were summed up by the journalist Aquiles Zonio, who had been part of the Maguindanao convoy but had turned back prior to the fatal checkpoint because he had forgotten his cell phone. "I believe that Justice will eventually be served to the victims," he said as he visited the massacre site, today a nondescript clearing overgrown with weeds. "Because if not, this country has no future."[27]

Fighting Back

On December 18, 2013, the UN General Assembly passed a resolution declaring November 2 "The International Day to End Impunity" of crimes against journalists.[28] The designation of the special international day to commemorate the anti-impunity struggle was the culmination of years of advocacy by global press groups, who had initially proposed November 23 to mark the Maguindanao massacre. That date was blocked by the Philippines, which did not want to draw attention to its failure to achieve justice. The November 2 date was a compromise commemorating the death of two French journalists, Ghislaine Dupont and Claude Verlon, who were kidnapped and murdered in 2013 while reporting in Mali.

The resolution called on member states "to do their utmost to prevent violence against journalists and media workers, to ensure accountability through the conduct of impartial, speedy and effective investigations into all alleged violence against journalists and media workers falling within their jurisdiction, and to bring the perpetrators of such crimes to justice and to ensure that victims have access to appropriate remedies."

As the Garcia-Esperat and Politkovskaya cases illustrate, such outcomes are exceedingly rare at a global level. Indeed, the problem of impunity seems intractable until you dig down into the data. CPJ's 2013 Impunity Index—which includes all countries in the world where there are at least five unsolved journalist murders over the preceding ten years—lists only twelve countries. While every media killing is a threat to the flow of information, those countries included on the index are the places around the world where the problem is sustained and systematic. Iraq and Somalia, which top the list, are both experiencing active conflicts, and the rule of law is so weak in both countries that the prospect for justice in the current environment is essentially nil. This does not mean that the fight for impunity should be abandoned in either country, or in Syria, which because of the recent spate of killings will be included on the 2014 index. But it must be contemplated as part of a longer-term effort to achieve transitional justice when the circumstances permit.

That leaves ten countries around the world that should be the focus of international attention and action. They are the Philippines,
Sri Lanka, Colombia, Afghanistan, Mexico, Pakistan, Russia, Brazil,
Nigeria, and India. As the case studies in Russia and the Philippines
make clear, each country must be approached differently. In Russia,
the authoritarian structures have made it possible to translate limited
political will into action, and violence has declined. In the Philippines,
where both the level of mobilization and government engagement is
higher, the weakness of the criminal justice system and lack of government control and influence in key areas of the country make concrete
progress more difficult.

The UN Plan of Action on the Issue of Impunity and Safety of Journalists seeks to address the issue in a systematic way. It was developed
with considerable input from civil-society and press-freedom groups
and emphasizes strategies both for achieving justice and mitigating
future risk. The plan states:

> Without freedom of expression, and particularly freedom of the
> press, an informed, active and engaged citizenry is impossible. In
> a climate where journalists are safe, citizens find it easier to ac-
> cess quality information and many objectives become possible as
> a result: democratic governance and poverty reduction; conserva-
> tion of the environment; gender equality and the empowerment
> of women; justice and a culture of human rights, to name a few.
> Hence, while the problem of impunity is not restricted to the failure
> to investigate the murders of journalists and media workers, the
> curtailment of their expression deprives society as a whole of their
> journalistic contribution and results in a wider impact on press
> freedom where a climate of intimidation and violence leads to self-
> censorship. In such a climate societies suffer because they lack the
> information needed to fully realize their potential.[29]

But like all UN plans, there are lots of proclamations and statements of good intentions and less clarity about how the ambitious
strategy will be put into action. The plan identifies four countries—
Iraq, South Sudan, Nepal, and Pakistan—which are the focus of initial
action. Pakistan has been the country of most urgent attention and

the increased visibility has resulted in the government formally accepting the UN action plan in October 2013 at a joint conference with media freedom groups.[30] But as in the Philippines, the weakness of the criminal justice system will need to be overcome. That challenge will be even more difficult because (as discussed in the introduction to this book) there is compelling evidence that the country's powerful spy service, the ISI, has been involved in a number of journalist murders.

Fighting impunity means not only applying political pressure. It means supporting governments that seek to build investigative capacity and develop legal infrastructure. In this regard, the case of Mexico is instructive. When I first joined CPJ in 1997, I undertook a reporting trip across Mexico to investigate a series of murders of journalists that had taken place over the previous several years. Because murder is a state crime, the investigations were being undertaken by state prosecutors who not only lacked resources but were often corrupt or threatened by the same people who had carried out the killings. When I met with federal authorities to push for more aggressive action, I was told that the federal government had no authority to intervene in the cases even though the killings represented a fundamental threat to the right to freedom of expression, guaranteed by the 1917 Mexican Constitution.

In July 2000, Vicente Fox Quezada from the conservative National Action Party was elected president of Mexico, ending the six-decade-long reign of the Institutional Revolutionary Party, or PRI. With violence against journalists continuing to escalate under his administration, the urgency of federal action became more acute. Under pressure from domestic and international groups, Fox agreed to appoint a special prosecutor for crimes against journalists to coordinate the state-level investigations. He also promised to support legislation making attacks on journalists a federal crime. While Fox followed through and named the special prosecutor in February 2006, without a legal framework for action the effectiveness of the new office was limited.

Throughout the Fox administration and government of Felipe Calderón that followed, the issue languished. Proposed legislation moved forward, then collapsed amid debate in Mexico's acrimonious Congress. It was not until April 2013—as Calderón's six-year term was nearing its end—that the legislation was finally passed.[31] It will be up to Mexico's current president, Enrique Peña Nieto, to ensure that the new federal authority is used to deliver justice.

In Sri Lanka, where the government of President Mahinda Rajapaksa has consolidated power following the defeat of the Tamil Tigers insurgency in a brutal 2009 military offensive, the immediate goal is necessarily more modest. The government there has shown zero interest in investigating the nine unsolved murders of journalists that have taken place over the last decade but has focused considerable energy on burnishing its international reputation following the defeat of the Tamil Tigers. When Sri Lanka hosted a meeting of the Commonwealth Heads of Government in November 2013, press freedom and human rights groups from around the world used the opportunity to highlight the country's terrible human rights and press freedom record. British prime minister David Cameron used the Commonwealth meeting to speak out about ongoing human rights issues and even visited besieged Tamil journalists in Jaffna, in the country's north.

In Colombia, where violence has declined dramatically and a comprehensive settlement to end the decades-long insurgency seems within reach, the goal is to ensure that those responsible for the wave of media killings are held accountable. While fear and self-censorship remain, Colombia's situation has undoubtedly improved. The attorney general's office won the first-ever conviction of the masterminds of a journalist's killing when three ex-officials, including the former mayor of the town of Barrancabermeja, were sentenced to twenty-eight years' imprisonment for the 2003 murder of a radio commentator.[32]

Ultimately, the battle against impunity is a long-term struggle. In lawless and violent societies where powerful groups fight to control information, journalists will continue to be killed. But it is possible to reduce the rate of violence or at least ensure that countries that fail to take aggressive steps to investigate the crimes and bring the killers to justice face a significant political cost. It is also important to recognize that in most cases the motive for killing a journalist is to use violence as a form of censorship. The best way to undermine this logic is by keeping the story itself alive after a journalist is killed. This means supporting journalists and media organizations that continue to cover sensitive issues. Or, in the poignant words of the Mexican investigative reporter Marcela Turati, who founded an organization, Periodistas de Pie, to defend the human rights of journalists covering the drug war, "Don't abandon us."[33]

Impunity must be addressed in the context of a universal right to freedom of expression. But governments also need to recognize that stemming the tide of violence against the press is essential to the creation of a society based on the rule of the law, one in which information and knowledge circulate freely, in which political differences are resolved through public debate, and in which accountability is assured through the public exposure of corruption, abuse, and malfeasance. Murdering journalists is the most brutal and primitive means of controlling information, information that benefits people within a particular society as well as those who seek to access it across borders. Fighting and winning the battle against impunity in the Philippines, Russia, Mexico and Pakistan ultimately requires the recognition of countries all around the world that they have a collective stake in justice.

EIGHT

Journalists by Definition

Journalists who report the news are exercising a fundamental human right. But they are also contributing to the creation of more informed societies. In the best cases, they are exposing corruption and human rights violations, making it possible to address these abuses and contributing to global peace and security. This is why their work must be protected.

The acceptance of this basic premise invites an inevitable question: Who, precisely, is a journalist? It's a question that has never been easy to answer. Journalists, unlike lawyers or doctors, don't require a license or in most cases a degree to practice their profession. They may work for an established media organization, but they don't have to. They may be objective and balanced—but then again they may not be. They may be highly ethical, professional, and committed to the truth. Or they may be sloppy, ignorant, and in extreme cases corrupt.

The question of who is a journalist surfaces nearly every day at CPJ, and many of the cases we grapple with are extremely thorny. Our experience has shown us that a rigid definition of what constitutes journalism is unhelpful for several reasons. First, because technology is constantly changing the way journalism is practiced, any understanding of who is a journalist must constantly evolve. Second, because judging what is and what is not journalism depends so much on the context. For example, CPJ has classified dissident bloggers in places like Cuba, China, and Burma as journalists precisely because access to the state-controlled media is closed. In more open societies, we might not make the same determination.

Making a judgment about who is and who is not a journalist is more straightforward when you look at individual cases of violations or abuses. At CPJ we ask ourselves some basic questions, such as: Was the person documenting facts or events? Was the person engaged in fact-based commentary? Were authorities seeking to suppress the events or issues in question? Is the individual's work being disseminated to the public? Then we look at specific work, relying on the expertise of regional staff to access and evaluate the material in the local language.

The easier question to answer is what is *not* journalism. Poetry, fiction, and political campaign speeches are all forms of expression but do not qualify as journalism. While CPJ does not make judgments about the point of the view or even quality in making a determination—after all, international law equally protects well-documented investigative pieces and shoddy, partisan rants—we do exclude any journalism that crosses the line into incitement to violence. What constitutes incitement to violence under international law is discussed in the next chapter, but these distinctions are among the most difficult and controversial.

In recent years, the challenge has been to differentiate journalism from activism, particularly in the Middle East where traditional media has become much more polarized and where activists have exploited new technologies to enter the journalistic fray. When I visited Cairo in March 2013, during the waning months of the Mohamed Morsi government, I found the lines thoroughly blurred. This was a time when mainstream journalists had turned against the regime and authorities had responded with lawsuits and intimidation. When I asked some of Egypt's most prominent media figures to explain the difference between journalism and activism, most described the exercise as futile. "As a journalist, your job is to seek the truth and defend your freedom, and that makes you an activist in this environment," said Ibrahim Eissa, one of Egypt's best-known editors and political commentators. "You will confront the government simply trying to defend your rights as a journalist. So you are not changing your description—you are just operating in a different state."[1]

Eissa has considerable authority on the issue. He was one of Hosni Mubarak's fiercest critics, twice convicted on journalism-related charges. After Mubarak was toppled, he and two partners established a new broadcaster appropriately named Tahrir TV. He eventually sold his shares in the station and later resigned as a commentator when it changed its editorial line. He continued to edit a newspaper, also called *Tahrir*, and to serve as a regular TV commentator despite an onslaught of threats and public denunciations from Morsi supporters. "There is no press freedom in Egypt, either before or after the revolution," Eissa said at the time. "There is simply the courage of journalists."

The journalist and talk show host Reem Maged agreed. She gained acclaim for standing with the protesters in Tahrir Square. In early 2013, she faced charges of "disseminating false information about judges through the media." She tried her best to draw a distinction between her on-air journalistic persona and her participation in political protests. "I consider myself a journalist, but in the street I'm an activist, and I have positions," she said. "It's really difficult to separate the two."

Meanwhile, one of the country's most prominent social media activists insisted that she was not a journalist at all. Esraa Abdel Fattah helped launch the April 6 Movement to support a celebrated workers' strike. The group's innovative use of social media, particularly Facebook, eventually helped galvanize opposition to the Mubarak regime among the young and wired and laid the groundwork for the Tahrir Square uprising. Abdel Fattah was arrested not long after the April 6 group launched when authorities tracked her down at an Internet café. She was held for two weeks and then released.

During the Morsi government, Abdel Fattah said social media had become "even more important." Her Twitter feed—followed by more than 220,000 people—consisted of a steady diet of outrage and documentation, photos and updates, commentary, and curated news. Abdel Fattah also published a regular newspaper column.

Despite this informational output, Abdel Fattah said she was not a journalist because she is not objective. "When I cover the women's march I support what the women are doing, so yes I have a point of view," she noted, as an example. But journalists like Eissa or Maged, despite their mainstream credentials, were hardly objective either, and I could not make a meaningful distinction between their role and hers.

The convergence of journalism with activism is a phenomenon not only in post-Mubarak Egypt but throughout the Middle East and the world. At a March 2013 meeting in Doha, Qatar, in which press freedom activists gathered to develop a collective strategy for responding to the violence in Syria, a heated discussion broke out about what constitutes journalism in an environment in which professional reporters work alongside a new generation of online communicators who dub themselves "media activists." Using social media and public platforms like YouTube, these activists have provided firsthand accounts of the fighting, the toll, and daily life in a war-ravaged country but make no claim to objectivity. Some are fairly journalistic in their approach, and others are essentially propagandists for the rebel forces. A few are armed and participate in combat.

To give a few additional examples from other parts of the world, in China, a leading blogger, Zhou Shuguang, who uses the online moniker Zola (a nod to the French writer-journalist), has traveled around the country with a video camera documenting injustice but insists, "I don't know what journalism is. I just record what I witness." In Vietnam, a blogger named Nguyen Van Hai who took a similar approach was given a twelve-year jail sentence. In Turkey, while mainstream media ignored the Gezi Park protesters, activists using Twitter and other social media became the essential source of independent news. Even New York police seeking to control access to the Occupy Wall Street protests struggled to differentiate between accredited journalists and sympathetic citizens who used smartphones to disseminate news and information to the public.

In an era in which technology has changed everything about the way news is gathered and delivered, is it possible to draw a line between journalism, activism, and other kinds of speech? And is it necessary to do so? The answer is extremely significant for several reasons. First, because it directly affects the way journalists themselves understand their role. Are the rights of journalists distinct from others who provide information and commentary? Is the ability of journalists to perform their role as media professionals dependent on preserving some sort of distinction? Second, because it goes to larger questions about the kind of global information environment that would best preserve and even expand the accountability, oversight, and transparency that have historically been the function of independent media.

Journalists Defending Journalists

In order to answer these questions it is helpful to understand the origins and evolution of the global press freedom movement, which emerged along two parallel tracks. In the late 1970s, media industry groups came together to fight a proposal from UNESCO to create what was termed the New World Information and Communication Order, or NWICO. The purported goal of NWICO was to address inequalities in global communications structures between the West and the developing world, for example the fact that news agencies based in New York, London, and Paris set the global news agenda. But the findings of the specially appointed McBride Commission, which developed the NWICO guidelines, fueled an intensive debate that reverberated across the ideological divide. The Soviet bloc and the nonaligned countries argued that NWICO justified state involvement in the media sector to correct imbalances. There was even talk of government-established ethical standards to guide media conduct. This was a prospect that industry groups like the World Association of Newspapers, the International Press Institute, and the Inter-America Press Association believed would compromise independent media, and they formed a lasting alliance under the World Press Freedom Committee that eventually helped defeat the NWICO proposal. The U.S. government opposed NWICO and in 1984 withdrew from UNESCO in protest. It rejoined the organization in 2003.

At the same time that industry groups were joining forces to fight NWICO, the emerging human rights movement was having a significant effect on international journalists and their coverage of global issues. Post–World War II foreign correspondence by the U.S. media had focused on war and diplomacy. This had started to change during the Carter administration, with its emphasis on the promotion of human rights. By the late 1970s and early 1980s, independent human rights groups like Amnesty International and the newly created Helsinki Watch (which became Human Rights Watch) had begun to raise awareness about the persecution of dissidents behind the Iron Curtain and the widespread use of torture and disappearance by the military governments in Latin America. Among those subjected to violent persecution were journalists themselves, over one hundred of whom were abducted and disappeared in Argentina alone. Journalists and media organizations in the United States were obviously alarmed about these abuses, but many felt that reporting on—much less embracing—human rights could undermine their status as impartial observers. They continued to view human rights as an activist cause.

This was the landscape in 1981 when a Paraguayan journalist named Alcíbiades González Delvalle toured the United States as a part of a State Department–sponsored visitors program. As a columnist for the Asunción-based daily *ABC Color*, González Delvalle had repeatedly clashed with the government of its dictator, Alfredo Stroessner. The U.S. visit was supposed to be a reprieve, and it was until González Delvalle learned that an arrest warrant had been issued against him in Paraguay in response to his critical columns. The Paraguayan government wanted to force him into exile, but González Delvalle was determined to go home and face the charges. "The other South American dictatorships were spectacular, but Stroessner was sneaky," González Delvalle recalled in an interview years later. "We needed to bring what was happening there to the attention of the world."[2]

Laurie Nadel, a writer for CBS News in New York, read a one-paragraph Reuters story about González Delvalle and was moved by his ordeal. Concerned, she made a call to Michael Massing, then the executive editor of *Columbia Journalism Review*, and asked him if he would be interested in a story. He was, but the two also decided they needed to do more. They alerted U.S. foreign correspondents based in Latin America of González Delvalle's imminent arrest. Not long after González Delvalle flew back to Paraguay in June 1980, Paraguayan plainclothes police grabbed him off a downtown street and hauled him by the belt into a waiting taxi. At that point, the network of international support that had been mobilized kicked into gear. Reuters and ANSA, the Italian news agency, filed stories on his arrest. Warren Hoge, the *New York Times* South America correspondent based in Brazil, flew to Paraguay. His June 27 report in the *New York Times* datelined Asunción began, "The government of Gen. Alfredo Stroessner has arrested a prominent Paraguayan journalist here just hours after he returned from a visit to the United States sponsored by the United States government."[3]

It took seventy days for the Paraguayan government to succumb to the international pressure. On September 2, González Delvalle was released from jail and went right back to writing his column. He did not hold back and was arrested once again on September 23, 1983, and jailed for more than two months. In March 1984, Paraguayan police raided *ABC Color*, ransacked the newspaper's offices, and arrested the publisher, Aldo Zuccolillo, who was jailed briefly. *ABC Color* remained closed for five years, until the Stroessner dictatorship collapsed in 1989, by which time the general had spent thirty-five years in power.

The response to González Delvalle's arrest suggested that by covering human rights abuses committed against their less-fortunate colleagues, international journalists could help keep them safe. This was a kind of activism that many journalists initially resisted. But for U.S. journalists especially—who were at the height of their power in the post-Watergate era—standing up for their colleagues facing persecution from authoritarian governments increasingly seemed like the right thing to do. Massing and Nadel institutionalized this kind of support when they founded the Committee to Protect Journalists in 1981. They also succeeded in bringing some of the most prominent names in American journalism onto the board. Among them were Victor Navasky, the editor of the weekly *Nation*; the *New York Times* columnist Anthony Lewis; Jane Kramer from the *New Yorker*; the CBS News anchor Dan Rather; and Peter Arnett, who had left the AP to join the newly launched CNN. Walter Cronkite agreed to serve as the honorary chairman. In March 1981, Arnett publicly announced the creation of CPJ, explaining that the goal of the new organization was "to gather and disseminate information about the plight of American and local reporters in foreign nations that are systematically abusing press rights. We want to be a link between journalists and human rights concerns where it involves abuses of reporters."

Four years later, in 1985, Robert Ménard and several colleagues founded Reporters sans frontières, or Reporters Without Borders, in Montpellier, France. The original goal of RSF was to promote media coverage of humanitarian emergencies, but after a shakeout that left Ménard the sole leader of the organization, he shifted its mandate and began to focus exclusively on press freedom and defense of journalists around the world.[4] In 1992, a dozen press freedom and freedom of expression organizations—including CPJ, RSF, Article 19, Index on Censorship, and the Canadian Committee to Protect Journalists (later Canadian Journalists for Free Expression)—met in Montreal, Canada, and together formed the International Freedom of Expression Exchange, or IFEX, whose initial purpose was to coordinate work and share information. IFEX soon expanded to become a network of organizations working on the global, regional, or national level to advocate for freedom of expression. IFEX also helped nurture new member groups around the world and today consists of more than eighty organizations, most of which operate at the national level.[5]

By the mid-1990s the original resistance on the part of journalists and global media organizations to covering press freedom violations around the world had been largely overcome, and attacks on journalists were seen as newsworthy events in their own right. Coverage of attacks on the media tended to emphasize the unique and critical role that journalists play as impartial observers. Such a framework worked reasonably well so long as it was possible to make distinctions between journalists and nonjournalists. But that challenge grew as new technologies began to transform the media industry. The advent of blogs and online media raised new questions. As the volume, complexity, and speed of information increased, the process of defining journalism has become more and more unwieldy. The trend has accelerated in the last several years, with the explosion of social media and its increasing use to accomplish basic journalism: documenting events and disseminating information to the public.

Some traditional journalists are deeply uncomfortable with the blurring of lines, which they feel undermines the integrity of the profession while also making coverage of conflict more dangerous. NBC's chief foreign correspondent Richard Engel told the U.N. Security

Council during its July 2013 briefing on journalist security, "Protecting journalists these days is hard, perhaps harder than ever, because one has to tackle the question of who is a journalist and who is an activist in a way that never existed before." Engel lamented the ways in which the advent of social media has eviscerated the special status that international correspondents once enjoyed, eliminating distinctions among professional journalists, activists, and "rebels with cameras" and "state broadcasters," who are "fundamentally different from journalists." "If one cannot or will not write an article that goes against one's cause, then one is not a journalist and does not deserve to be treated like one," Engel explained. He proposed that the diplomats on the Security Council make a distinction between the broad defense of freedom of expression and the defense of "dedicated and trained professionals who take risks to deliver the kind of information council members need to make their decisions."

But inviting governments to differentiate journalists from nonjournalists would set a dangerous precedent. Many governments—Turkey, Egypt, China, and Venezuela, to cite some examples—seem to believe "journalists" support government policies while "activists" oppose them. Journalists and media freedom organizations have long resisted any effort by governments or government-controlled bodies like the United Nations to define who is and who is not a journalist, arguing that such a distinction is tantamount to licensing, which is anathema to the journalism profession.

Indeed, journalists themselves are divided on the issue, with opinion writers and columnists tending to take a more expansive view. The *New York Times* columnist Nick Kristof argues that a press freedom group needs to be "as broad as possible when thinking about its mission and role." "It would be pusillanimous if they helped only full-time journalists and let everyone else take the heat," he argued. "You need to speak up for everyone even if you don't call them journalists."

In the last three decades, the way in which journalists define their role has evolved considerably. Defending the human rights of persecuted colleagues, once viewed as activist special pleading, is now widely accepted. But today, precisely because the distinction between journalists and nonjournalists has broken down so dramatically, journalists are confronting a new dilemma: Should journalists more broadly embrace the freedom-of-expression cause? Or should they speak out—as Engel suggests—only in defense of their professional colleagues?

The Assange Conundrum

This debate played out in dramatic fashion beginning in April 2010, when WikiLeaks released a video provocatively labeled "Collateral Murder." The video showed the crew of a U.S. helicopter gunship in Iraq opening fire on a group of Iraqi men who had been identified as insurgents, some of them armed. A journalist and media assistant from Reuters who were with the group were both killed. A van that tried to rescue the wounded media worker also came under fire. Two children inside the van were wounded, and their father, the driver, was killed.[6]

WikiLeaks was cofounded by Julian Assange in 2006, with the goal of making public documents of "political, ethical, diplomatic, or historical significance," a description that of course covers just about everything. It was originally conceived of as a "wiki," meaning anyone could contribute, but that approach was later abandoned in favor of a format in which confidential documents were submitted through a secure electronic drop box, then evaluated before publication. In its first years, WikiLeaks scored several major "scoops," with the release of confidential documents ranging from Swiss banking records to the personal e-mails of Sarah Palin.[7]

But it wasn't until the "Collateral Murder" video that WikiLeaks garnered widespread public attention. The video—which Reuters had tried to obtain unsuccessfully from the Pentagon under the Freedom of Information Act—was provided to WikiLeaks by a disgruntled low-level military intelligence analyst named Bradley Manning. Manning also shared with WikiLeaks hundreds of thousands of confidential State Department cables that WikiLeaks began publishing in November 2010 under the heading "Cablegate." While Assange has never publicly acknowledged that Manning was the source of the leaks,

Manning pleaded guilty in February 2013 to leaking classified information to WikiLeaks. Military prosecutors, however, continued to pursue more serious charges against Manning, and in July 2013 they won a conviction on six counts of violating the Espionage Act (Manning was acquitted on the most serious charge, aiding the enemy). The day after being sentenced to thirty-five years in prison, Manning announced that he was female and would be known henceforth as Chelsea.[8]

To maximize public interest and attention, Assange made deals with leading international media organizations, including *Der Spiegel*, *El País*, *Le Monde*, and the *Guardian*, all of which were provided with advance copies of the leaked cables. Fearing legal consequences for publishing the cables in the United Kingdom, the *Guardian* decided to share them with the *New York Times*. As the *Guardian* editor Alan Rusbridger described the arrangement he made with the *Times* editor Bill Keller: "You've got the First Amendment, we've got the memory stick."[9]

The publication of the cables set off a firestorm, with various U.S. political figures denouncing Assange as a "high-tech terrorist" (Mitch McConnell and Joe Biden) and "an enemy combatant" (Newt Gingrich). Sarah Palin, perhaps still smarting over the public release of her personal e-mails, posted a rant on Facebook on which she asserted that Assange "had blood on his hands" and should be hunted down with the same urgency as Osama bin Laden. Under intensive political pressure—notably from former Connecticut Senator Joe Lieberman—MasterCard and PayPal said they would not process online donations to the organization, and Amazon announced it would no longer support the WikiLeaks site through its commercially available webhosting service. WikiLeaks was able to find a new home, and hundreds of groups around the world launched "mirror sites" that duplicated the published material and made it almost impossible to take offline. Lieberman also called for Assange to be prosecuted under the 1917 Espionage Act, which criminalizes obtaining, copying, or communicating documents related to the defense of the United States. A grand jury was convened in Virginia to consider a possible indictment against Assange, and the U.S. Congress held hearings in December 2010 to discuss the implications.

The response of media organizations and press freedom groups regarding Assange and WikiLeaks was confused and ambivalent. On August 12, 2010, RSF's secretary general Jean-François Julliard and Washington, D.C., representative Clothilde Le Coz sent an open letter to Assange accusing him of "incredible irresponsibility" in failing to redact the names of Afghan informants included in the release of the 91,000 military documents that WikiLeaks had released a month earlier under the banner of "The Afghan War Diaries."[10]

"The argument with which you defend yourself, namely that WikiLeaks is not made up of journalists, is not convincing. WikiLeaks is an information outlet and, as such, is subject to the same rules of publishing responsibility as any other media," the letter noted. After coming under withering and sustained criticism from WikiLeaks, highly organized and motivated supporters (who accused RSF of being both smug and self-righteous and of carrying water for the U.S. government), RSF posted a clarification on August 17 noting, "We reaffirm our support for WikiLeaks, its work, and its founding principles. It is thanks in large part to WikiLeaks that the world has seen the failures of the wars waged by the United States in Iraq and Afghanistan. . . . The U.S. authorities would be very mistaken if they tried to use our criticism as support for a decision to silence WikiLeaks." When pressure mounted on WikiLeaks in the aftermath of the "Cablegate" release, RSF offered a vigorous defense, even hosting a mirror site.

The public statements from other press freedom and media groups were even more tortured. The president of the U.S.-based Society of Professional Journalists Hagit Limor acknowledged on her blog that the organization was deeply conflicted. "If you're looking for consensus on WikiLeaks, don't ask a group of journalists," she wrote. "Several of our committees have been batting around the ramifications all week, and we can't even agree on the most basic question: Is WikiLeaks journalism?"[11]

The faculty of Columbia University's School of Journalism split, with half signing a letter to President Obama in support of Assange and half abstaining. "While we hold varying opinions of WikiLeaks' methods and decisions, we all believe that in publishing diplomatic cables WikiLeaks is engaging in journalistic activity protected by the First Amendment," the letter noted.[12]

CPJ did not initially take a position on WikiLeaks as we carried out a divisive internal review. Many on the staff felt that failure to confront the United States and condemn the overheated rhetoric from members of Congress and other public figures undermined CPJ's global credibility. In November 2010, Raushan Yesergepova, the wife of a journalist jailed in Kazakhstan for disclosing "state secrets," confronted Hillary Clinton during an event in Astana, the capital, and asked the secretary of state to intercede. Yesergepova was reprimanded by a senior Kazakh official who pointed to the U.S. position on WikiLeaks. "Didn't you hear what Clinton said?" he told her. "Publishing state secrets is dangerous and wrong."[13]

CPJ board members, who set policy for the organization, were reluctant to speak out in response to statements by public officials calling for Assange's head, no matter how distasteful those remarks. Partly this was because as an organization that defends free speech—including some pretty outrageous views expressed through the media—it would be hypocritical for CPJ to condemn politicians for expressing their views publicly. But there was also a wariness about—as one board member, put it—embracing Assange in a "journalistic bear hug." While the view was not universal on the board, many members didn't believe that WikiLeaks constituted journalism, arguing that Assange functioned more as "source" or even a "conduit."

But after reports emerged that the grand jury was considering an indictment of Assange under the Espionage Act, we were able to forge a compromise position opposing prosecution of Assange because of the threat this posed to the media as a whole. "Our concern flows not from an embrace of Assange's motives and objectives," CPJ's chairman Paul Steiger and I noted in a letter to President Obama and Attorney General Eric Holder. "But the Constitution protects the right to publish information of important interest to the public. That right has been upheld through decades of American jurisprudence and has served the people well."[14]

The tepid embrace by the media community was based in large measure on the fact that most professional journalists did not identify with Assange or his methods. And Assange did not help matters at all with his dissembling and obfuscation. Assange presented himself as a journalist at times, but his justifications for WikiLeaks' actions ranged from disrupting government communications, to ending war, to "crushing bastards." These are not necessarily journalistic motives.[15] He also violated the most basic of journalistic ethics by failing to remove the names of human rights activists and journalists who had interacted with U.S. authorities in repressive counties, putting these individuals at grave risk. After reviewing the first tranche of leaked cables in December 2010, CPJ provided to WikiLeaks the names of a number of vulnerable journalists, and their names were promptly redacted from the cables. Later, WikiLeaks released thousands of additional cables without redacting names. An Ethiopian journalist identified in one cable, Argaw Ashine, was threatened and forced to flee the country.[16]

Even journalists who supported the WikiLeaks project were disturbed by Assange's personal behavior, particularly after Swedish authorities began a criminal investigation into allegations of rape.[17] Without making a judgment about the veracity of the claims, it is fair to say that Assange's response to the charges was disgraceful. In a December 2010 interview with the BBC, Assange dismissed charges brought by two women—one of whom claimed he had used force and the other of whom claimed that he had initiated unprotected sex while she was asleep. "I've never had a problem before with women. Women have been extremely helpful and generous," Assange claimed. He said his accusers had been bamboozled by police and that one "of the women has written many articles on taking revenge against men for infidelity and is a notorious radical feminist." He complained without apparent irony about the *Guardian*'s leaked police files about his case, calling the decision "disgusting" and describing it as part of an organized effort by Swedish prosecutors to undermine his legal defense.[18]

After fighting and losing a legal battle to avoid extradition from the United Kingdom to Sweden, where he would likely face formal criminal charges, Assange sought refuge in the Ecuadoran embassy in London. He was eventually granted asylum by the country's president Rafael Correa, a man with a history of intimidating and suing critical journalists. When pressed about Ecuador's record by the CNN anchor Erin Burnett, Assange could not bring himself to utter one word in favor of free speech in Ecuador, dismissing the issue and Ecuador itself as "not significant" in a global context.[19]

Should Assange be disqualified from support from journalists and press freedom organizations because of his lack of journalistic ethics and his generally loathsome behavior? I don't think so. While I was outraged that WikiLeaks did not make a greater effort to remove the names of vulnerable individuals from the leaked cables, it is an exaggeration to suggest, as some have, that this carelessness led to journalists and human rights activists being killed or imprisoned (although several were forced into exile). Assange's personal behavior—while deplorable—is irrelevant in terms of a determination as to whether he is a journalist.

On the other side of the equation, WikiLeaks has tried to suggest that it functions as a journalistic entity. I'm skeptical. Even though Assange has taken the title of "editor-in-chief" and describes other WikiLeaks volunteers as a "journalists," this seems a largely opportunistic ploy to reposition the organization and claim the mantle of press freedom. WikiLeaks lacks a journalistic outlook. It provides limited context or analysis and does not generally seek to independently confirm the accuracy of the information it publishes (other than to verify the authenticity of leaked documents). WikiLeaks is best described as an anti-secrecy advocacy group that uses journalistic strategies to advance its goals.

Although the question of whether Julian Assange is a journalist is interesting, it's not ultimately resolvable or even that relevant. The real question is whether Assange and WikiLeaks are part of the new global information ecosystem in which journalists operate. Here the answer is clearly yes. And the other important question is whether prosecuting Assange under the Espionage Act would threaten that system. Here again the answer is yes.

The 1917 Espionage Act, as noted, makes it a crime to obtain, copy, or publicize documents relating to the defense of the United States. The language is both broad and vague and could be construed to apply to the media. However, journalists have not been previously charged for a number of reasons. The first is that legislative history suggests that Congress never intended that the law be used to prosecute the press. To obtain a conviction, prosecutors must prove bad faith criminal intent—a legal concept known as scienter. This would be very difficult to do in the case of a traditional journalist. A prosecution would also almost certainly have to overcome a First Amendment challenge. Finally, the Justice Department has resisted prosecuting journalists because of the likely adverse public reaction and the damage that such a prosecution would do to the country's international reputation.[20]

There are several sections of the act that could conceivably be used to bring charges against Assange. Section 793(e) criminalizes communication of national security information. To win a case against Assange under this provision, prosecutors would either have to argue that the dissemination of information to the public is covered by the act or that Assange operates so clearly outside a journalistic framework that even though the act does not apply to traditional journalists it does apply to him. Either argument—if successful—would undermine the work of the press. Prosecutors could also try to make a case under section 793(c), which makes it a crime to receive or obtain documents connected with national defense. But to prevail under this provision, prosecutors would have to demonstrate that Assange acted in bad faith. Since Assange disseminated the information to the public—which is precisely what journalists do—it would be difficult to draw a distinction between his approach and that of traditional journalists. Finally, prosecutors could argue that Assange violated section 793(g), which makes it a crime to conspire to violate the act, if it could somehow prove that Assange encouraged Manning to disclose to him the confidential documents. But if that case were successful, any journalist who persuaded a source to provide confidential or classified material could face legal jeopardy. The issue in fact emerged in an extremely troubling way after it was revealed that a Fox television reporter, James Rosen, was named in court papers as a coconspirator in a leak investigation for encouraging a source to provide him with a confidential report on North Korea.[21]

In other words, a successful prosecution of Assange under the Espionage Act would mean that any journalist anywhere in the world would be vulnerable to prosecution under U.S. law. If a journalist in Kenya, or Colombia, or Egypt, or Pakistan published information from classified documents in the local media they could, at least theoretically, be charged under the act and brought to trial if arrested in the United States or extradited.

Journalists may find Assange personally distasteful and generally disapprove of the reckless way in which the information was released. But WikiLeaks has in fact made an extraordinarily valuable contribution to the work of the media. The initial revelations from Cablegate were, of course, reported simultaneously in mainstream media outlets, from the *Guardian* to *Le Monde*. But the cables have also served as an invaluable resource that has enriched day-to-day coverage from Pakistan to Mali. Global citizens have benefitted tremendously as a result. Holed up in the Ecuadoran embassy in London, Assange seems a reduced figure. But if the U.S. government should ever proceed with prosecuting him under the Espionage Act, journalists around the world should rush to his defense, and the outcry should be loud and sustained. Not only would the prosecution threaten traditional journalists, but it would erode the new system of information distribution on which global citizens all depend. In other words, Julian Assange may not be a journalist, but journalists should defend him as if he were.

Journalism and Free Expression

As the Assange case illustrates, journalists can no longer protect their own interests by advocating solely for press freedom. Instead, journalists must embrace the broader struggle for freedom of expression and make it their own.

This does not mean that journalism is going to disappear or that professional journalists are indistinguishable from bloggers, social media activists, or human rights advocates. And it certainly does not mean that the quality and accuracy of the information is irrelevant. Precisely because the line is growing blurrier by the day, those who define themselves as professional journalists need more than ever to maintain standards and report with seriousness and objectivity. However, it is up to journalists themselves to make distinctions between journalism and other kinds of speech, and these distinctions will always be fluid and subject to debate. Governments should not be participants in these discussions any more than they should be expected to weigh in on the debate about what constitutes poetry. Governments must protect all speech, whether journalistic or not. Respect for freedom of expression is the enabling environment for global journalism.

Aside from the political and practical considerations, there is also a legal question. Are journalists or the press as an institution entitled to special protection under law? Article 19 of the Universal Declaration of Human Rights makes no distinction between journalistic and non-journalistic speech. It states, "Everyone has the right to freedom of opinion and expression; this right includes freedom to hold opinions without interference and to seek, receive, and impart information and ideas through any media and regardless of frontiers." Other global and regional treaties and conventions, including the International Covenant on Civil and Political Rights, the European Convention of Human Rights, and the American Convention on Human Rights, use similar language. Journalists are not singled out for any special protections or privileges, with one notable exception, and that is the right under certain circumstances not to testify in international legal proceedings. A 2002 decision from the International Criminal Tribunal for the Former Yugoslavia determined that "war correspondents" should only be required to testify if they have evidence "of direct and important value in determining a core issue in the case" and if the information "cannot reasonably be obtained elsewhere." [22]

The issue, generally, is one of definitions. If the law is to protect journalists, then they must be defined. Journalists have been reluctant to grant governments or courts the authority to make a determination about who is and who is not a member of the press. For example, when the Geneva Conventions were ratified in 1949 special protections were extended to "war correspondents" who accompany military forces with their explicit authorization. If captured, war correspondents are entitled to prisoner-of-war status, meaning, for example, that they cannot be executed as spies. This provision clearly reflected the prevailing reality during World War II, when many journalists wore military uniforms. However, during the Vietnam War, journalists operated independently throughout the conflict zone without formally attaching themselves to a military unit. In the 1970s governments began discussions about how best to extend protections under international humanitarian law to this class of independent reporters.

Negotiations eventually reached an impasse over the question of who would be entitled to claim the title "journalist" and thus the mantle of protection. Having some sort of formal accreditation for journalists would allow governments—or belligerents—to use the accreditation process to limit media access to the conflict zone. This was unacceptable to the media, and in the end Article 79 of the Additional Protocol to the Geneva Conventions ratified in June 1977 merely reaffirmed the civilian status of journalists, meaning they cannot be targeted so long as they do not participate directly in hostilities. Article 79 also provided to journalists the opportunity to obtain an identity card "issued by the government of the State of which the journalist is a national or in whose territory he resides or in which the news medium employing him is located" but made clear that such accreditation is not required. In other words, journalists working in conflict zones have the exact same status as bloggers, documentarians, human rights activists, truck drivers, bakers, librarians, and teachers. All are civilians. While they cannot be targeted, journalists do not have the special legal status of representatives of the Red Cross, who are given protected access to the battlefield.[23]

Some national constitutions do make explicit reference to press freedom, most notably the First Amendment of the U.S. Constitution, which states, "Congress shall make no law respecting an establishment of religion, or prohibiting the free exercise thereof; or abridging the freedom of speech, or of the press; or the right of the people peaceably to assemble, and to petition the Government for a redress of grievances." In constitutional legal circles, there is an active debate about whether the "free press" clause confers any special rights on the institutional media, with the prevailing view being that it does not. The most active debate revolves around whether journalists can be compelled in legal proceedings to reveal their confidential sources.[24] While most states have "shield laws" on the books, a journalist facing a federal subpoena enjoys no special legal protection. The public outcry that erupted in the summer of 2013 after U.S. investigators seized phone records from the Associated Press as part of a leak investigation forced the Justice Department to issue new internal guidelines limiting the circumstances in which it would seek to obtain information from the media. But a proposed federal shield that would institutionalize the new standards has languished in Congress partly as a consequence of a failure to agree on a definition of journalism.

Those who believe that the press is entitled to special protection—such as the former Supreme Court Justice Potter Stewart—argue that the press serves as an "institution outside of government," a watchdog and a check on power, a fourth estate. The debate is important in the U.S. domestic context, but if any special legal status afforded to the press is derived from the unique role it plays in a democratic society, then what happens if the press fails to perform this role effectively? Does this mean the press would be entitled to less protection?

This framing is even more problematic from an international perspective since the "fourth estate" argument can be distorted by repressive governments to justify restrictions on the media. Take the case of Singapore, whose laws define what kind of criticism is permitted and provide a framework to ensure that the press plays its proper role as defined by the Singaporean authorities. Speaking at a conference on global press freedom at Columbia University in 2010, Singapore's Home Affairs minister K. Shanmugam explained it this way: Press freedom exists in order to ensure free and open debate about issues of public interest. But because the media is increasingly partisan, irresponsible, and sensational, this ideal is seldom realized. Press freedom, therefore, does not serve the public interest unless the media is guided by responsible government.[25]

The media, Shanmugam argued, "should be a neutral medium for conveying news—with commentary clearly separate from news; it should report fully and fairly what goes on." Singaporean authorities believe the media "can probe, ask inconvenient questions, and expose wrongdoing; it should not join the political fray and become a political actor. It should not campaign for or against a policy position." Journalists who in the government's view fail to meet these standards can be subject to legal action, including prosecution under Singapore's punitive libel laws.

Journalists and press freedom organizations seeking to advance their position with individual governments can and should make all sorts of pragmatic arguments. They can argue with clear justification that a free media is necessary to limit corruption, ensure government accountability, improve the delivery of government services, ensure efficient administration of justice, increase transparency, mediate internal conflict, improve investor confidence, and enhance economic performance. All of these arguments are supported by numerous studies. But the problem with any press freedom argument based on positive outcomes is that it opens the door for governments to impose restrictions if the desired outcomes are not achieved and meanwhile blame the failure to achieve results on poor performance by the media.

To suggest that journalists are entitled to special legal protections is even more problematic in countries around the world where the media as an institution is historically compromised and the boundaries between journalism and other forms of expression are rapidly breaking down. In many countries "traditional" journalists who would be the beneficiaries of greater "press freedom" are hardly the most trustworthy or independent sources of news. Take Egypt during the Tahrir Square uprising. Most professional journalists in Egypt—coddled by decades of government largesse—continue to take their marching orders from the authorities. It was a relatively small number of independent journalists working with bloggers and activists who broke Mubarak's information blockade.[26] Throughout 2013, as street demonstrations erupted in Russia, Turkey and Brazil, the institutional media performed woefully, forcing protesters to turn to bloggers and social media activists for independent information. Independent journalists working in these sorts of environments operate in a "freedom of expression" environment that they share with other independent voices seeking to document and disseminate information.

Historically, even if journalists did not enjoy any special legal status, they have been treated with some deference by governments because of their perceived political clout. The logic is summed up by the maxim "Never pick a fight with someone who buys ink by the barrel," a phrase that has been attributed by a top aide to President Gerald Ford but whose origin is in dispute.[27] What it meant was that while governments would take on leakers and others who disclosed confidential information, they were less likely to challenge the media that published the information. This is still true, but the distinction is breaking down as the media fractures and its power diminishes. Prosecutors in the Chelsea Manning case who argued that she should have been convicted of espionage and "aiding the enemy" because she knew that the documents she leaked, once public, would be accessed by al-Qaeda acknowledged that they would have presented the same argument had the materials been published by the *New York Times*. Meanwhile, British investigators are considering laying terrorism charges against the *Guardian* editor Alan Rusbridger for publishing accounts of the documents leaked by Edward Snowden.

Journalists play a unique and pivotal role in every society and must be able to do their work without interference from the state. But as the boundaries between journalists and nonjournalists continue to erode and any meaningful definition of journalism becomes more and more elusive, journalists have to recognize that their rights are best protected not by the special realm of "press freedom" but rather by ensuring that guarantees of free expression are extended to all. While it is natural and normal for journalists and press freedom organizations to give special emphasis to their journalistic colleagues, they can't stand on the sidelines of the broader struggle for freedom of expression, both online and off, and must actively defend the rights of all people everywhere to gather news, express their opinions, and disseminate information to the public. This is a difficult adjustment for journalists, but no more difficult than the one professional journalists made thirty years ago when they decided they could defend their media colleagues without compromising their professional standing. For journalists around the world, standing up for freedom of expression is a matter both of principle and of self-interest. While journalists can be objective when it comes to covering the news, they cannot be objective when the legal and physical barriers to their work continue to mount. In the final analysis, they have to roll up their sleeves and fight alongside the various and diverse constituencies that share their common interests.

NINE

News of the Future
(and the Future of News)

Just as struggles over trade routes and natural resources defined previous eras, control over information will grow as a source of conflict and strife in the decades ahead. The battles will be fought among governments and also between governments and institutions, corporations, and individuals. As technology makes information more and more accessible to people everywhere, political struggles—from elections to civil uprisings—will take place in both the physical and virtual space. It is likely that journalists will continue to be jailed and killed in record numbers. This is alarming, of course, but the news, as it were, is not all bad.

Journalists are increasingly threatened precisely because governments and other powerful institutions are finding it more difficult to manage and manipulate information. They are lashing out as a result. The outcome in the struggle to control information in the Internet age is not predetermined and will not be decided simply by who dominates the technology, although that will certainly be a factor. The outcome will also depend on the international political environment and the ability to strengthen and protect freedom of expression at a global level.

In previous chapters we've taken a careful look at some of the challenges to the global flow of information: a new generation of autocrats that is more adept at masking repression, terror and criminal groups that target the media directly, and governments that are asserting greater control over the Internet. This chapter looks at some steps that can be taken to meet these emerging threats.

In order to develop strategies that preserve and strengthen the global flow of information we need to make some assumptions about how global news will be delivered in the future. This is exceedingly difficult, as the only certainty is that technology will continue to transform the way news is gathered and disseminated, as well as the underlying economics of the news industry. But there are some reasonable assumptions that can be used to predict future challenges and develop responses.

As technology makes it easier for individuals and smaller outlets to gather and distribute information, power will continue to shift away from the larger media organizations that were once dominant because only they had the resources and infrastructure to maintain bureaus and field correspondents. However, this legacy media will continue to be the most important way to reach mass audiences, particularly during periods of crisis. Consolidation will slow, leaving perhaps a dozen major global brands that will compete directly for readers and viewers. The distinction between print outlets and broadcasters will continue to erode as more and more people around the world get their news online.

Many people, particularly those living in parts of the world with low connectivity and under the sway of repressive regimes, will continue to rely on radio for their international news for the time being. Government-funded networks like the BBC World Service and Voice of America will remain the dominant means to reach these individuals in their native language. However, as production becomes less expensive and distribution easier, and as the cost of smart phones plummets, making them accessible throughout the developing world, Internet radio and audio downloads will become pervasive. In Africa, where the use of cell phones is growing at an incredible rate, people without access to global media are using SMS messaging to generate and distribute original content. In the future, villagers in Zimbabwe who come together to fight for a land title will instantly form their own Internet audio channel to coordinate action and keep one another informed. They will broadcast "news" in their own language, making it accessible to the entire village via the mobile devices that they will all use.

Translation tools will also become more powerful, making the original language of publication less relevant. All Web content will be instantly and automatically translated into the language of the user, and in the future even audio translations will become routine. This will make it even easier for interested people around the world to access local news sources. For example, a businessperson in Canada planning a trip to Brazil will read the local Portuguese-language media to find if there are any protest marches planned through the streets of Rio. Students in Iran who are following protests in Cairo will be able to access Farsi translations of Egyptian and international media websites.

Internet utopians will continue to insist that information wants to be free. But in the future, you're going to have to pay for it more often. This will be an incremental shift, affecting high-frequency users or people who need information immediately. But global news providers will develop better systems of charging for content, and this will become an increasingly important source of revenue. Foreign bureaus will not necessarily expand as a result. Instead, international news organizations will build larger networks of local stringers and correspondents. Those journalists will be vulnerable to pressure from national governments and other forces that object to the way they are being depicted to an international audience. Global media will also improve its use of technology to carry out reporting, including mining social media and using media drones that could, for example, fly above a street demonstration. These strategies will give an on-the-ground feel to stories that were once reported at a distance. More coverage will also be data driven, reducing the role of anecdotal story telling. Since virtually everyone will carry a smart phone and as photo technology continues to improve, frontline images, both video and still, will increasingly be captured by eyewitnesses rather than professional photographers.

These ongoing disruptions to the traditional media will be compounded by the continued growth of regional media networks, many financed by governments. These stations will seek to amplify the influence of the governments underwriting them. Some states have a sophisticated understanding of what those interests are, but a portion of these new networks will be provocative, inflammatory, and irresponsible. Many will publish and broadcast in English in an effort to reach the largest possible audience and to influence global public opinion. Those media outlets that are able to meet a successful information need—like al-Jazeera in the Middle East or CCTV in parts of Africa—will gain a foothold, reducing the influence of Western media organizations in these regions.

Smaller media organizations, along with advocacy groups that use journalistic techniques to provide comprehensive information on relevant topics, will continue to refine their ability to deliver news to a specialized audience. This category includes media nonprofits and global NGOs, particularly in the human rights field. Of course, political factions, separatist groups, and terror and criminal groups will also continue to use technology to deliver information directly to their own supporters and followers.

A handful of highly placed and highly trained freelance journalists will provide specialized coverage, particularly of conflict. Their work will be supplemented by fledging freelancers, "citizen journalists," and partisan "media activists" who will distribute information through social media or specialized websites. These groups will increasingly provide breaking news and firsthand accounts from conflict zones.

The Internet will bend but not break as a global system of information delivery. The Web will increasingly be censored and restricted at the national level, with sophisticated users working their way around the censors. As more and more people access news and information via mobile devices—and rely more on them for everything they do—government surveillance will become even more sophisticated and sweeping, and there will be a growing information gap between those who access the uncensored Web and those whose information is restricted.

If these assumptions are correct, then the global media environment will remain highly vulnerable for the foreseeable future. Meanwhile, the need for independent information at a global level will grow, as economies integrate and improved communication fuels the growth of transnational communities. What specific steps can be taken to ensure that information continues to circulate freely in the decades ahead? Here are ten strategies.

Expose the Democratators

One of the most troubling political developments of the post–Cold War era is the rise of sophisticated autocrats who are able to hide their repressive strategies. But the democratators can only reap the benefits of their subterfuge if they are able to claim some sort of democratic legitimacy. Journalists, human rights groups, civil society activists, and even governments must do everything in their power to document and expose the means of repression and must make sure that their findings affect global institutions.

This is an approach that has been shown to be effective. For example, detailed reports on Turkey's media crackdown eroded the legitimacy of the government of Prime Minister Erdoğan. (His legitimacy was further compromised by the harsh crackdown on the Gezi Park protesters.) The actions that governments take in response to such pressure are often limited and self-serving, as, for example, Russia's renewed commitment to investigate journalist murders. But such gestures are not insignificant. They can be exploited to leverage more meaningful action, for example successful prosecutions that reduce the likelihood of future violence.

Producing reports documenting and exposing hidden repression is a laborious and time- consuming process. Such documentation often requires specialized knowledge and deep contacts. And no number of reports—no matter how exhaustive—will change the fundamental nature of these regimes. The democratators will continue. But such strategies can be used to ensure that governments that engage in systematic human rights violations, including limiting free expression and the rights of the media, cannot as easily claim the mantle of democracy. They can be made to endure the consequences of their actions, at least in terms of their international standing. Pressure must be applied not only to the governments themselves but the full range of institutions that confer international legitimacy. Advocacy targets should include the IMF, the World Bank, and the United Nations; regional institutions and bodies like the European Union and the Organization of American States; and even quasi-independent organizations like the International Olympic Committee and FIFA, the international soccer federation that oversees the World Cup. Human rights and press freedom groups effectively used the 2008 Beijing Olympics to push the Chinese government to ease restrictions on free expression in the run-up to the games. Similar strategies were used to highlight Russia's press freedom shortcomings in advance of the 2013 Winter Olympics in Sochi.

Increase Safety for Conflict Reporters

Covering war and conflict has long been one of the most essential tasks that journalists perform—and one of the most dangerous. But in recent years the risk has reached an intolerable level. Terrorist and sectarian groups have deliberately targeted media professionals, and national militaries have demonstrated a callous indifference to the work of journalists, resulting in numerous unnecessary deaths.

The notion that journalists are neutral observers to war and serve all sides by publicizing their grievances and concerns has been shattered by the proliferation of new technologies that allow the warring parties to communicate directly. The old paradigm cannot be restored. And there is virtually no way to influence terrorist groups, especially those aligned with al-Qaeda, that deliberately target the media.

The onus thus falls on media organizations to do more to protect the safety of the reporters and support staff they employ. Hostile environment training for journalists working for major media organizations has become routine, but the training is not sufficiently specialized to meet the needs of all reporters. Data compiled over two decades make clear that journalists working in conflict zones are much more likely to be murdered than step on a landmine. Safety training should more adequately address this specific risk, teaching journalists how to detect surveillance and respond to threats, not just how to take cover in a firefight.

Because hostile environment training is extremely expensive, it is not generally available to freelancers, much less stringers, fixers, and local reporters, who face the greatest risk. When considering risk and responsibility media organizations must take the broadest possible view of the information ecosystem in which they operate and develop specific policies and practices to mitigate risk to informal support staff, including drivers and translators. Information security must also be a greater focus of training. A smart phone that falls into the wrong hands endangers not only journalists but all of their sources.

Increasingly, some of the most dangerous conflicts are covered not by trained and seasoned professionals but freelancers with smart phones and even local "media activists." There are many reasons why this trend is troubling, ranging from the heightened risk to those gathering the news to the quality of the information itself. But lamenting the change accomplishes nothing; the trend is not reversible. Moreover, the value of the information that these informal journalists bring the world cannot be denied. The only way to improve the safety and security for this category of journalist is to carry out aggressive outreach, create a community of freelancers who share information and tips and to make accessible to them appropriate training at low cost. This is being done, but informally and at a modest level.[1]

Governments and militaries can obviously do much more to reduce the risk to conflict reporters. We can exclude for the moment rogue states like Syria that routinely target and detain journalists and are largely impervious to international pressure. But militaries that profess adherence to international humanitarian law have engaged in grave abuses that endanger journalists on an ongoing basis. This includes the U.S. military, whose overly liberal rules of engagement led to the killing of at least sixteen journalists by U.S. forces in Iraq.[2] It is unconscionable that media facilities are routinely targeted in conflict, despite clear prohibitions in international humanitarian law. Recent examples include Israel's assault on media facilities in Gaza during the December 2012 Operation Cast Lead and the NATO airstrike in Libya in July 2011. U.N. Security Council Resolution 1738, ratified in December 2006, reiterated the civilian status of journalists in conflict zones, affirming that "media equipment and installations constitute civilian objects, and in this respect shall not be the object of attack or of reprisals, unless they are military objectives." This is a crucial standard that must be upheld to ensure that conflict reporters can carry out their work with some modicum of safety.

Break the Cycle of Impunity

After years of indifference, the international community has begun to tackle the issue of impunity. There is a good reason for this. The systematic murder of journalists has staunched the flow of information from areas experiencing conflict, allowing violent actors to exercise censorship and dictate what the world knows. In 2013, the UN Security Council held two separate discussions on the topic, and the UN General Assembly passed a resolution declaring November 2 the International Day to End Impunity in crimes against journalists. UNESCO is implementing a UN Plan of Action on the Safety of Journalists and Issue of Impunity, targeting initially a handful of countries in which the violence is persistent.

But what does all this attention mean in practical terms? Ultimately, the crimes will have to be prosecuted by national governments that have demonstrated neither the political will nor the capacity to reduce the violence. As noted in chapter 7, the problem of impunity seems intractable. But focusing attention on the relative handful of countries where the situation is particularly acute can produce progress. The challenge is to create the political will to solve the crimes and then support the development of judicial and investigative infrastructure in those countries that have demonstrated a commitment to bringing the killers of journalists to justice. UN agencies can also play a valuable role by supporting efforts of national governments to protect journalists under threat.

The existing data on impunity—including CPJ's Impunity Index, first created in 2008—show clearly that progress is incremental but can be measured over a period of time. The best example is Colombia, which has seen the rate of killing of journalists decline in the last five years. In fact, Colombia's Impunity Rating, which is the number of unsolved killings divided by the total population, dropped from .439 in 2008 to .171 in 2013.[3] There are three fundamental reasons for this.

First, the overall political environment improved, with the violence associated with the ongoing civil war and the drug trade more contained. This had led to a pronounced decline in the number of new killings. Second, prosecutors have won convictions in at least three journalist murders, reducing the number of unsolved cases and creating a disincentive for those who might consider the use of the targeted violence against the press.[4] Third, Colombia has implemented a highly regarded journalist protection program, a government-NGO partnership in which journalists under threat are provided with security, bodyguards, and internal relocation.[5]

Despite the reduction in violence, Colombia remains an exceedingly difficult and dangerous environment for the press. Journalists are routinely threatened, and self-censorship is rife. Still, it is probably the best model for other countries looking to tackle the issue of violence against the press in an effective way. For the international community—including the United Nations—the goal must be to raise the cost of inaction by ensuring that those countries that fail to stem the tide of violence against the press face international opprobrium. The issue should be a frequent topic in bilateral discussions with donor nations and others in a position to exercise influence. Those countries that demonstrate a willingness to tackle the problem should expect support in developing the investigative and judicial resources they need to solve the crimes. The culture of impunity can only be defeated by ensuring that those who carry out the killings of journalists face justice. Progress can be objectively measured. Currently the global rate of impunity for journalists' killings stands at a staggering 88 percent. If the scourge of violence against the press is to be defeated, that number must decline over time.

Keep the Internet Open and Free

The Internet has become the primary means through which information is disseminated at a global level. Online communication has transformed the way that news and critical opinion are shared within repressive societies. Put another way, there is no press freedom without Internet freedom. Yet as we have seen, the decentralized system that makes the Internet so difficult to control is threatened by the actions of a number of countries around the world that are more effectively restricting online speech within their own societies and seeking to create a new Internet governance structure that will give greater power to governments.

The battle to preserve the multistakeholder model of Internet governance and keep the Internet open is being waged by civil society groups, Internet companies with a clear commercial stake in preserving the existing system, and governments with a tradition of support for freedom of expression. Journalists and media companies have been largely absent from the debate, although some press freedom groups, including CPJ and Reporters Without Borders, have become increasingly involved. The global media has a tremendous stake in the outcome; if the Internet becomes fragmented or balkanized the ability to gather information and disseminate to a global audience will be deeply impaired. Direct participation by global media companies in advocating for and supporting an open Internet does not compromise their responsibility to report the news fairly and objectively since the Internet is merely the medium through which the information is delivered and has no bearing on the content itself. Journalists and global media companies need to participate more actively in defending Internet freedom, recognizing their own stake in the outcome.

Limit Government Surveillance

In an April 2013, UN Special Rapporteur for Freedom of Expression Frank La Rue released a report on the effect of surveillance on freedom of expression. La Rue concluded,

> States cannot ensure that individuals are able to freely seek and receive information or express themselves without respecting, protecting and promoting their right to privacy. Privacy and freedom of expression are interlinked and mutually dependent; an infringement upon one can be both the cause and consequence of an infringement upon the other. Without adequate legislation and legal standards to ensure the privacy, security and anonymity of

communications, journalists, human rights defenders and whistle-blowers, for example, cannot be assured that their communications will not be subject to States' scrutiny.[6]

La Rue's report was published before documents provided by the former NSA contractor Edward J. Snowden demonstrated that a global surveillance effort is being carried out on an unprecedented—perhaps unimaginable—scale. There is limited evidence thus far to suggest that journalists are specific targets of NSA surveillance, yet it would be prudent for all reporters to assume that their electronic communication is actively monitored. Even if that is not currently the case, the staggering ability of the NSA to store massive amounts of data indefinitely means that communications information could be accessed at some point in the future.

Journalists who are not U.S. citizens are even more vulnerable since they have no constitutional protections against NSA spying. Reporting on national security issues requires that journalists be able to promise confidentiality to their sources. The scope and uncertainty of the NSA spying program has compromised their ability to do so, according to Janine Gibson, editor-in-chief of the *Guardian* US. "You can't guarantee anonymity to a source," Gibson stated. "That's a terrifying thing for the journalists we work with and a profound shift."[7] Gibson could have added that editors and reporters can no longer communicate securely. Gibson frequently found herself on a plane to Rio, where the then *Guardian* reporter Glenn Greenwald resides, just to have a conversation or review and edit one of his stories on the Snowden leaks. Gibson, prudently, did not trust phones or e-mail, even when it was encrypted.

In July 2013, a coalition of Internet freedom and privacy groups led by the San Francisco–based Electronic Frontier Foundation came together to develop a set of principles on human rights and surveillance for the Internet age. As noted in the preamble to the principles,

The explosion of digital communications content and information about communications, or "communications metadata"—information about an individual's communications or use of electronic devices—the falling cost of storing and mining large sets of data, and the provision of personal content through third party service providers make State surveillance possible at an unprecedented scale.[8]

Signatories called on all states to comply with thirteen principles that include ensuring due process, judicial oversight, transparency, and user notification when carrying out surveillance.

Beyond the broad objections to the sweeping scope of the NSA surveillance program journalists have specific concerns. These were laid out in a detailed October 2013 letter prepared by the Washington-based Reporters Committee for Freedom of the Press and signed by dozens of media organizations. The letter, addressed to the high-level Review Group convened by President Obama to examine U.S. government surveillance programs, called on the government to limit the scope of leak investigations so as not to impede legitimate news gathering, to ensure that communication between journalists and their sources are protected, and generally to be more open and forthcoming about the scope and nature of government surveillance.[9] While nothing rivals the scale of the NSA surveillance program, these principles of course need to apply globally.

End Censorship

In the Internet age—when information moves at the speed of light—censorship should be a thing of the past. But it isn't. Around the world information is censored for a variety of reasons. In China, "subversive" websites are routinely blocked, and critical comments are routinely removed from social media platforms. In the advanced democracies of Europe, censorship is practiced under a different and obviously more legitimate rubric. Those who engage in "hate speech" can be legally prosecuted, and the expression of certain ideas, including support for Nazism and Holocaust denial, is subject to prior restraint.

But there is one region of the world where censorship is prohibited by law. Article 13 of the American Convention on Human Rights states that the people of the hemisphere have the right "to seek, receive, and impart information and ideas of all kinds, regardless of frontiers, either orally, in writing, in print, in the form of art, or through any other medium of one's choice" and that the right to freedom of expression "shall not be subject to prior censorship but shall be subject to subsequent imposition of liability."[10]

What does this mean in practical terms? The American Convention of Human Rights is an international treaty that is legally binding, superseding domestic law in countries in which it has been ratified. This includes nearly all of the countries of Latin America with the exception of Cuba. (The American Convention has been signed but not ratified by the United States.)[11] While the clearly stated prohibition on censorship in the Americas does not mean that prior restraint has been abolished, it does make it more difficult for governments in the region to justify such measures. And it makes it easier for advocates of freedom of expression to fight such restrictions through the use of regional human rights mechanisms, like the Inter-American Court of Human Rights. Indeed, in 2001 the Inter-American Court ruled that Chile had violated the prohibition on censorship when it banned the showing of Martin Scorsese's film *The Last Temptation of Christ*.[12]

Each region of the world has its own traditions and its own challenges especially with regards to hate speech and incitement to violence. But limiting government response to "the subsequent imposition of liability" is always the preferred approach. Articulating a prohibition of censorship in international law would be an important step in the creation of a global standard for freedom of expression. While countries like China, Vietnam, and Saudi Arabia will continue to censor the news, such actions will appear increasingly illegitimate and outside the international mainstream. An explicit prohibition on censorship at the international level would also make it easier to campaign around a variety of freedom-of-expression issues including, for example, impunity.

Catalina Botero, the special rapporteur for freedom of expression of the Organization of American States, has argued that threats and violent attacks on journalists constitute a form of "indirect censorship" and therefore violate Article 13 of the Inter-American Convention of Human Rights. Botero's interpretation could help define the systematic government failure to stem the killing of journalists as a violation of international law.

Redrafting international legal instruments to include a specific prohibition of censorship is not in the cards in the current political environment. In fact, any effort to open international human rights treaties and conventions to revision would almost certainly result in a weakening, rather than a strengthening, of existing protections. Instead, advocates of freedom of expression should seek to create a new norm through jurisprudence, interpretation of existing standards, public debate, and campaigns. A global campaign to end censorship will resonate with a generation that grew up online and who recognize that while people need to be accountable for what they say, governments should not be moderating the global conversation.

Clearly Define Incitement to Violence

Within the contours of the global freedom of expression movement, there must be zero tolerance for speech that incites violence. The problem is that international law is a muddle on this issue. The vagueness of the standards not only makes it difficult for well-intentioned governments to understand and act on their responsibilities; they also make it easier for repressive leaders to justify suppression of speech that is merely critical by citing their obligation to stem incitement.

Article 19 of the International Covenant on Civil and Political Rights (ICCPR)—which has been formally ratified by 167 countries around the world and is legally binding—echoes the language of the Universal Declaration of Human Rights. It states that "Everyone shall have the right to hold opinions without interference" as well as "freedom of expression," which includes the right "to seek, receive and impart information and ideas of all kinds, regardless of frontiers either orally, in writing or in print, in the form of art, or through any other media of his choice." However, this right is subject to certain restrictions so long as they "are provided by law and are necessary . . . for respect of the rights or reputations of others" or "the protection of national security or of public order . . . or of public health or morals." Article 20 of the ICCPR puts the onus on governments to take action. It states that "any propaganda for war shall be prohibited by law" along with "any advocacy of national, racial or religious hatred that constitutes incitement to discrimination, hostility or violence."

The limitations on speech permitted under Article 19 and 20 have been the subject of extensive debate and discussion for decades. In August 2011 the UN Human Rights Committee issued a "General Comment" on Article 19 based on input from leading experts. While not legally binding, the General Comment serves as an authoritative interpretation of international law. The General Comment emphasized that any restriction imposed on freedom of expression must be both "necessary" and "proportionate" to achieve a limited aim and that governments must take extreme care when imposing such restrictions because "when a State party imposes restrictions on the exercise of freedom of expression, these may not put in jeopardy the right itself."[13] The 1995 Johannesburg Principles on National Security, Freedom of Expression, and Access to Information, drafted by leading experts convened by the global freedom of expression organization Article 19, state, "Expression shall not be subject to prior censorship in the interest of protecting national security, except in time of public emergency which threatens the life of the country."[14]

In December 2012, Article 19 (the group) published a policy brief on how governments should interpret their responsibility to prohibit "incitement to discrimination, hostility and violence." Noting that "in the absence of an agreed uniform definition, 'hate speech' is the subject of a great deal of confusion, globally as well as nationally" the report recommended that national courts apply a six-part test to determine if speech constitutes incitement and give preference to civil remedies over criminal sanctions in all but the most severe cases. Among the factors courts should consider are the context of the expression; the position of the speaker; and the likelihood that the speech will result in action, with "imminence" requiring the most aggressive response.[15]

But few governments apply these commonsense guidelines, and the issue of incitement is highly emotional. This is particularly true in parts of the world in which the media has been used to incite mass violence. As has been well documented, radio played a key role in both inspiring and facilitating the 1994 Rwandan genocide, during which an estimated eight hundred thousand Rwandans were killed. In December 2003, the UN International Criminal Tribunal for Rwanda

(ICTR) convicted three media executives of genocide, incitement and conspiracy to commit genocide, and crimes against humanity, and they were sentenced to terms ranging from thirty-five years to life. Two of those convicted, Ferdinand Nahimana and Jean-Bosco Barayagwiza, were executives of Radio Télévision des Mille Collines (RTLM), the notorious radio station that was used by the genocidal government not only to poison the minds of Rwanda but also to mobilize the population and direct the actual killing. The third defendant, Hassan Ngeze, the owner of the newspaper *Kangura*, was convicted based largely on inflammatory writing his paper had published several years before the genocide commenced.

In Europe as well, media has been used to inspire ethnic killing. Fears that expressions of hate can quickly escalate to violent actions in a European context are based not only on the experience of World War II but also more recent history. During the 1990s in the Balkans, state-sponsored Radio Television Serbia (RTS) broadcast a steady diet of programming that denigrated Muslim Bosnians, inspired fear, and rallied support for the campaign of ethnic cleansing.

These examples make clear why governments and the international community must have the legal authority to intervene directly when incitement to violence threatens communities with genocide, ethnic violence, war crimes, or other mass atrocities. Under the Responsibility to Protect Doctrine—which affirms that governments and the international community have an obligation to protect vulnerable populations—military action to knock RTLM off the air would have been legal and appropriate. UN forces operating inside Bosnia repeatedly jammed RTS in order to forestall ethnic killing.

It is precisely because governments and the international community must have the authority to punish and in the most dire cases censor speech that incites violence that clear and concise standards are essential. In the Nahimana case, the ICTR conflated vague national laws outlawing incitement to hatred with prohibitions on incitement to genocide, an international crime.[16] While that legal reasoning was refined by the Appeals Tribunal, the vagueness of definition allows governments to redefine critical speech as incitement and restrict it on that basis. In Africa, dozens of journalists from Rwanda to Ethiopia have been arrested and prosecuted on trumped-up charges like "divisionism," "incitement to tribal hatred," and "incitement to geno-cide" merely for criticizing those in power. In Putin's Russia, "extrem-ism" is a criminal offense, and journalists are routinely prosecuted for advocating unpopular views.[17]

As a free-speech absolutist, I'm not a big fan of laws prohibiting hate speech or discrimination because these offences are exceedingly difficult to define and enforce. But as a practical matter, Article 20 of the ICCPR not only empowers government to enact such laws; it requires that they do so.[18] Incitement to violence is a much clearer concept, and the necessity of international action to stop incitement that threatens whole communities is obvious. The current muddled understanding of what constitutes incitement not only makes it more difficult for governments and the international community to act de-cisively when lives are at stake; it also makes it easier for governments to exploit the fear of violence to justify suppression of legitimate criti-cism. In the current environment, developing a unified global stan-dard of what constitutes incitement and what actions governments may legitimately take will not be easy. But it must be a priority.

Make Access to Independent
Information a Development Goal

In 2000, the United Nations established the Millennium Develop-ment Goals, eight specific targets intended to guide development as-sistance and set global priorities through 2015. The goals range from halving global poverty; to achieving universal primary education; to reducing child mortality, HIV/AIDS, and malaria. The process for setting, achieving, and measuring the MDGs, as they are called, has been much debated. But one thing is clear: When the next round of development goals are established in 2015 expanding freedom of ex-pression must be among them.

In May 2013 a High-Level Panel of Eminent Persons chaired by Indonesian President Susilo Bambang Yudhoyono, Liberian President Ellen Johnson Sirleaf, and UK Prime Minister David Cameron pre-sented a report on *A New Global Partnership* to UN Secretary General Ban-Ki Moon. The report, which is intended to lay the groundwork for the establishment of the next round of MDGs, recommended that one of the goals should be to "ensure people enjoy freedom of speech, association, peaceful protest and access to independent media and information."[19]

The process for finalizing the 2015 MDGs will play out throughout 2014, and many governments can be expected to resist the establishment of any goal centered around free expression. This is precisely why an MDG that expands access to independent media and information would be a milestone. Its inclusion would mobilize resources to develop global news networks and would disarm governments that view independent information as a threat to their power and control.

Support Ethical Standards and Quality Media

Those fighting for global freedom of expression should resist being drawn into debates with governments on how to ensure that the media is "responsible" or that the information circulating on social media is "accurate" or "truthful" or "constructive." This means engaging with governments on their own terms and risks legitimating state intervention and control. The goal instead should be to build a global information environment in which all voices are heard, constrained only by legally defined prohibitions against incitement to violence.

Of course, there is no guarantee that thoughtful, responsible, or moderate perspectives will emerge from the global cacophony. But the lack of an assured outcome can never be used to justify control over news, information, or thought.

That said, it is of course the goal to all those who support freedom of expression to nurture an environment in which people around the world have access to high-quality, accurate information. There are a variety of groups supporting such efforts by carrying out media development, investing in journalism education, training journalists in ethical standards, working to improve the quality and accuracy of citizen journalists, or seeking to ensure access to appropriate technology. This is critically important work that must be supported. Ethical, high-quality journalism improves the press freedom environment. While it in no way justifies the violence, I have seen over and over that journalists who compromise their ethical standards, sometimes at the point of a gun, are more vulnerable. To give one example, journalists in Mexico are often approached by one cartel and told that if they do not agree to "work" for them they will be killed. With no other option, they agree to do so, only to then be targeted by a competing cartel that now views the journalist as a threat to its interests.

The existence of ethical journalism also removes a common pretext that governments use to justify state intervention and control. We see this most clearly in the case of the democratators, particularly in Venezuela, where Chávez took measures to contain the "corrupt," "oligarchic" media that openly supported the political opposition. One growing tactic that governments use in this environment is to build a parallel media structure loyal to the state and staffed with journalists who parrot the government line and rail against its opponents.

While efforts to improve media performance are absolutely essential, there is no guarantee that they will succeed, often because they are subverted by governments themselves. In many instances I have seen investments in media training and development squandered because newly trained journalists are not given the opportunity to practice their profession in an ethical manner. Journalists trained in objective, balanced reporting are often unable to find a job in an environment in which every media outlet is allied with the government or opposition forces. Governments often then exploit the partisan media environment to impose further restrictions.

Build a Free Expression Coalition

There are many powerful constituencies that benefit from the circulation of ideas and information at a global level. They include civil society and advocacy groups, especially those fighting to protect human rights and to safeguard the environment; business and financial institutions that operate in international markets; communications and technology companies that move information across borders; and governments and intergovernmental institutions making foreign policy, evaluating security threats, and promoting trade. And of course there are journalists and media organizations that operate internationally or report on global developments. The interests of these groups do not always align. Yet they all benefit from expanding the flow of information.

Together, they must build a grand coalition to advance the shared goal of expanding global freedom of expression. One way to bring these diverse constituencies together would be to develop a freedom-of-expression charter articulating their shared goals. The Internet and other modern communication technologies have made real the ideals expressed in Article 19 of the Universal Declaration of Human Rights: the right to freedom of expression transcends borders. Governments that accepted Article 19 when it was an abstract ideal are less comfortable in a world in which the vision could be realized. They are pushing back, asserting that freedom of expression is not a universal right but must be adapted to national circumstances. A global charter affirming this basic right would not have the force of law, but it would be a critical way to stand up and assert the importance of freedom of expression in an interconnected world.

While there are various statements, principles, and declarations on freedom of expression and Internet freedom, many are technical, legal, regional, or narrow in scope. What is needed is a new document that does not merely restate principles that are long established in international law but that translates those principles into concrete and verifiable terms. The freedom-of-expression charter should ban censorship, condemn those who use violence or the threat of violence to suppress ideas and information, call for a free and open Internet and clear limits on surveillance, and demand that people all over the world be given access to the information they need to make informed decisions about their lives.

The charter should be formally endorsed by participants in the freedom-of-expression coalition: human rights and press freedom groups, international NGOs, global businesses and independent financial institutions, and prominent individuals in the freedom-of-expression field. Governments should be asked to declare their public commitment to its principles. Some leaders will readily embrace them, others can be compelled to do so, and many others will resist. The goal must be eventually to build broad enough support that governments refusing to endorse the charter will be perceived as outliers.

Governments that commit to the principles, meanwhile, should also agree to undergo a periodic independent assessment to evaluate compliance.[20]

Even if these principles are realized, the international media environment will continue to be a messy, tumultuous place in which no single force is dominant. Global media organizations will compete with regional and national outlets, bloggers, activists, citizen journalists, and political organizations to meet the world's information needs. People in every corner of the world will be able to access a range of independent information in their own language. Of course there will continue to be challenges. State secrets will be published and confidential documents exposed; provocative and destabilizing ideas will be put forward; the voices of violent groups will be heard; people's religious views will be mocked; and myriad ideas, good, bad, and otherwise, will all compete for public attention. This is the necessary reality determined by the role of information in a global community united as never before by a set of common interests and experiences. It is only when information is democratized and decentralized, when news is truly harder to control and manage, and when the voices of the marginalized and disenfranchised are heard that the full potential of the information revolution unleashed by technological innovation can fully and finally be realized.

Notes

Introduction: A Murder in Pakistan

1. For background on CPJ's May 2011 mission to Pakistan, see Committee to Protect Journalists, "Pakistan Vows to Pursue Justice in Journalist Murders" (May 3, 2011), http://www.cpj.org/2011/05/pakistan-president-vows-to-pursue-justice-in-journ.php.

2. CPJ's "Dossier of Death"—the list of fifteen journalists murdered in Pakistan that was presented to President Zardari—is available at http://www.cpj.org/pakistan_killings.pdf. See also Joel Simon, "Mission Journal: CPJ Tackles Impunity in Pakistan," Committee to Protect Journalists (May 6, 2011), http://www.cpj.org/blog/2011/05/mission-journal-cpj-tackles-impunity-in-pakistan.php.

3. During the meeting with President Zardari, I cited Brazil as a country that had made progress in the fight against impunity. But the country has been backsliding since then, with escalating incidents of violence against the press. For more, see Committee to Protect Journalists, "Getting Away with Murder," CPJ special report (May 2, 2013), http://www.cpj.org/reports/2013/05/impunity-index-getting-away-with-murder.php.

4. For background on the abduction and murder of the journalist Hayatullah Khan, see Bob Dietz, "The Last Story: Hayatullah Kahn," CPJ special report (September 20, 2006), http://cpj.org/reports/2006/09/khan.php.

5. I visited Najam Sethi and Jugnu Moshin at their home in Lahore, Pakistan, May 7–9, 2011, and interviewed both of them over the course of several days. Quotations are transcribed from this meeting.

6. On Saleem Shahzad, see Dexter Filkins, "The Journalist and the Spies: The Murder of a Reporter Who Exposed Pakistan's Secrets," *New Yorker* (September 19, 2011). For the U.S. reaction to Saleem Shahzad's killing, see Jane Perlez and Eric Schmitt, "Pakistan's Spies Tied to Slaying of a Journalist," *New*

York Times (July 4, 2011). Perlez notes: "The anger over Mr. Shahzad's death followed unprecedented questioning in the media about the professionalism of the army and the ISI, a military-controlled spy agency, in the aftermath of the Bin Laden raid."

7. See also Elizabeth Rubin, "Roots of Impunity: Pakistan's Endangered Press," CPJ special report (May 23, 2013), http://www.cpj.org/reports/2013/05/pakistan-roots-impunity.php. Chapter 3, "Intimidation, Manipulation and Retribution," chronicles the media environment in the aftermath of the bin Laden raid and the threats and pressure prominent journalists confronted.

8. Sethi and Mohsin returned to their home in Lahore in 2012 after the threats subsided and continued to pursue journalism. In March 2013, Sethi was named the caretaker chief minister of Punjab. He stepped down in June after elections were held and later went on to become chairman of the Pakistan Cricket Board.

1. Informing the Global Citizen

1. For CPJ's 2012 Imprisoned Census, see http://www.cpj.org/imprisoned/2012.php.

2. For CPJ's list of journalists killed in 2012, see http://www.cpj.org/killed/2012/.

3. For a discussion of the deaths in Syria, see "Journalist Deaths Spike in 2012 Due to Syria, Somalia," CPJ special report (December 18, 2012), http://www.cpj.org/reports/2012/12/journalist-deaths-spike-in-2012-due-to-syria-somal.php.

4. For more on Freedom House's press freedom index, see Karin Deutsch Karlekar, "Freedom of the Press 2011: Signs of Change Amid Repression," 2011, http://www.freedomhouse.org/report/freedom-press/freedom-press-2011.

5. Peter Maas, "The Toppling: How the Media Inflated a Minor Moment in a Long War," *New Yorker* (January 10, 2011).

6. Personal interview with Rajiv Chandrasekaran, July 5, 2012.

7. For data on journalists killed in Iraq, see http://cpj.org/killed/mideast/iraq/.

8. Mae Azango, "Growing Pains: Sande Tradition of Genital Cutting Threatens Liberian Women's Health," *Front Page Africa* (March 8, 2012), http://www.frontpageafricaonline.com/old/health/54-health-matters/2691-growing-pains-sande-tradition-of-genital-cutting-threatens-liberian-womens-health.html. For background on Mae Azango, see Kristin Jones, "Harnessing Power in the Stories of Ordinary People," in *Attacks on the Press: Journalism on the World's Front Lines*, 2013 ed., Committee to Protect Journalists (New York: Wiley/Bloomberg, 2013), 59–68.

9. See also Jina Moore, "Mae Azango Exposed a Secret Ritual in Liberia, Putting Her Life in Danger," *Christian Science Monitor* (May 29, 2012), http://www.csmonitor.com/World/Making-a-difference/2012/0529/Mae-Azango-exposed-a-secret-ritual-in-Liberia-putting-her-life-in-danger.

10. See "China Has World's Largest New Media Market," Xinhua (May 15, 2013), http://www.globaltimes.cn/content/781766.shtml.

11. For the list of thirty-two imprisoned journalists in China in CPJ's December 2012 census, see http://www.cpj.org/imprisoned/2012.php#china. Of them, imprisoned journalists from the minority Tibetan and Uyghur ethnic groups accounted for nineteen of the cases.

12. On China's social media policies, see Sharon Lafraniere, Michael Wines, and Edward Wong, "China Reins in Entertainment and Blogging," *New York Times* (October 26, 2011); and Tania Branigan, "China to Step up Social Media Censorship," *Guardian* (October 26, 2011), http://m.guardian.co.uk/world/2011/oct/26/china-social-media-censorship?cat=world&type=article. In August 2011, three dissident Chinese writers who had been jailed filed a lawsuit in Maryland against Cisco alleging that technology that the company supplied to China led to their arrest and imprisonment. Cisco denied the allegations, saying that its products were not customized to allow the Chinese government to censor or track users more effectively. See Madeline Earp, "In Lawsuit, Chinese Writers Allege Cisco Aids Government," Committee to Protect Journalists (August 24, 2011), http://www.cpj.org/blog/2011/08/in-lawsuit-chinese-writers-allege-cisco-aids-gover.php.

13. I interviewed Adela Navarro Bello and other *Zeta* editors at the newspaper's Tijuana office on April 7, 2011. The quotes from Navarro Bello are taken from that interview. For background on *Zeta*, see also the 2012 documentary *Reportero*, directed by Bernardo Ruiz.

14. For more on the death toll of the Mexican Drug War, see Damian Cave, "Mexico Updates Death Toll in Drug War to 47,515, but Critics Dispute the Data," *New York Times* (January 12, 2012).

15. See CPJ's November 2003 investigative report on the murder of *Zeta*'s editor Francisco Ortiz Franco, *Free Fire Zone*, which I coauthored with America's program coordinator Carlos Lauría: http://www.cpj.org/reports/2004/11/tijuana.php. After my April 2011 visit to *Zeta*'s newsrooms I blogged about developments in the Ortíz Franco investigation, citing a new report from *Zeta* that "described how a cartel enforcer named Luis Alberto Salázar Vega ('El Bolas'), who had been captured by the Mexican Army . . . had declared in a written statement that cartel leader Javier Arellano Félix had personally ordered the killing of Ortiz Franco because he had published photographs of cartel members." That story, published May 14, 2004, included headshots taken from fake police credentials used by cartel members, including some of its leaders. The photos had been released by the FBI in

San Diego the week before. See http://www.cpj.org/blog/2011/04/in-mexico
-a-chance-for-justice.php.

16. For background on Julian Leyzaola, the controversial police commander in Tijuana, see Richard Marosi, "Tijuana's Security Chief Needs All
of It He Can Get," *Los Angeles Times* (December 20, 2009), http://articles
.latimes.com/2009/dec/20/world/la-fg-tijuana-police20-2009dec20. Leyzaola
later left Tijuana to become chief of police in Ciudad Juárez.

17. See National Southwest Border Counternarcotics Strategy, Office
of National Drug Control Policy, June 2009, Appendix A, Tunnel Strategy,
pp. 45–49. The report notes, "There were 24 tunnels discovered in Calendar
Year 2008 alone. One tunnel—the longest crossborder tunnel discovered in
United States history—had ventilation, drainage, and lighting systems, as well
as a cement floor and a pulley system. . . . The marked increase in the number
and sophistication of tunnels along the Southwest border could likely be a
result of increased CBP pressure against narcotraffickers and their traditional
surface mobility corridors into the homeland. More aggressive enforcement
on established overland routes since the 9/11 attacks probably has resulted
in Mexican drug trafficking organizations turning more and more to tunnel
construction. The length, number, and sophistication of the tunnels, as well
as the extensive time and labor that go into their construction, suggest that
smugglers consider tunnels to be a useful investment despite the risk of dis-
covery and interdiction."

18. For further background on the smuggling tunnels, see Rebecca Cath-
cart, "Second Rail-Equipped Drug Tunnel Found at Mexican Border," *New
York Times* (November 26, 2010). See also John Burnett, "Drug Tunnel Dis-
covery Signals New Cartel in Town," *NPR.com* (November 28, 2010), which
notes that the two recently discovered drug tunnels in Tijuana, "were under
the control of the Sinaloa Cartel, which is run by Joaquin 'Chapo' Guzman,
the world's most wanted drug lord." http://www.npr.org/2010/11/28/131647387
/drug-tunnel-discovery-signals-new-cartel-in-town.

19. On the murder of the social media activist and journalist María Elizabeth Macías Castro, see Sara Rafsky, "Mexico Murder May Be Social Media
Watershed," Committee to Protect Journalists (September 30, 2011), http://
www.cpj.org/blog/2011/09/mexican-murder-may-mark-grim-watershed-for
-social.php.

2. The Democratators

1. For CPJ data on journalist arrests in Turkey in December 2011, see
"Turkey Must Justify Widespread Arrests of Journalists" (December 20, 2011),
http://cpj.org/2011/12/turkey-must-justify-widespread-arrests-of-journali
.php.

2. For a Turkish group's tally, see "104 Journalists and 30 Distributors in Prison," *Bianet* (January 31, 2012), http://www.bianet.org/english/freedom -of-expression/135831–104-journalists-and-30-distributors-in-prison.

3. For CPJ's review of the journalists' indictment, see "Turkey's Press Freedom Crisis," CPJ special report (October 22, 2012), http://www.cpj.org/ reports/2012/10/turkeys-press-freedom-crisis.php.

4. Personal interview at *Özgür Gündem.*

5. "PM Erdoğan Compared Journalist Şık's Book to a Bomb," *Bianet* (April 14, 2011), http://bianet.org/english/minorities/129243-pm-erdogan -compared-journalist-siks-book-to-a-bomb.

6. Personal interview in Istanbul, October 15, 2013.

7. Erdoğan's alliance with the Gülen movement was critical to his power in Turkey, but by late 2013 the relationship had fractured. Many of the convictions were then reversed. See Piotr Zaleski, "Turkey's Erdogan Battles Country's Powerful Religious Movement," *Time* (December 4, 2013), http:// world.time.com/2013/12/04/turkeys-erdogan-battles-with-countrys-most -powerful-religious-movement/?iid=gs-main-lead.

8. CPJ was criticized after it listed only eight journalists in prison in Turkey in its 2011 census released on December 8, 2011. In response to the criticism, the organization carried out a detailed examination of all of the outstanding cases, including a review of the indictments. See the 2011 imprisoned journalist list at http://www.cpj.org/imprisoned/2011.php. A special report, *Turkey's Press Freedom Crisis: Dark Days of Jailing Journalists and Criminalizing Dissent*, was released in October 2011 and based on the updated information listed sixty-one journalists imprisoned for their work. See http://cpj.org /reports/Turkey2012.English.pdf.

9. For more, see Dexter Filkins, "The Deep State," *New Yorker* (March 12, 2012); and Stephen Kinzer's books *Crescent and Star: Turkey Between Two Worlds* (New York: Farrar, Straus and Giroux, 2008) and *Reset: Iran, Turkey, and America's Future* (New York: Times, 2010).

10. From CPJ's special report "Turkey's Press Freedom Crisis."

11. For a full transcript of Christiane Amanpour's interview with Prime Minister Erdoğan see http://transcripts.cnn.com/TRANSCRIPTS/1209/07 /ampr.01.html.

12. See Özgür Öğret and Nina Ognianova, "Erdoğan Tells Media Not to Cover Kurdish Conflict," CPJ blog (September 12, 2012), http://cpj.org /blog/2012/09/erdogan-tells-media-not-to-cover-kurdish-conf.php.

13. Özgür Öğret, "Turkey Peace Talks Positive; Press Freedom Still in Peril," CPJ blog (April 8, 2012), http://www.cpj.org/blog/2013/04/turkey -peace-talks-positive-but-press-freedom-stil.php.

14. "Turkish Mayor Harasses BBC Journalist on Twitter" (June 24, 2013), CPJ alert, http://www.cpj.org/2013/06/turkey-mayor-harasses-threatens-bbc -journalist-on.php.

15. Personal communication with Daniel Dombey, *Financial Times* Turkey correspondent.

16. On Chávez's cancer allegations, see Andrew Cawthorne, "Venezuela to Probe Chavez Cancer Poisoning Accusation," Reuters (March 12, 2013), http://www.reuters.com/article/2013/03/12/us-venezuela-election-idUSBRE92 BoMM20130312.

17. For background on Hugo Chavez, see Bart Jones, *Hugo! The Hugo Chavez Story from Mud Hut to Perpetual Revolution* (Hanover, N.H.: Steerforth, 2007).

18. For general background on Latin America press, see my article "Hot on the Money Trail," *Columbia Journalism Review* (January 1998) and Silvio Waisbord, *Watchdog Journalism in South America by Silvio Waisbord* (New York: Columbia University Press, 2000).

19. For background on Peru and Alberto Fujimori, see my pieces "Danger Signs: Fujimori's Secret War Against the Press," CPJ special report (September 10, 1998), https://cpj.org/Briefings/1999/1996–8/9_10_98/fujimori.html; and "Fujimori Stomps a Station," *Columbia Journalism Review* (November 1997).

20. For background on press freedom in Venezuela, see four CPJ special reports: Marylene Smeets, "Radio Chávez" (February 1, 2001); Sauro González Rodríguez, "Cannon Fodder" (August 1, 2002); Carlos Lauria and Sauro González Rodríguez, "Static in Venezuela" (April 24, 2007); and Monica Campbell, "Venezuela's Private Media Wither Under Chávez Assault" (August 29, 2012). For links to all reports, see my piece "In Venezuela, a Media Landscape Transformed" (August 29, 2012), http://www.cpj.org/reports /2012/08/in-venezuela-a-media-landscape-transformed.php. See also two reports from Human Rights Watch, "Tightening the Grip: Concentration and Abuse of Power in Chávez's Venezuela" (July 17, 2012), http://www .hrw.org/reports/2012/07/17/tightening-grip; and "A Decade Under Chávez: Political Intolerance and Lost Opportunities for Advancing Human Rights in Venezuela" (September 22, 2008), http://www.hrw.org/reports/2008/09/22 /decade-under-ch-vez.

21. On the Globovisión sale, see John Otis, "Globovisión Quickly Eases Combative Stance After Sale" (May 30, 2013), http://www.cpj.org/blog/2013 /05/globovision-quickly-eases-combative-stance-after-s.php.

22. William Dobson, *The Dictator's Learning Curve: Inside the Global Battle for Democracy* (New York: Doubleday, 2012), 96.

23. For background on Russia media, see my piece "Muzzling the Media: How the New Autocrats Threaten Press Freedoms," *World Policy Journal* (Summer 2006).

24. For Babitsky's background see "Babitsky's 'Crime' and Punishment," CPJ special report (February 2000), http://cpj.org/reports/2000/02/main.php.

25. In David Hoffman's book *Citizens Rising: Independent Journalism and the Spread of Democracy* (New York: CUNY Journalism Press, 2013), he argues that in fact the radio station B92 helped mobilize the population to topple Milošević.

26. The quote from Masha Lipman on Beslan is from a talk by Lipman at CPJ on March 24, 2006, titled "Constrained or Irrelevant: The Media in Putin's Russia." Lipman published an article with the same title in *Current History* (October 2005).

27. For more on Putin, see John Kampfner, *Freedom for Sale: Why the World Is Trading Democracy for Security* (New York: Basic Books, 2010), chap. 3, "Russia: Angry Capitalist."

28. See CPJ's 2012 Impunity Index, special report (April 17, 2012), http://cpj.org/reports/2012/04/impunity-index-2012.php.

29. On Ekho Moskvy, see David Remnick, "Echo in the Dark: A Radio Station Strives to Keep the Airwaves Free," *New Yorker* (September 22, 2008), http://www.newyorker.com/reporting/2008/09/22/080922fa_fact_remnick.

30. See Nina Ognianova, "Ekho Moskvy Board Shuffled Ahead of Russian Election" (February 14, 2012), http://cpj.org/blog/2012/02/ekho-moskvy-board-shuffled-ahead-of-russia-preside.php.

31. On Russia's Internet, see Danny O'Brien, "Internet Law: A Good Bad Example of Russia's Backsliding" (July 13, 2012), https://www.cpj.org/internet/2012/07/internet-bill-highlights-russias-divergence-on-hum.php; and "Internet Censorship 'Useless'—Medvedev," *RT* (April 18, 2012), http://rt.com/politics/internet-users-help-reforms-347/. On the rise of netizens in Russia, see Leon Aron, "Nyetizdat: How the Internet Is Building Civil Society in Russia," *American Enterprise Institute Russian Outlook* (June 28, 2011), http://www.aei.org/article/nyetizdat-how-the-internet-is-building-civil-society-in-russia/.

32. Julia Ioffe, "Oleg Kashin's Horrible Truth," *Foreign Policy* (November 6, 2010), http://www.foreignpolicy.com/articles/2010/11/06/the_horrible_truth_about_oleg_kashin. See also Elena Milashina, "Impunity Still Reigns in Beating of Oleg Kashin" (December 15, 2011), http://www.cpj.org/blog/2011/12/impunity-still-reigns-in-beating-of-oleg-kashin.php.

33. See Elena Malashina, "Russia Steps up Crackdown on Rights Groups, Internet" (March 26, 2013), http://cpj.org/blog/2013/03/russia-steps-up-crackdown-on-rights-groups-interne.php.

3. The Terror Dynamic

1. Giuliana Sgrena, *Friendly Fire: The Remarkable Story of a Journalist Kidnapped in Iraq, Rescued by an Italian Secret Service Agent, and Shot by U.S. Forces* (New York: Haymarket, 2006). See also Giuliana Sgrena, "Freedom at a

Price," *Guardian* (March 5, 2009), http://www.theguardian.com/media/2005 /mar/09/pressandpublishing.italy.

2. Richard A. Oppel Jr. and Robert F. Worth, "Ex-Hostage's Italian Driver Ignored Warning, U.S. Says," *New York Times* (May 1, 2005).

3. "Dueling Views of the Sgrena Shooting," *Christian Science Monitor* (May 5, 2005), http://www.csmonitor.com/2005/0505/p07s01-woiq.html.

4. For more on journalists killed in Iraq, see http://cpj.org/killed/mideast /iraq/.

5. For CPJ's census of journalists killed since 1992, see http://cpj.org/killed/.

6. See the joint letter to Secretary of State Donald Rumsfeld, "CPJ, Human Rights Watch Urge Checkpoint Safety" (June 17, 2005), http://cpj.org /2005/06/joint-letter-from-human-rights-watch-and-the-commi.php.

7. Accounts of Daniel Pearl's kidnapping are taken from *The Truth Left Behind: Inside the Kidnapping and Murder of Daniel Pearl*, http://pearlproject. georgetown.edu/pearlproject_march_2013.pdf; and Mariane Pearl and Sarah Crichton, *A Mighty Heart: The Brave Life and Death of My Husband, Danny Pearl* (New York: Scribner, 2003) See also Bernard Henri Lévy, *Who Killed Daniel Pearl?* (Hoboken, N.J.: Melville House, 2003).

8. Morris Davis: "Osama bin Laden was angry that KSM had slaughtered Pearl so publicly and brutally, arguing that the murder brought unnecessary attention on the network." *The Truth Left Behind*, 18.

9. Personal interview with Peter Bergen, April 25, 2013.

10. Lawrence Wright, *The Looming Tower: Al-Qaeda and the Road to 9/11* (New York: Vintage, 2007), 262.

11. The statistics on journalists killed in Iraq are taken from CPJ's special report, "Iraq: Journalists in Danger" (July 23, 2008), http://cpj.org /reports/2008/07/journalists-killed-in-iraq.php.

12. For Atwar Bhajat's background, see Megan Stack, "I Have Seen Death," *Los Angeles Times* (March 15, 2006): http://articles.latimes.com/2006/mar/15 /world/fg-bahjat15. A tribute to Atwar Bhajat from Mhamed Krichen can be found at http://cpj.org/awards/2006/bahjat-article.php.

13. Jill Carroll and Peter Grier, "Hostage: The Jill Carroll Story—Part 8: A New Enemy," *Christian Science Monitor* (August 23, 2006), http://www .csmonitor.com/2006/0823/p01s01woiq.html.

14. The statistics on kidnappings in Iraq are taken from CPJ's special report, "Iraq: Journalists in Danger" (July 23, 2008), http://cpj.org/reports/2008/04 /abducted.php.

15. For background on Zarqawi, see Mary Anne Weaver, "The Short, Violent Life of Abu Musab al-Zarqawi," *Atlantic* (July/August 2006), http:// www.theatlantic.com/magazine/archive/2006/07/the-short-violent-life-of -abu-musab-al-zarqawi/4983/1/.

16. There were tensions between Zarqawi and the al-Qaeda leadership over the use of ultraviolent tactics, including mass attacks on Shiite civilians

and hostage beheadings. In a July 2005 letter to Zarqawi, al-Qaeda's number two, Ayman al-Zawahiri, noted pointedly that captives can just as easily be killed with a gun as a knife.

17. For more on George Malbrunot and Christian Chesnot's abduction, see Jody K. Biehl, "Abducted In Iraq: Four Months on Planet bin Laden," *Spiegel Online* (January 21, 2005), http://www.spiegel.de/international/0,1518,337867,00 .html.

18. For more on the payment of ransom, see "Western Countries Reject Claims of Iraq Ransom Payments," Deutsche Presse-Agentur (May 22, 2006).

19. Personal interview with Rajiv Chandrasekaran, July 5, 2012.

20. See Daniel Kimmage and Kathleen Ridolfo, "Iraqi Insurgent Media: The War of Images and Ideas," Radio Free Europe/Radio Liberty special report (June 26, 2007), http://www.rferl.org/content/article/1077316.html; See also Daniel Kimmage, "The al-Qaeda–Media Nexus," RFE/RL special report (May 2008).

21. See Michael Moss and Souad Mekhennet, "An Internet Jihad Aims at U.S. Viewers," *New York Times* (October 15, 2007); "Tracking Al-Qaida's Media Production Team," NPR (July 11, 2006), http://www.npr.org/templates /story/story.php?storyId=5548044.

22. See also CPJ's report on the Palestine Hotel incident, Joel Campagna and Rhonda Roumani, "Permission to Fire" (May 27, 2003), which concluded that the attack on the hotel, which killed two journalists, resulted from a breakdown in military communication and while "not deliberate, was avoidable." http://cpj.org/reports/2003/05/palestine-hotel.php.

23. General Brooks's quote is from "U.S. Attacks Kill Three Journalists," CNN (April 8, 2003), http://www.cnn.com/2003/WORLD/meast/04/08/sprj .irq.hotel/.

24. CPJ data on journalists killed by U.S. military in Iraq can be found in an April 26, 2010, letter to U.S. Secretary of Defense Robert Gates: http://cpj .org/2010/04/cpj-seeks-pentagon-investigations-in-iraq-journali.php.

25. For more on the three Iraqi journalists working for Reuters who were detained near Fallujah in January 2004, see Joel Campagna and Hani Sabra, "Under Threat—Iraqi Journalists Frequently Face Hazardous Conditions on the Job," CPJ special report (May 17, 2004), http://cpj.org/reports/2004/05 /iraq-journ-5–04.php.

26. Bilal Hussein was the owner of an electronics store in Fallujah when he was hired by the AP to escort a photographer around the city. Eventually he was brought to the AP's Baghdad bureau, where he was given equipment and training. During the November 2004 siege of Fallujah by U.S. Marines, Hussein photographed insurgents as they fought U.S forces. Several of the photos were included in a package that was awarded a Pulitzer Prize. After the Fallujah offensive, Hussein was transferred to Ramadi, where he continued to

work for the AP. He was picked up in April 2006 by U.S. forces in what may have been a deliberate operation to capture him.

Throughout the course of his detention, U.S. military authorities made a series of unsubstantiated allegations, including that he had ties to insurgents, that he had advance knowledge of U.S. attacks, and that he had participated in the kidnapping of fellow journalists. An AP investigation determined that all of the allegations were unfounded, and the agency eventually concluded that Hussein was arrested in reprisal for his work as a journalist. See Charles Layton, "Behind Bars," *American Journalism Review* (December 2006/January 2007), http://www.ajr.org/article.asp?id=4225. See also "AP Photographer Walks Free After Two-Year Detention," http://www.cpj.org/2008/04/-ap -photographer-walks-free-after-twoyear-detentio.php.

27. For more on the use of terrorism allegations against journalists, see "9-11: Looking Back, Looking Forward," special report by the staff of the SPJ (September 11, 2002), http://cpj.org/reports/2002/09/9-11-essay.php.

28. Rohde spoke at a meeting of the Security Council in Arria Format on Protecting Journalists that took place on December 13, 2013.

4. Hostage to the News

1. The account of Micah Garen's kidnapping is taken from Micah Garen and Marie-Helene Carleton, *American Hostage: A Memoir of a Journalist Kidnapped in Iraq and the Remarkable Battle to Win His Release* (New York: Simon and Schuster, 2007).

2. Jill Carroll's account of her kidnapping published in the *Monitor* gave some insight into the kind of "journalism" the militants professed to admire, which were the propaganda videos of their operations showing Humvees and tanks being hit with improvised explosive devices, snipers shooting soldiers, and interviews with suicide bombers. Carroll's abductors also bragged about kidnapping Florence Aubenas and Giuliana Sgrena—who they claimed was given a gold necklace as a token of appreciation upon her release. They also claimed responsibility for the killing of the Iraqi journalist Atwar Bahjat, whom they murdered because "she had said the mujahedeen are bad." See Jill Carroll and Peter Grier, "The Jill Carroll Story," *Christian Science Monitor* (August 14, 2006), http://www.csmonitor.com/2006/0814/p01s01 -woiq.html.

3. Dexter Filkins' quote was condensed from an in-depth discussion at CPJ's New York headquarters in 2006: http://cpj.org/Briefings/2006/anniversary /IraqMP3.mp3.

4. Mullah Dadullah was killed in a firefight with U.S. forces on May 12, 2007, a month after the Naqshbandi execution. See also the documentary

film *Fixer: The Taking of Ajmal Naqshbandi*, http://www.fixerdoc.com; and Daniele Mastrogiacomo and Michael Reynolds, *Days of Fear: A Firsthand Account of Captivity Under the New Taliban* (New York: Europa, 2010).

On fixers in Afghanistan, see Monica Campbell, "In Afghanistan, International Coverage Relies on Local Links" in *Attacks on the Press 2011*, http://cpj.org/2012/02/fixers-on-front-lines-in-afghanistan.php. In another major case involving the death of a fixer, CPJ sent a letter to Prime Minister Gordon Brown on November 5, 2009, requesting a comprehensive investigation into the operation that rescued Stephen Farrell but then led to the death of Sultan Munadi. The letter was referred to the Ministry of Defense, which declined to carry out an investigation. CPJ sent a follow-up letter to Brown on March 5, 2010. See the November 2009 letter: http://cpj.org/2009/11/pm-brown-urged-to-probe-farrell-rescue.php; and the March 2010 letter: http://cpj.org/2010/03/cpj-calls-for-uk-to-investigate-munadi-death-in-fa.php.

5. CBC interview with Mellissa Fung, "Mellissa Fung Discusses Her Abduction in Afghanistan": http://www.cbc.ca/archives/categories/arts-entertainment/media/bringing-the-world-home-international-correspondents/abducted-in-afghanistan.html.

6. Rohde's account is from David Rohde and Kristen Mulvihill, *A Rope and a Prayer: A Kidnapping from Two Sides* (New York: Viking, 2010).

7. A discussion of Bill Keller's position on the news blackout in Rohde's case can be found in Clark Hoyt, "Journalistic Ideals, Human Values" *New York Times* (July 4, 2009); see also Richard Perez-Pena, "Keeping News of Kidnapping off Wikipedia," *New York Times* (June 28, 2009).

8. For more on Gawker's refusal to comply with the media blackout in Engel's kidnapping, see John Cook, "Fifteen Ways of Looking at the Media Blackout of Richard Engel's Abduction," *Gawker* (December 19, 2012), http://gawker.com/5969842/fifteen-ways-of-looking-at-the-media-blackout-of-richard-engels-abduction-vol-i-for.

9. Zeina Karam, "Journalists in Syria Face Growing Risk of Kidnap" (November 9, 2013), http://bigstory.ap.org/article/journalists-syria-face-growing-risk-kidnap.

5. Web Wars

1. *Southern Weekly* is sometimes translated as *Southern Weekend*. For more on *Southern Weekly*, including the quote from Zuo Fang, see Qian Gang, "*Southern Weekly* 'Not Tell Lies,'" China Media Project (February 18, 2013), http://cmp.hku.hk/2013/02/18/31257/.

2. See David Bandurski, "A New Year's Greeting Gets the Axe in China," China Media Project (January 3, 2013), http://cmp.hku.hk/2013/01/03/30247/.

3. See Bob Dietz's CPJ blog, "*Southern Weekly* Journalists Air Anger with Chinese Censors" (January 4, 2013), https://www.cpj.org/blog/2013/01/in-china -southern-weekly-journalists-air-anger-wit.php; see also Sophie Beach's CPJ blog, "In China, Rebellion Grows Over *Southern Weekly*" (January 8, 2013), https:// www.cpj.org/blog/2013/01/in-china-online-rebellion-grows-over-southern -week.php; and Madeline Earp's blog in the *Guardian*, "Can China's Journalists Win the Fight Against Censorship?" (January 9, 2013), http://www.guardian .co.uk/commentisfree/2013/jan/09/china-journalists-fight-censorship.

4. See Ai Weiwei's op-ed in the *Guardian*, "China's Censorship Can Never Defeat the Internet" (April 15, 2012), http://www.guardian.co.uk/comment isfree/libertycentral/2012/apr/16/china-censorship-internet-freedom.

5. The quote from Nicholas Kristof comes from his May 24, 2005, column for the *New York Times*, "Death by a Thousand Blogs"; Kristof's column was also cited in Jack Goldsmith and Tim Wu, *Who Controls the Internet? Illusions of a Borderless World* (New York: Oxford University Press, 2006), which gives an authoritative account of how governments have asserted control over the Internet.

6. Human Rights in China's translation of Wang's April 29, 2010, speech, "Concerning the Development and Administration of Our Country's Internet," http://www.hrichina.org/crf/article/3241; HRIC's analysis, "How the Chinese Authorities View the Internet," *China Rights Forum* 2 (2010), http:// www.hrichina.org/content/3240.

7. Rebecca MacKinnon, *Consent of the Networked: The Worldwide Struggle for Internet Freedom* (New York: Basic Books, 2012), 32.

8. For more on Google's China pullout, see "China Hackers Hit Media Companies and Activists Online" (January 13, 2010), http://cpj.org/2010/01 /hackers-hit-media-companies-and-activists-online-f.php; and Sophie Beach, "Google's Chinese Wake-up Call" (March 24, 2010), http://cpj.org/blog/2010/03 /googles-wake-up-call.php.

9. For more on the Jasmine Revolution, see "China Detains, Censors Bloggers on 'Jasmine Revolution'" (February 25, 2011), http://cpj.org/2011/02 /china-detains-censors-bloggers-on-jasmine-revoluti.php.

10. For more on China's Internet blackout in Xinjiang, see "China Restores Internet to Xinjiang," *Guardian* (May 14, 2010), http://www.guardian.co.uk /world/2010/may/14/china-restores-internet-access-xinjiang; See also "Internet Reopened in East Turkestan, but Uyghur Webmasters and Bloggers Remain Behind Bars," Uyghur Human Rights Project (May 14, 2010), http://uhrp .org/press-releases/internet-reopened-east-turkestan-uyghur-webmasters -and-bloggers-remain-behind-bars-0.

11. For an analysis of CPJ's statistics of jailed journalists in China, see the March 2013 CPJ special report "Challenged in China: The Shifting Dynamics of Censorship and Control," http://cpj.org/reports/2013/03/challenged -china-media-censorship.php.

12. For background on Dhondup Wangchen, see CPJ's profile for the 2012 International Press Freedom Awards: http://cpj.org/awards/2012/dhondup -wangchen-china.php.

13. For restrictions on quake reporting in Sichuan in May 2008, see "China Steps up Checks on Quake Reporting" (June 6, 2008), http://cpj.org/2008/06 /china-steps-up-checks-on-quake-reporting.php.

14. For more on restrictions on Wenzhou crash reporting, see Madeline Earp's essay "Amid Change, China Holds Fast to Information Control," in *Attacks on the Press in 2011*, http://www.cpj.org/2012/02/throughout-change -china-holds-fast-to-information.php.

15. On devastating flooding in Beijing, see Madeline Earp, "Propaganda Officials Miss the Boat on 'China's Katrina'" (July 26, 2012), http://cpj.org /blog/2012/07/propaganda-officials-miss-the-boat-on-chinas-katri.php.

16. The statistic that China has 597 million active social media users comes from Simon Kemp, "Internet Users Social, Digital, Mobile China," *We Are Social* (January 17, 2013), http://wearesocial.sg/blog/2013/01/social-digital -mobile-china-jan-2013/.

17. The quote from Liu Jianfeng comes from a video Jonah Kessel created for CPJ, "A Chinese Journalist's Inside View of Censorship" (March 11, 2013), http://www.cpj.org/tags/jonah-kessel. For more on the Wukan story, see the Reuters special report by James Pomfret (February 13, 2012), http://www .reuters.com/article/2013/02/28/us-china-wukan-idUSBRE91R1J020130228.

18. Regarding the new regulations of SARFT (State Administration of Radio, Film, and Television), see Liz Carter, "SARFT to Enhance Control Over Editors' Online Activities," A Big Enough Forest Blog (April 16, 2013), http:// www.abigenoughforest.com/blog/2013/4/16/sarft-to-enhance-control-over -editors-online-activities.html.

19. See the *People's Daily* article "US Must Hand Over Internet Control to the World" (August 18, 2012), http://english.peopledaily.com.cn/90777 /7915248.html.

20. Personal interview with Danny O'Brien, April 5, 2013.

21. On six principles of cyber order, see Mai Jun, "To Establish a Just, Reasonable, and Secure Cyber Order," CCTV (June 28, 2013), http://english.cntv .cn/20130628/102629.shtml.

22. A transcript of Hillary Clinton's speech on U.S. Internet policy at the Newseum in Washington, D.C., is available at http://www.state.gov /secretary/rm/2010/01/135519.htm.

23. *Rappler* covered the IGF forum: Ayee Macaraig, "US, China, Google on the Spot Over Spying," *Rappler* (October 24, 2013), http://www.rappler.com /world/regions/asia-pacific/42080-us-china-google-spying.

24. Personal interview with Rebecca MacKinnon, October 21, 2013.

25. UN Special Rapporteur for Freedom of Expression Frank La Rue's report on Internet freedom and international law, May 16, 2011, can be

found at http://www2.ohchr.org/english/bodies/hrcouncil/docs/17session /A.HRC.17.27_en.pdf.

26. Timothy Garton Ash's quote is from a personal interview cited in my essay for *Attacks on the Press in 2012*, "Beyond Article 19, a Global Press Freedom Charter," http://cpj.org/2013/02/attacks-on-the-press-beyond-article -19.php.

27. Andrew Jacobs, "Pursuing Soft Power, China Puts Stamp on Africa's News," *New York Times* (August 17, 2012); See also Mohamed Keita, "Africa's Free Press Problem" (op-ed), *New York Times* (April 15, 2012); and Madeline Earp, "China Not Most Censored, but May Be Most Ambitious" (May 2, 2010), http://cpj.org/blog/2012/05/china-not-most-censored-but-may-be-most -ambitious.php.

28. Tom Rhodes' blog on CCTV in Kenya, "China's Media Footprint in Kenya" (May 7, 2012), http://www.cpj.org/blog/2012/05/chinas-media -footprint-in-kenya.php.

29. "Challenged in China: The Shifting Dynamics of Censorship and Control," http://cpj.org/reports/2013/03/challenged-china-media-censorship.php.

30. Allegation of the removal of Iraq's top-level domain from the *People's Daily* article "US Must Hand Over Internet Control to the World."

31. The list of signatories to the ITU treaty: http://www.itu.int/osg/wcit-12 /highlights/signatories.html.

32. Ellen Nakashima, "U.S. Refuses to Back UN Treaty, Saying It Endorses Restricting the Internet," *Washington Post* (December 13, 2012); see also a CPJ blog by Danny O'Brien, "In Internet Freedom Fight, Why the ITU Matters (for Now)" (December 14, 2012), http://www.cpj.org/internet/2012/12/why -the-itu-matters.php; Ethan Zuckerman, "Good and Bad Reasons to Be Worried About WCIT" (December 5, 2012), http://www.ethanzuckerman.com /blog/2012/12/05/good-and-bad-reasons-to-be-worried-about-wcit/;Rebecca MacKinnon, "The United Nations and the Internet: It's Complicated," *Foreign Policy* (August 8, 2012), http://www.foreignpolicy.com/articles/2012/08/08 /the_united_nations_and_the_internet_it_s_complicated.

33. Personal communication with Marietje Schaake, October 29, 2013.

34. ICANN declaration, Montevideo, April 5, 2013: http://www.icann.org /en/news/correspondence/elac2015-to-icann-05apr13-en.

35. Edward Wyatt, "U.S. to Cede Its Oversight of Addresses on Internet," *New York Times* (March 14, 2014).

36. Personal interview of Dan Gillmor, October 3, 2013.

37. On China's surplus production, see Keith Bradsher, "China Confronts Mounting Piles of Unsold Goods," *New York Times* (August 23, 2012).

38. The review of food safety issues is taken from Madeline Earp's essay "Amid Change, China Holds Fast to Information Control" in *Attacks on the Press in 2011*, http://www.cpj.org/2012/02/throughout-change-china-holds -fast-to-information.php.

39. Personal interview with Issac Mao, cited in my essay "The Next Information Revolution: Abolishing Censorship" in *Attacks on the Press in 2011*, http://cpj.org/2012/02/attacks-on-the-press-in-2011-the-global-citizen.php.

6. Under Surveillance

1. Gustavo Guillén, "Indignación por las Actividades del DAS Colombiano," *Nuevo Herald* (June 3, 2009), http://www.elnuevoherald.com/2009/06/02/465506/indignacion-por-actividades-del.html. On interception of e-mail in Ethiopia, see "Ethiopian Blogger, Journalists Convicted of Terrorism," CPJ alert (January 19, 2012), http://www.cpj.org/2012/01/three-journalists-convicted-on-terrorism-charges-i.php.

2. *Der Spiegel* article: http://www.spiegel.de/international/world/nsa-spied-on-al-jazeera-communications-snowden-document-a-919681.html.

3. UN Special Rapporteur for Freedom of Expression Frank La Rue's report on surveillance and press freedom, April 17, 2013: http://www.ohchr.org/Documents/HRBodies/HRCouncil/RegularSession/Session23/A.HRC.23.40_EN.pdf.

4. Joel Simon, "How United States' Spying Strengthens China's Hand," in *Attacks on the Press*, 2014 ed. (New York: Bloomberg/Wiley, 2014).

5. On the use of social media for crackdown in Iran, see Farhad Manjoo, "The Revolution Will Not Be Digitized," *Slate* (June 25, 2009), http://www.slate.com/articles/technology/technology/2009/06/the_revolution_will_not_be_digitized.html; On the censoring of the press and blocking of certain websites, see "Iran Censors Newspapers Amid Unrest" (June 18, 2009), http://cpj.org/2009/06/iran-censors-newspapers-amid-unrest.php.

6. On use of spyware in Syria see Ben Brumfield, "Computer Spyware Is Newest Weapon in Syrian Conflict," CNN (February 17, 2012), http://www.cnn.com/2012/02/17/tech/web/computer-virus-syria.

7. On "Halal Internet," see Eric Schmidt and Jared Cohen, *The New Digital Age* (New York: Knopf, 2013), 95. See also Neal Ungerleider, "Iran Cracking Down Online with 'Halal Internet,'" *Fast Company* (April 18, 2011), http://www.fastcompany.com/1748123/iran-cracking-down-online-halal-internet.

8. Sherif Mansour, "As Election Nears, Iran's Journalists Are in Chains," CPJ Iran special report (May 8, 2013), http://www.cpj.org/reports/2013/05/as-election-nears-irans-journalists-are-in-chains.php.

9. Christopher Soghoian, "When Secrets Aren't Safe With Journalists," op-ed, *New York Times* (October 26, 2011).

10. ProPublica wrote about encryption in Jeff Larson, Nicole Perlroth, and Scott Shane, "Revealed: The NSA's Secret Campaign to Crack, Undermine Internet Security" (September 5, 2013), http://www.propublica.org/article/the-nsas-secret-campaign-to-crack-undermine-internet-encryption.

11. On commercially available surveillance products, see Schmidt and Cohen, *The New Digital Age*, 77.

12. On Syria and Rami Nakhle, see Danny O' Brien, "When a Bug Fix Can Save a Journalist's Life" (September 29, 2011), http://cpj.org/internet/2011/09 /when-a-bug-fix-can-save-a-journalists-life.php.

13. On its withdrawal for Iran, see Nokia's September 28, 2010, press statement, "Clarification on Nokia Siemens Networks' Business in Iran," http:// www.nokiasiemensnetworks.com/news-events/press-room/clarification-on -nokia-siemens-networks-business-in-iran.

14. For more on the Shi Tao case, see Rebecca MacKinnon, *Consent of the Networked: The Worldwide Struggle for Internet Freedom* (New York: Basic Books, 2012), 133–136.

15. Joint letter from ICT companies, October 31, 2013: http://apps .washingtonpost.com/g/page/business/facebook-google-apple-and-others -write-letter-urging-lawmakers-to-reform-nsa-programs/545/?fg.

16. Rebecca MacKinnon's discussion of Facebookistan is from *Consent of the Networked*, 32.

17. Rebecca MacKinnon, *Consent of the Networked*, 151–152.

7. Murder Central

1. Official Security Council transcript: http://www.un.org/ga/search/view _doc.asp?symbol=S/PV.7003, http://www.un.org/ga/search/view_doc.asp? symbol=S/PV.7003%28Resumption1%29.

2. UN Interagency plan: http://www.unesco.org/new/en/communication -and-information/freedom-of-expression/safety-of-journalists/un-plan-of -action/.

3. CPJ database on journalists killed: http://www.cpj.org/killed/; RSF database on journalists killed: http://en.rsf.org/press-freedom-barometer- journalists-killed.html?annee=2008. Also see "Where Are the Deadliest Places for Journalists?" DATABLOG, *Guardian* (January 7, 2014), http:// www.theguardian.com/news/datablog/2014/jan/07/where-deadliest-most -dangerous-place-journalists-syria.

4. The CPJ database on journalist murders show that 88 percent have complete impunity, 7 percent partial justice, and only 5 percent have full justice: http://www.cpj.org/killed/murdered.php.

5. The Impunity Index calculates the number of unsolved journalist murders as a percentage of each country's population. It includes only countries in which at least five murders have occurred over the previous ten years. Murder is defined as a deliberate attack against a specific journalist in relation to the victim's work. Cases are considered unsolved when no convictions have been

obtained. For more on the index, see http://www.cpj.org/reports/2013/05/impunity-index-getting-away-with-murder.php#index.

6. For background on IAPA's Impunity campaign, including statistics see http://www.sipiapa.org/en/service/impunity.

7. See http://daytoendimpunity.org/take_action/?day=05.

8. Some of Anna Politkovskaya's books are translated into English: *The Dirty War: A Russian Reporter in Chechnya* (London: Harvill Seckler, 2001), *Putin's Russia: Life in a Failing Democracy* (London: Harvill Seckler, 2004), and *A Small Corner of Hell: Dispatches from Chechnya* (Chicago: University of Chicago Press, 2003). Posthumously, three books were released, *A Russian Diary: A Journalist's Final Account of Life, Corruption, and Death in Putin's Russia* (London: Harvill Seckler, 2007), *Nothing but the Truth: Selected Dispatches* (New York: Vintage, 2011), and *Is Journalism Worth Dying For? Final Dispatches* (New York: Melville House, 2011).

9. On Paul Klebnikov, see "Russia Should Disclose Information on Klebnikov Murder" (July 9, 2010), http://www.cpj.org/2010/07/russia-should-disclose-information-on-klebnikov-mu.php. Project Klebnikov, a global alliance devoted to investigating the journalist's murder and continuing his work, was founded in July 2005. Numerous journalists are involved, including the executive director, Richard Behar. See the group's website: http://www.projectklebnikov.org/.

10. The claim was made by Politkovskaya herself; see Lucy Popescu and Claire Seymour-Jones, eds., *Writers Under Siege: Voices of Writers from Around the World* (New York: New York University Press, 2007), 220.

11. CPJ press release on the Malakhov meeting, "Chechnya Police May Be Behind Politkovskaya Murder, Russian Officials Tell CPJ" (January 23, 2007), http://cpj.org/2007/01/chechnya-police-may-be-behind-politkovskaya-murder.php; and the *New York Times's* coverage of the Malakhov meeting, C. J. Chivers, "Chechen Police Under Scrutiny in Journalist's Killing, Group Says," *New York Times* (January 24, 2007).

12. Nina Ognianova and I met with Ambassador Ustinov in Washington, D.C., in the spring of 2007. Ustinov informed us of a struggle between elements in the Russian government who were determined to investigate Kadyrov and other forces determined to block it.

13. More on Kadyrov's denial can be found in "CPJ: Chechen Police Targeted in Politkovskaya Murder Probe," *North Caucasus Analysis* 8, no. 4 (January 25, 2007), http://www.jamestown.org/single/?no_cache=1&tx_ttnews%5Btt_news%5D=3437#.Ucucuz6GonI.

14. On Putin's press conference, see: "Putin Pledges to Protect Journalists" (February 1, 2007), http://cpj.org/2007/02/putin-pledges-to-protect-journalists.php.

15. Following the 2008 sentencing of five gang members for Domnikov's murder, in May 2013 a Moscow businessman, Pavel Sopot, was arrested and

charged of "intentional infliction of a grave injury," also in relation to the Domnikov murder. See "Russia Charges Suspect in Igor Domnikov Murder" (May 8, 2013), http://www.cpj.org/2013/05/russia-arrests-indicts-suspect-in -igor-domnikov-mu.php.

16. See the statement from Memorial issued July 17, 2009, which quotes Oleg Orlov, head the Memorial board, as saying: "I know for sure who is responsible for the killing of Natalia Estemirova. We all know that man. It is Ramzan Kadyrov, president of Chechen Republic. Ramzan threatened Natalia, insulted her, believed her to be his personal enemy. We don't know whether it was Ramzan himself who ordered to kill Natalia or his close associates did it to please the ruling authority. And President Medvedev seems satisfied to have a murderer as a head of one of Russia's republics." The release further alleges: "When Natasha made a statement about young women of Chechnya being almost forced to wear head scarves in public she was invited to an almost private talk with Ramzan Kadyrov. Natalia later shared that Kadyrov threatened her and quoted him, 'My hands are indeed covered in blood. And I'm not ashamed of it. I was killing and will be killing bad people. We fight against enemies of our republic.'" See http://www.memo.ru/eng/news/2009/07/17/1707091.htm. Based on the statement, Kadyrov sued Orlov for defamation but lost.

17. See CPJ's press release on the Investigative Committee meeting, "Russia Pledges to Pursue Journalist Murder Probes" (September 30, 2010), http://www.cpj.org/2010/09/russia-pledges-to-pursue-journalist-murder -probes.php.

18. Sean Walker, "Chechens Face Second Trial in Anna Politkovskaya Murder Case," *Independent* (June 20, 2013), http://www.independent.co.uk/news /world/europe/chechens-face-second-trial-in-anna-politkovskaya-murder -case-8667415.html.

19. "Former Police Colonel Indicted in Politkovskaya Murder" (July 16, 2012), http://www.cpj.org/2012/07/former-police-colonel-indicted-in-polit kovskaya-mu.php.

20. Account of Marlene Garcia-Esperat from Terry Gould, *Marked for Death: Dying for the Story in the World's Most Dangerous Places* (Berkeley, Calif.: Counterpoint, 2009), 59–102.

21. See CPJ's special report "Marked for Death: The Five Most Murderous Countries for Journalists" (May 2, 2005), http://cpj.org/reports/2005/05 /murderous-05.php.

22. The quote from Reynato Puno can be found in my piece for the magazine *Index on Censorship*, "Impunity: Stopping the Killers" (January 26, 2010), http://www.indexoncensorship.org/2010/01/impunity-cpj-politkovskaya -journalists/.

23. See the timeline in Madeline Earp and Mayuri Mukherjee, "In Garcia-Esperat Murder, a Twisting Path to Justice" (March 24, 2010), http://www.cpj .org/blog/2010/03/philippine-impunity-in-garcia-esperat-murder.php.

24. CPJ records on journalists killed go back to 1992. For records prior, see the database of journalists killed on the website of the Newseum: http://www.newseum.org/scripts/journalist/main.htm.

25. International Crisis Group, "The Philippines: After the Maguindanao Massacre," *Asia Briefing* 98 (December 21, 2009), http://www.crisisgroup.org/~/media/Files/asia/south-east-asia/philippines/b98%20The%20Philippines%20After%20the%20Maguindanao%20Massacre.pdf.

26. I paid tribute to the Philippine prosecutor Leo Dacera in a CPJ blog post, "Remembering Philippine Prosecutor Leo Dacera" (November 8, 2010), http://cpj.org/blog/2010/11/remembering-philippine-prosecutor-leo-dacera.php.

27. See CPJ's reports, "Makings of a massacre: Impunity fostered Philippine killings," by Shawn Crispin, February 16, 2010: http://www.cpj.org/2010/02/makings-of-a-massacre.php; and "Impunity on trial in the Philippines," by Shawn Crispin, November 10, 2010: http://www.cpj.org/reports/2010/11/impunity-on-trial-in-the-philippines.php; See also, an accompanying CPJ video report: "In Pursuit of Justice," November 24, 2010: http://www.cpj.org/reports/2010/11/video-philippines-pursuit-of-justice.php.

28. See http://www.unesco.org/new/en/media-services/single-view/news/un_general_assembly_adopts_resolution_on_journalist_safety_and_pro claims_2_november_as_international_day_to_end_impunity/.

29. For the full text of the UN Plan Against Impunity, see: http://www.unesco.org/new/fileadmin/MULTIMEDIA/HQ/CI/CI/pdf/official_documents/un_plan_action_safety_en.pdf.

30. See "Pakistan to Support UN Plan to Fight Impunity Against Media," *Freedom Network* (October 13, 2013), http://www.freedomnetwork.org.pk/?p=2133.

31. On federalization in Mexico, read Mike O'Connor's blow-by-blow account on how it came to pass: "In Mexico, a Movement and a Bill Against Impunity" (April 26, 2013), http://www.cpj.org/blog/2013/04/in-mexico-a-movement-and-law-against-impunity.php.

32. For more on the January 2009 convictions in Columbia, see "In Landmark Case, Ex-Officials Convicted in Slaying" (January 22, 2009), http://cpj.org/2009/01/in-landmark-case-ex-officials-convicted-in-slaying.php.

33. From June 25, 2013, keynote speech at Investigative Reporters and Editors Annual Conference in San Antonio, Texas. http://gijn.org/2013/07/03/mexican-journalist-marcela-turati-dont-abandon-us/.

8. Journalists by Definition

1. I visited Cairo in March 2013 with the CPJ's Middle East and North Africa program coordinator, Sherif Mansour. While there, I met with and

interviewed Esraa Abdel Fattah, Ibrahim Eissa, and Reem Maged. Mansour provided interpretation for the interviews. I blogged about the challenge of differentiating between journalists and activists in post-Revolutionary Egypt: "Mission Journal: Who Is a Journalist in Egypt?" (March 14, 2013), https://www.cpj.org/blog/2013/03/mission-journal-who-is-a-journalist-in-egypt.php.

2. I interviewed Alcíbiades González Delvalle on February 1, 2005. Information in this section also comes from personal interviews with Laurie Nadel, Michael Massing, and Aryeh Neier. CPJ's history is described in detail in a documentary made for its thirtieth anniversary in March 2011: http://vimeo.com/33421645. See also my CPJ blog, "Walter Cronkite's Press Freedom Legacy" (July 17, 2009), http://www.cpj.org/blog/2009/07/walter-cronkites-press-freedom-legacy.php; Michael Massing, "Dangerous Assignments Twentieth Anniversary: In the Beginning," CPJ special report (May 1, 2001), http://cpj.org/reports/2001/05/massing.php; and my article "Muzzling the Media," *World Policy Journal* 23, no. 2 (2006): 51–61.

3. Warren Hoge, "Paraguay Imprisons a Columnist, Critic of Regime, for Second Time; Arrested Outside Court," *New York Times* (June 27, 1980).

4. For more on the background of Reporters Without Borders, see: http://en.rsf.org/who-we-are-12-09-2012,32617.html.

5. For more on the background of IFEX, see http://www.ifex.org/history/.

6. On the leaked video of the attack that killed the Reuters staff members Namir Noor-Eldeen and Saeed Chmagh, see "Video Shows U.S. Attack That Killed Reuters Staffers in Iraq" (April 5, 2010), http://cpj.org/2010/04/wikileaks-video-iraq-attack-killed-reuters-staffers.php.

7. For background on WikiLeaks, see Danny O'Brien, "Technicalities: Ten Questions on WikiLeaks" (April 8, 2010), http://cpj.org/internet/2010/04/technicalities-10-questions-on-wikileaks.php.

8. See my CPJ blog on the Manning prosecution, "Transparency, accountability at stake in Manning trial," May 16, 2013: http://www.cpj.org/blog/2013/05/transparency-accountability-at-stake-in-manning-tr.php.

9. The quote from Alan Rusbridger comes from a CPJ panel discussion event at the Paley Center for International Media, "Newsgathering and Its Vulnerabilities Today: A Conversation with Alan Rusbridger" (November 19, 2012). A video from the event is online: http://www.paleycenter.org/mc-cpj-alan-rusbridger-nov-19/; see also Rusbridger's acceptance speech for CPJ's 2012 Burton Benjamin Award in honor of a lifetime achievement for press freedom: https://www.cpj.org/awards/2012/alan-rusbridger-award-acceptance-speech.php.

10. RSF letter to Julian Assange, "Open Letter to Wikileaks Founder Julian Assange: 'A Bad Precedent for the Internet's Future'" (August 12, 2010), http://en.rsf.org/united-states-open-letter-to-wikileaks-founder-12-08-2010,38130.html.

11. Hagit Limor, "The Consensus on WikiLeaks: There Is No Consensus. But Consider the Ethics," Society of Professional Journalists Blog (December 2, 2010), http://blogs.spjnetwork.org/president/2010/12/02/the-consensus-on-wikileaks-there-is-no-consensus-but-consider-the-ethics/.

12. On the Columbia petition, see Jim Romenesko, "Columbia J-School Staff: WikiLeaks Prosecution 'Will Set a Dangerous Precedent,'" Poynter Institute (December 14, 2010), http://www.poynter.org/latest-news/mediawire/110885/columbia-j-school-staff-wikileaks-prosecution-sets-dangerous-precedent/.

13. The incident involving Raushan Yesergepova and Hillary Clinton is cited in my introduction to *Attacks on the Press in 2010*, "International Institutions Fail To Defend Press Freedom," http://www.cpj.org/2011/02/attacks-on-the-press-2010-introduction-joel-simon.php.

14. CPJ's letter to President Barack Obama and Attorney General Eric Holder: "CPJ Urges U.S. Not to Prosecute Assange" (December 17, 2010), http://www.cpj.org/2010/12/cpj-urges-us-not-to-prosecute-assange.php.

15. On Assange's motives see Theo Brainin, "Just What Does Julian Assange Want?" *Guardian* (December 5, 2010), http://www.guardian.co.uk/commentis free/cifamerica/2010/dec/05/wikileaks-julian-assange; and Steve Coll, "Leaks," *New Yorker* (November 8, 2010). For a defense, see David Samuels, "The Shameful Attacks on Julian Assange," *The Atlantic* (December 3, 2010). Assange argued that governments are essentially conspiracies and that disrupting their ability to operate depends on "reduc[ing] or eliminating important communication." See "State and Terrorist Conspiracies," attributed to Julian Assange (November 10, 2006), http://cryptome.org/0002/ja-conspiracies.pdf.

In a July 26, 2010, interview in *Der Spiegel*, Assange said, "We all only live once. So we are obligated to make good use of the time that we have and to do something that is meaningful and satisfying. This is something that I find meaningful and satisfying. That is my temperament. I enjoy creating systems on a grand scale, and I enjoy helping people who are vulnerable. And I enjoy crushing bastards. So it is enjoyable work."

16. The Ethiopian journalist Argaw Ashine was forced into exile after WikiLeaks released his name: see my CPJ blog post, "In Ethiopia Case, a Response to WikiLeaks" (September 19, 2011), http://www.cpj.org/blog/2011/09/in-ethiopia-case-a-response-to-wikileaks.php.

17. On the Assange rape allegations, see Nick Davies, "Ten Days in Sweden: The Full Allegations Against Julian Assange," *Guardian* (December 17, 2010), http://www.guardian.co.uk/media/2010/dec/17/julian-assange-sweden.

18. For a transcript from Julian Assange's December 21, 2010, interview with the BBC, see http://news.bbc.co.uk/today/hi/today/newsid_9309000/9309320.stm.

19. See Julian Assange's interview with Erin Burnett: "Assange Dodges Question on Ecuador" (November 28, 2012), http://www.cnn.com/video/#/video/bestoftv/2012/11/28/exp-erin-preview-assange.cnn.

20. On the Espionage Act, see James Goodale's *Fighting for the Press: The Inside Story of the Pentagon Papers and Other Battles* (New York: CUNY Journalism Press, 2013).

21. On Julian Assange's prosecution under the Espionage Act, see: "Why the WikiLeaks Grand Jury Is So Dangerous: Members of Congress Now Want to Prosecute *New York Times* Journalists Too," Electronic Frontier Foundation (July 23, 2012), https://www.eff.org/deeplinks/2012/07/why-wikileaks-grand -jury-important-some-members-congress-want-prosecute-new-york. On the Rosen case, see Ann Marimow, "A Rare Peek Into a Justice Department Leak Probe," *Washington Post* (May 19, 2013).

22. See "Prosecutor v. Radoslav Brdjanin Decision on Prosecution's Second Request for a Subpoena of Jonathan Randal" (January 2003), http://www .icty.org/x/cases/brdanin/tdec/en/030630.htm.

23. For the protection of journalists under international humanitarian law, see "How Does International Humanitarian Law Protect Journalists in Armed-Conflict Situations?" International Committee on the Red Cross, interview with ICRC legal expert Robin Geiss (July 27, 2010), http:// www.icrc.org/eng/resources/documents/interview/protection-journalists -interview-270710.htm.

24. For a summary of the debate over the press freedom clause in the U.S. Constitution, see Lee Bollinger, *Uninhibited, Robust, and Wide Open: A Free Press for a New Century* (New York: Oxford University Press, 2010), 7–12.

25. See K. Shanmugam's speech at Columbia University, November 4, 2010: http://www.mlaw.gov.sg/news/speeches/speech-by-minister-for-home-affairs -and-minister-for-law-k-shanmugam-at-the-inaugural-forum-a.html.

26. On the impact of social media during the Tahrir Square protests, see my *Huffington Post* article, "A Twitter Revolution for Journalists" (February 14, 2011), http://www.huffingtonpost.com/joel-simon/a-twitter-revolution-for-_ b_823113.html.

27. As with virtually every aphorism worth its salt, the phrase has even been attributed to Mark Twain. But this blog, published on Freakonomics. com, traces it to a 1964 quote from an Indianapolis congressman, Charles Brownson. http://freakonomics.com/2011/05/12/ink-by-the-barrel/.

9. News of the Future (and the Future of News)

1. One important example is RISC (Reporters Instructed in Saving Colleagues), which provides no-cost training in combat first aid to freelance journalists. It was founded by Sebastian Junger in response to the death of his good friend Tim Hetherington, who bled to death while reporting in Libya after being hit with shrapnel. See http://risctraining.org/.

2. See CPJ's April 26, 2010, letter to U.S. Secretary of Defense Robert Gates regarding journalists killed in Iraq: http://cpj.org/2010/04/cpj-seeks -pentagon-investigations-in-iraq-journali.php.

3. See 2013 CPJ Impunity Index, "Getting Away with Murder," CPJ special report (May 23, 2013), http://www.cpj.org/reports/2013/05/impunity-index -getting-away-with-murder.php; and 2008 CPJ Impunity Index, "Getting Away with Murder 2008," CPJ special report (April 30, 2008), http://cpj.org/reports /2008/04/getting-away-with-murder.php.

4. The Colombian press freedom organization FLIP has created a database of journalist killings showing the status of all investigations: http://flip.org.co /cifras-indicadores/periodistas-asesinados.

5. For more information on the journalist protection program in Colombia see "Violence and Impunity: Protecting Journalists in Colombia and Mexico," Inter-American Dialogue (March 2010), http://www.thedialogue.org /PublicationFiles/English%20PDF,%20final.pdf.

6. See Report of the Special Rapporteur on the promotion and protection of the right to freedom of opinion and expression, by Frank La Rue, http://www.ohchr.org/Documents/HRBodies/HRCouncil/RegularSession /Session23/A.HRC.23.40_EN.pdf, p. 20.

7. Personal communication from Gibson, quoted in my essay "How United States' Spying Strengthen China's Hand," in *Attacks on the Press* (Bloomberg/ Wiley, 2014), http://cpj.org/2014/02/attacks-on-the-press-surveillance-press -freedom.php.

8. Necessary and Proportionate Principles (July 10, 2013), https://en .necessaryandproportionate.org/text.

9. "Media Coalition Urges Better Protection of First Amendment Rights in NSA, FISA Court Matters," Reporters Committee for Freedom of the Press press release (October 11, 2013), http://www.rcfp.org/media -coalition-urges-better-protection-first-amendment-rights-nsa-fisa-court -matters.

10. See the American Convention on Human Rights, "Pact of San-Jose, Costa Rica (B-32)," http://www.oas.org/dil/treaties_B-32_American_Conven tion_on_Human_Rights.htm.

11. For a list of ratifications see http://www.oas.org/dil/treaties_B-32 _American_Convention_on_Human_Rights_sign.htm.

12. See the Inter-American Court of Human Rights document "Case of *The Last Temptation of Christ* (Olmedo-Bustos et al. v. Chile), Judgment of February 5, 2001," http://www.corteidh.or.cr/docs/casos/articulos/seriec_73 _ing.pdf.

13. See General Comment 34 from the UN Human Rights Committee meeting in Geneva (July 11–29, 2011), http://www2.ohchr.org/english/bodies /hrc/docs/GC34.pdf.

14. Johannesburg Principles on National Security, Freedom of Expression and Access to Information: http://www.article19.org/data/files/pdfs/standards /joburgprinciples.pdf.

15. See "Prohibiting Incitement to Discrimination, Hostility, or Violence," Article 19 Policy Brief (December 2012), http://www.article19.org/data/files /medialibrary/3548/ARTICLE-19-policy-on-prohibition-to-incitement.pdf.

16. See Joel Simon, "Murder by Media," *Slate* (December 11, 2003), http:// www.slate.com/articles/news_and_politics/foreigners/2003/12/murder_by _media.1.html; see also Joel Simon, "In Africa, Exploiting the Past," *Columbia Journalism Review* (January/February 2006), http://cpj.org/2006/01/of-hate- and-genocide.php.

17. On Russia's 2007 extremism law see, "In Russia, Putin Signs Restrictive Amendments on 'Extremism,'" CPJ alert (July 26, 2007), http://cpj.org/2007/07 /in-russia-putin-signs-restrictive-amendments-on-ex.php. In 2008, Nadira Isayeva, then the editor of the leading independent newspaper *Chernovik*, was charged with making public calls for extremism and inciting hatred based on her interview with a separatist leader. See "Independent Weekly Editor Charged with Extremism in Dagestan," CPJ alert (August 7, 2008), https://cpj .org/2008/08/independent-weekly-editor-charged-with-extremism-i.php.

18. In ratifying the ICCPR the U.S. Senate expressed the following reserva- tion: "That Article 20 does not authorize or require legislation or other action by the United States that would restrict the right of free speech and associa- tion protected by the Constitution and laws of the United States." See "U.S. Reservations, Declarations, and Understandings, International Covenant on Civil and Political Rights, 138 Cong. Rec. S4781–01" (April 2, 1992), available at the University of Minnesota Human Rights Library, http://www1.umn.edu /humanrts/usdocs/civilres.html.

19. "A New Global Partnership: Eradicate Poverty and Transform Econo- mies Through Sustainable Development," report of the High-Level Panel of Eminent Persons on the Post-2015 Development Agenda (May 30, 2013), http://www.un.org/sg/management/pdf/HLP_P2015_Report.pdf.

20. The section on a global press freedom charter is adapted from my essay, "Beyond Article 19, a Global Press Freedom Charter," in *Attacks on the Press in 2012*, http://cpj.org/2013/02/attacks-on-the-press-beyond-article-19.php.

Selected Bibliography

Anderson, Jon Lee. *The Fall of Baghdad*. London: Penguin. 2005.

Article 19. "Prohibiting incitement to discrimination, hostility or violence," *Policy Brief,* December 2012. http://www.article19.org/data/files/media library/3548/ARTICLE-19-policy-on-prohibition-to-incitement.pdf.

Auletta, Ken. *Googled: The End of the World As We Know It.* London: Penguin. 2010.

Azango, Mae. "Growing Pains: Sande Tradition of Genital Cutting Threatens Liberian Women's Health." *Front Page Africa* (March 8, 2012). http://www .frontpageafricaonline.com/old/health/54-health-matters/2691-growing -pains-sande-tradition-of-genital-cutting-threatens-liberian-womens -health.html.

Bahari, Maziar, with Aimee Molloy. *Then They Came For Me.* New York: Random House. 2011.

Bollinger, Lee C. *Uninhibited, Robust, and Wide-Open: A Free Press for a New Century.* New York: Oxford University Press, 2010.

Campagna, Joel, and Rhonda Roumani. "Permission to Fire." Committee to Protect Journalists. May 27, 2003. http://cpj.org/reports/2003/05/palestine -hotel.php.

Campagna, Joel, and Hani Sabra. "Under Threat—Iraqi Journalists Frequently Face Hazardous Conditions on the Job." Committee to Protect Journalists. May 17, 2004. http://cpj.org/reports/2004/05/iraq-journ-5–04.php.

Campbell, Monica. "In Afghanistan, International Coverage Relies on Local Links." In *Attacks on the Press in 2011.* Baltimore: United Book Press. http://cpj.org/2012/02/fixers-on-front-lines-in-afghanistan.php.

——. "Venezuela's Private Media Wither Under Chávez Assault." Committee to Protect Journalists. August 29, 2012. http://www.cpj.org/reports/2012 /08/after-years-of-assault-venezuelas-independent-pres.php.

Clark, Wesley K. *Waging Modern War: Bosnia, Kosovo, and the Future of Combat*. New York: Public Affairs, 2001.

Cohen, Jared, and Eric Schmidt. *The New Digital Age: Reshaping the Future of People, Nations, and Business*. New York: Knopf, 2013.

Coll, Steve. *Ghost Wars: The Secret History of the CIA, Afghanistan, and bin Laden, from the Soviet Invasion to September 10, 2001*. New York: Penguin, 2004.

Collings, Anthony C. *Words of Fire: Independent Journalists Who Challenge Dictators, Drug Lords, and Other Enemies of a Free Press*. New York: NYU Press, 2001.

Committee to Protect Journalists. "Babitsky's 'Crime' and Punishment." Special reports. February 2000. http://cpj.org/reports/2000/02/main.php.

———. "9-11: Looking Back, Looking Forward." September 11, 2002. http://cpj.org/reports/2002/09/9-11-essay.php.

———. "Marked for Death: The Five Most Murderous Countries for Journalists." May 2, 2005. http://cpj.org/reports/2005/05/murderous-05.php.

———. "Getting Away with Murder 2008." April 30, 2008. http://cpj.org/reports/2008/04/getting-away-with-murder.php.

———. "Turkey's Press Freedom Crisis." October 22, 2012. http://www.cpj.org/reports/2012/10/turkeys-press-freedom-crisis.php.

———. "Journalist Deaths Spike in 2012 Due to Syria, Somalia." December 18, 2012. http://www.cpj.org/reports/2012/12/journalist-deaths-spike-in-2012-due-to-syria-somal.php.

———. "Challenged in China: The Shifting Dynamics of Censorship and Control." March 2013. http://cpj.org/reports/2013/03/challenged-china-media-censorship.php.

———. "Getting Away with Murder." Special Report. May 2, 2013. http://www.cpj.org/reports/2013/05/impunity-index-getting-away-with-murder.php.

Crispin, Shawn. "Makings of a Massacre: Impunity Fostered Philippine Killings." Committee to Protect Journalists. February 16, 2010. http://www.cpj.org/2010/02/makings-of-a-massacre.php.

———. "Impunity on Trial in the Philippines." Committee to Protect Journalists. November 10, 2010. http://www.cpj.org/reports/2010/11/impunity-on-trial-in-the-philippines.php.

Dobson, William J. *The Dictator's Learning Curve: Inside the Global Battle for Democracy*. New York: Doubleday, 2012.

Domscheit-Berg, Daniel. *Inside WikiLeaks: My Time with Julian Assange at the World's Most Dangerous Website*. New York: Crown, 2011.

Earp, Madeline. "Amid Change, China Holds Fast to Information Control." In *Attacks on the Press in 2011*. http://www.cpj.org/2012/02/throughout-change-china-holds-fast-to-information.php.

Erlick, June Carolyn. *Disappeared: A Journalist Silenced—the Irma Flaquer Story*. Emeryville, Calif.: Seal, 2004.

Feitlowitz, Marguerite. *A Lexicon of Terror: Argentina and the Legacies of Torture*. New York: Oxford University Press, 1998.

Filkins, Dexter. *The Forever War*. New York: Knopf, 2008.

———. "The Journalist and the Spies: The Murder of a Reporter Who Exposed Pakistan's Secrets." *New Yorker* (September 19, 2011).

Garen, Micah, and Marie-Helene Carleton. *American Hostage: A Memoir of a Journalist Kidnapped in Iraq and the Remarkable Battle to Win His Release*. New York: Simon and Schuster, 2007.

Ghonim, Wael. *Revolution 2.0: The Power of the People Is Greater Than the People in Power: A Memoir*. Boston: Houghton Mifflin Harcourt, 2012.

Goldsmith, Jack, and Tim Wu. *Who Controls the Internet? Illusions of a Borderless World*. New York: Oxford University Press, 2006.

Goodale, James. *Fighting for the Press: The Inside Story of the Pentagon Papers and Other Battles*. New York: CUNY Journalism Press, 2013.

González Rodríguez, Sauro. "Cannon Fodder." Committee to Protect Journalists. August 1, 2002. http://www.cpj.org/reports/2002/08/ven-aug02.php.

Gould, Terry. *Marked for Death: Dying for the Story in the World's Most Dangerous Places*. Berkeley, Calif.: Counterpoint, 2009.

Hoffman, David. *Citizens Rising: Independent Journalism and the Spread of Democracy*. New York: CUNY Journalism Press, 2013.

Huffman, Alan. *Here I Am: The Story of Tim Hetherington, War Photographer*. New York: Grove, 2013.

Human Rights in China. "How the Chinese Authorities View the Internet." *China Rights Forum* 2 (2010). http://www.hrichina.org/content/3240.

Human Rights Watch. "A Decade Under Chávez: Political Intolerance and Lost Opportunities for Advancing Human Rights in Venezuela." September 22, 2008. http://www.hrw.org/reports/2008/09/22/decade-under-ch-vez.

———. "Tightening the Grip: Concentration and Abuse of Power in Chávez's Venezuela." July 17, 2012. http://www.hrw.org/reports/2012/07/17/tightening-grip.

International Crisis Group. "The Philippines: After the Maguindanao Massacre." *Asia Briefing* 98 (December 21, 2009). http://www.crisisgroup.org/~/media/Files/asia/south-east-asia/philippines/b98%20The%20Philippines%20After%20the%20Maguindanao%20Massacre.pdf.

Jones, Alex S. *Losing the News: The Future of the News That Feeds Democracy*. Institutions of American Democracy. New York: Oxford University Press, 2011.

Jones, Bart. *Hugo! The Hugo Chavez Story from Mud Hut to Perpetual Revolution*. Hanover, N.H.: Steerforth, 2007.

Jones, Kristin. "Harnessing Power in the Stories of Ordinary People." In *Attacks on the Press: Journalism on the World's Front Lines*, Committee to Protect Journalists, 59–68. New York: Wiley/Bloomberg, 2013.

Kampfner, John. *Freedom for Sale: Why the World Is Trading Democracy for Security*. New York: Basic Books, 2010.

Karlekar, Karin Deutsch. "Signs of Change Amid Repression." In *Freedom of the Press 2011*. http://www.freedomhouse.org/report/freedom-press /freedom-press-2011.

Katovsky, Bill, and Timothy Carlson. *Embedded: The Media at War in Iraq.* Guilford, Conn.: Lyons, 2003.

Kinzer, Stephen. *Crescent and Star: Turkey Between Two Worlds.* New York: Farrar, Straus and Giroux, 2008.

———. *Reset: Iran, Turkey, and America's Future.* New York: Times, 2010.

Knightley, Phillip. *The First Casualty: From the Crimea to Vietnam: The War Correspondent as Hero, Propagandist, and Myth Maker.* New York: Harcourt Brace Jovanovich, 1975.

Laurìa, Carlos, and Sauro González Rodríguez. "Static in Venezuela." Committee to Protect Journalists. April 24, 2007. https://cpj.org/reports/2007/04 /venezuela-07.php.

Layton, Charles. "Behind Bars." *American Journalism Review* (December 2006/January 2007). http://www.ajr.org/article.asp?id=4225.

Lessig, Lawrence. *The Future of Ideas: The Fate of the Commons in a Connected World.* New York: Vintage, 2002.

LeVine, Steve. *Putin's Labyrinth: Spies, Murder, and the Dark Heart of the New Russia.* New York: Random House, 2008.

Lévy, Bernard Henri. *Who Killed Daniel Pearl?* Hoboken, N.J.: Melville House, 2003.

Lewis, Anthony. *Freedom for the Thought That We Hate: A Biography of the First Amendment.* New York: Basic Books, 2010.

Lipman, Masha. "Constrained or Irrelevant: The Media in Putin's Russia." *Current History* (October 2005). http://www.currenthistory.com/Article .php?ID=359.

Maas, Peter. "The Toppling: How the Media Inflated a Minor Moment in a Long War." *New Yorker* (January 10, 2011).

MacKinnon, Rebecca. *Consent of the Networked: The Worldwide Struggle for Internet Freedom.* New York: Basic Books, 2012.

Mansour, Sherif. "As Election Nears, Iran's Journalists Are in Chains." Committee to Protect Journalists. May 8, 2013. http://www.cpj.org/reports /2013/05/as-election-nears-irans-journalists-are-in-chains.php.

Marinovich, Greg, and João Silva. *The Bang-Bang Club.* London: Heinemann, 2000.

Massing, Michael. "Dangerous Assignments 20th Anniversary: In the Beginning." CPJ Special Report. May 1, 2001. http://cpj.org/reports/2001/05 /massing.php.

Mastrogiacomo, Daniele, and Michael Reynolds. *Days of Fear: A Firsthand Account of Captivity Under the New Taliban.* New York: Europa, 2010.

Miles, Hugh. *Al-Jazeera: The Inside Story of the Arab News Channel That Is Challenging the West.* New York: Grove, 2006.

Morozov, Evgeny. *The Net Delusion: The Dark Side of Internet Freedom*. New York: PublicAffairs, 2011.

Moyn, Samuel. *The Last Utopia: Human Rights in History*. Boston: Belknap, 2012.

Neier, Aryeh. *Taking Liberties: Four Decades in the Struggle For Rights*. New York: PublicAffairs, 2003.

——. *The International Human Rights Movement: A History*. Human Rights and Crimes Against Humanity. Princeton, N.J.: Princeton University Press, 2012.

Nicks, Denver. *Private: Bradley Manning, WikiLeaks, and the Biggest Exposure of Official Secrets in American History*. Chicago: Chicago Review Press, 2012.

Packer, George. *The Assassins' Gate: America in Iraq*. New York: Farrar, Straus and Giroux. 2006.

Pearl, Mariane, and Sarah Crichton. *A Mighty Heart: The Brave Life and Death of My Husband, Danny Pearl*. New York: Scribner, 2003.

Politkovskaya, Anna. *Putin's Russia: Life in a Failing Democracy*. New York: Metropolitan, 2005.

——. *Is Journalism Worth Dying For? Final Dispatches*. Translated by Arch Trait. Brooklyn: Melville House, 2011.

——. "Essay Translated by Arch Tait." In *Writers Under Siege: Voices of Writers from Around the World*, edited by Lucy Popescu and Claire Seymour-Jones. New York: New York University Press, 2007.

Power, Samantha. *A Problem from Hell: America and the Age of Genocide*. New York: Basic Books, 2002.

Rashid, Ahmed. *Pakistan on the Brink: The Future of America, Pakistan, and Afghanistan*. New York: Viking, 2012.

Remnick, David. *Lenin's Tomb: The Last Days of the Soviet Empire*. New York: Random House, 1993.

——. "Echo in the Dark: A Radio Station Strives to Keep the Airwaves Free." *New Yorker* (September 22, 2008).

Rohde, David, and Kristen Mulvihill. *A Rope and a Prayer: A Kidnapping from Two Sides*. New York: Viking, 2010.

Rubin, Elizabeth. "Roots of Impunity: Pakistan's Endangered Press." Committee to Protect Journalists. May 23, 2013. http://www.cpj.org/reports /2013/05/pakistan-roots-impunity.php.

Saberi, Roxana. *Between Two Worlds: My Life and Captivity in Iran*. New York: Harper, 2010.

Sgrena, Giuliana. *Friendly Fire: The Remarkable Story of a Journalist Kidnapped in Iraq, Rescued by an Italian Secret Service Agent, and Shot by U.S. Forces*. New York: Haymarket, 2006.

Shane, Scott. *Dismantling Utopia: How Information Ended the Soviet Union*. Chicago: I. R. Dee, 1994.

Silber, Laura, and Allan Little. *The Death of Yugoslavia.* London: Penguin, 1995.

Simon, Joel. "Fujimori Stomps a Station," *Columbia Journalism Review* 36, no. 4 (1997): 58.

———. "Hot on the Money Trail." *Columbia Journalism Review* 36, no. 5 (1998): 50.

———. "Muzzling the Media: How the New Autocrats Threaten Press Freedoms." *World Policy Journal* 23, no. 2 (2006): 51–61.

———. "In Africa, Exploiting the Past." *Columbia Journalism Review* 44, no. 5 (2006): 9.

———. "Impunity: Stopping the Killers." *Index on Censorship* (January 26, 2010). http://www.indexoncensorship.org/2010/01/impunity-cpj-politkovskaya -journalists/.

———. "International Institutions Fail to Defend Press Freedom." In *Attacks on the Press in 2010.* http://www.cpj.org/2011/02/attacks-on-the-press -2010-introduction-joel-simon.php.

———. "The Next Information Revolution: Abolishing Censorship." In *Attacks on the Press in 2011.* http://cpj.org/2012/02/attacks-on-the-press-in -2011-the-global-citizen.php.

———. "Beyond Article 19, a Global Press Freedom Charter." In *Attacks on the Press in 2012.* http://cpj.org/2013/02/attacks-on-the-press-beyond -article-19.php.

———. "How the United States' Spying Strengthen China's Hand." In *Attacks on the Press 2014.* New York: Bloomberg/Wiley, 2014.

Simon, Joel, and Carlos Lauría. "Free Fire Zone." Committee to Protect Journalists. November 2003. http://www.cpj.org/reports/2004/11/tijuana .php.

Slpašak, Svetlana. *The War Started at Maksimir: Hate Speech in the Media: Content Analyses of Politika and Borba Newspapers, 1987–1991.* Beograd: Media Center, 1997.

Smeets, Marylene. "Radio Chávez." Committee to Protect Journalists. February 1, 2001. http://cpj.org/reports/2001/02/ven-feb01.php.

Snyder, Jack L. *From Voting to Violence: Democratization and Nationalist Conflict.* New York: Norton, 2000.

Smith, Jeffery Alan. *War and Press Freedom: The Problem of Prerogative Power.* New York: Oxford University Press, 1999.

Temple-Raston, Dina. *Justice on the Grass: A Story of Genocide and Redemption.* New York: Free, 2005.

Timerman, Jacobo. *Prisoner Without a Name, Cell Without a Number.* New York: Knopf, 1981.

Todd, Barbara Feinman, and Asra Nomani. "The Truth Left Behind: Inside the Kidnapping and Murder of Daniel Pearl." The Pearl Project. http:// pearlproject.georgetown.edu/pearlproject_march_2013.pdf.

Verbitsky, Horacio. *The Flight: Confessions of an Argentine Dirty Warrior.* New York: New Press, 1996.

Waisbord, Silvio R. *Watchdog Journalism in South America: News, Accountability, and Democracy.* New York: Columbia University Press, 2000.

Wright, Lawrence. *The Looming Tower: Al-Qaeda and the Road to 9/11.* New York: Vintage, 2007.

Zakaria, Fareed. *The Future of Freedom: Illiberal Democracy at Home and Abroad.* New York: Norton, 2004.

Zittrain, Jonathan. *The Future of the Internet—and How to Stop It.* New Haven, Conn.: Yale University Press, 2009.

Zuckerman, Ethan. *Rewire: Digital Cosmopolitans in the Age of Connection.* New York: Norton, 2013.

Index